CAN GOD INTERVENE?

CAN GOD INTERVENE?

HOW RELIGION EXPLAINS NATURAL DISASTERS

Gary Stern

PRAEGER

Westport, Connecticut
London

Library of Congress Cataloging-in-Publication Data

Stern, Gary, 1964–
    Can God intervene? : how religion explains natural disasters / Gary Stern.
        p. cm.
    Includes bibliographical references and index.
    ISBN 978-0-275-98958-3 (alk. paper)
1. Natural disasters—Religious aspects. 2. Indian Ocean Tsunami, 2004—Religious aspects. 3. Natural disasters—Religious aspects—Christianity. 4. Indian Ocean Tsunami, 2004—Religious aspects—Christianity. 5. Theodicy. I. Title.
BL65.N33S74 2007
202'.118—dc22   2007000067

British Library Cataloguing in Publication Data is available.

Library of Congress Catalog Card Number: 2007000067
ISBN: 978-0-275-98958-3
ISBN: 0-275-98958-5

First published in 2007

Praeger Publishers, 88 Post Road West, Westport, CT 06881
An imprint of Greenwood Publishing Group, Inc.
www.praeger.com

Printed in the United States of America

The paper used in this book complies with the
Permanent Paper Standard issued by the National
Information Standards Organization (Z39.48-1984).

10 9 8 7 6 5 4 3 2 1

To my parents,
Martin and Paulette Stern

CONTENTS

ACKNOWLEDGMENTS

First off, I have to thank the scholars, theologians, and clergy who agreed to speak with me for this project. They are extremely busy people who face all kinds of demands on their time. Nearly all were gracious and forthcoming. Most were willing to speak honestly, take some risks, and leave themselves vulnerable during our talks. Sometimes the hardest admission to make is that you just don't know.

I want to thank Anthony Chiffolo at Praeger Press, who thought I could pull this book off.

I've spent most of my career at the *Journal News,* the daily newspaper covering the northern suburbs of New York City, where I've been given mostly free reign to cover religion for the past decade. There have been too many good people at the paper for me to acknowledge them all. But I have to thank Henry Freeman, CynDee Royle, and Bob Fredericks for supporting my work for so long. I've been lucky to have editors, past and present, I could count on when I'm in a bind: John Alcott, Dan Greenfield, and Laurel Babcock. I have to thank some of my senior colleagues at the paper, longtime friends, for listening to my worries while working on this project: Rich Liebson, Jorge Fitz-Gibbon, Leah Rae, Noreen O'Donnell, Melissa Klein, Bruce Golding, Glenn Blain, Zana Varner, Seth Harrison, and Phil Reisman. Yes, there are others.

I also have to thank Reisman, our columnist extraordinaire, for a piece of advice he gave me when I started on the religion beat: "Write about it like you would anything else." The best possible advice.

Thanks to former editor Robert Ritter, who first suggested that the *Journal News* needed a religion reporter.

Thanks to my sister, Mindy Stern, my in-laws, George and Martina Brunner, the Ingrassias and the Brunners.

Finally, and this has been a long time coming, I have to thank my wife, Anne, and our sons, Raymond and Henry. When you have a demanding full-time job with no set hours, like I do, and when you take on a project like this book, everyone else in the house has to make big-time sacrifices. For over a year, I was not available on Saturdays, Sundays, and many evenings. To make things worse. I was grumpy much of the time. But Anne said she wanted me to write this book and that she would do whatever it took. She did, without complaint, while working as an elementary school teacher and shuttling the boys around White Plains. I will always be grateful. My wife is the best.

Ray and Hank got tired of sharing me with the book. "Dad, do you have to work on the book?" they would ask. "Who made you do the book?" But they're troopers and great kids and gave me space when I needed it. I couldn't be more proud of them.

INTRODUCTION

It's safe to say that most Americans knew nothing about tsunamis before December 26, 2004.

Earthquakes we know. A 1989 San Francisco quake collapsed bridges and freeways and delayed the World Series. We've heard about how the great San Francisco quake of 1906 unleashed fires throughout the city. Most of us have a vague understanding of the Richter scale—at least that a quake that measures 7 or 7.5 is something serious. Every now and then, news of a small quake, a tremor, gets our attention, and the TV news shows pull out their old files on the "Big One." We all know about the Big One. It's the quake that will someday change the course of history by sinking the West Coast. The Big One is part of the American consciousness, part of the vernacular. Predictions of when it will strike arise whenever there is "seismic activity" out west. East Coasters who are jealous of or bemused by Californians like to joke about it. But anyone who is remotely aware of the science behind earthquakes (or has seen a movie about one) has to wonder now and then when the Big One will strike. If an *Act of God* is going to take out the Land of Hope and Dreams, you have to hope that neither you nor anyone you love will be there to see it.

But who knew anything about tsunamis before December 26, 2004? The worst tsunami ever to hit the American mainland slammed into scenic Crescent City, California, in 1964. It was born of a major earthquake in Alaska and took the lives of eleven residents of Crescent City. Four decades later, this event was mostly lost to history. The worst tsunami on record took place in 1883, when a volcanic eruption on Krakatoa, an island in Southeast Asia, blew the island to bits. The eruption set off tsunamis that washed away more than 36,000 people. How many have heard of Krakatoa?

Today, we know something about tsunamis. We know that they are caused by earthquakes, that they come without warning, and that they can produce towering waves that wipe out the boundary between land and sea. Anyone who has seen some of the herky, jerky video shot by handheld cameras on December 26, 2004, will remember images of people holding onto trees and floating debris as the ocean tugged at their bodies and the threat of death rose all around them. Most shocking of all were scenes of parents clutching their children while fighting to stay above the tide. There is one scene that I can't get out of my mind: Two adults and seven or eight children were huddled together by a large object that I couldn't identify. The picture went black for some time, maybe a few seconds, maybe a couple of minutes. When it came back on, there was one adult left. He was holding onto the object, too far away to see his eyes.

The tsunami that hit southern Asia on the second day of Christmas stunned the whole world. It wasn't just the death count. Some 230,000 people would die, at least a third of them children, making the tsunami one of the worst natural disasters in recorded history. It was the way the victims died. People were going about their business, villagers and tourists alike, when the sea rose up to wash away entire communities. Just like that. To read the descriptions of what took place was to get the impression that the whole thing was somehow planned, a vicious sneak attack designed to take as many lives as possible.

The question was asked early and often: Where was God?

It was inevitable. Throughout history, the role of God or divine powers has been debated whenever humankind has encountered catastrophe. The greater the suffering, the more human beings have invoked God's name—sometimes for strength, sometimes in anger. For centuries, millennia really, God was seen as the *deliverer* of violence, a cosmic grim reaper. He was believed to be delivering his will in the form of earthquakes or floods or armies (which armies he favored, of course, was open to debate). He did so to punish the wicked or to deliver a message to humankind, in all or part. The perceived message was usually the same: Change your ways. This view became less universal after the Enlightenment, but it is still widely shared among followers of many religions around the world.

Whether or not one believes in divine punishment, people of faith face some of the most difficult, anguishing questions that can be asked about their God whenever innocent people suffer and die. Even if you believe that God is not responsible for a natural disaster, that he did not consciously make it happen, a believer has to wonder whether God could have stopped it. If God is all-powerful, shouldn't he be able to still an earthquake or calm a tsunami? If he can, then why doesn't he? Theodicy is the philosophy of trying to explain the existence of evil in a world that is overseen by an all-loving, all-powerful God. Nothing awakens ancient questions of theodicy like a history changing *Act of God*.

For a period of about one month after the tsunami, the United States, Europe, and much of the world engaged in a sometimes sober, sometimes hysterical dialogue about the religious meaning of the tsunami. Leaders of many faiths spoke out in the media, some making controversial statements that provoked further debate. It is this period of public dialogue and confrontation—which quietly fizzled like a candle splashed with water as the media lost interest—that I aim to reopen with this book. Unfortunately, the subject of natural disasters would only become more prominent as I worked on this project. Every few months, as if on cue, an *Act of God* would strike and raise new questions about the relationship between humankind and the divine. Hurricane Katrina hit the Gulf Coast in August 2005, drowning an American city and provoking an emotional national debate that swayed between theology and politics and back again. Two months later, an earthquake in northern Pakistan took 80,000 lives and left more than 3 million homeless. This disaster received scant attention in the United States, perhaps because there was little video of the quake itself and perhaps because of what I'll call "disaster fatigue." Four months after that, in February 2006, mudslides in the eastern Philippines buried a village and killed at least 1,800 people. Over the next two months, several rounds of tornadoes touched down in the American Midwest, killing about 50 people and tearing homes and churches from the ground. Only weeks later, in June 2006, Indonesia got hit again. A 6.3-magnitude earthquake on Java island took about 7,000 lives and injured more than 30,000. Each of these disasters touched this project in ways I will get to later.

Dialogue is probably too formal a word for what took place in January 2005, in the wake of the tsunami. What happened is that a variety of people—some religious, some not; some famous, some not—felt compelled to speak or write about God's role, or lack of one, in the horror that the world had just witnessed. Much of what came out was passionate and heated and inspired equally passionate responses. I would guess that many, many people read or heard bits of what was written and said. Some probably found themselves wondering, however briefly, about God's presence in this world.

As details first emerged on the scope of the tsunami's devastation, the initial, raw reactions from many religious leaders were dripping with emotion—anger, guilt, despair. Azizan Abdul Razak, a Muslim cleric in Malaysia, said the tsunami was God's message that "he created the world and can destroy the world."[1] Israel's Sephardic Chief Rabbi Shlomo Amar called the tsunami "an expression of God's great ire with the world."[2] Pandit Harikrishna Shastri, a Hindu priest in New Delhi, said it was caused by "a huge amount of pent-up man-made evil on earth."[3] Rowan Williams, the Archbishop of Canterbury and leader of the worldwide Anglican Church, drew international attention by writing honestly in a British newspaper about the theological difficulties posed by any attempt to paint the tsunami as part of God's plan. "If some religious genius did come up with an explanation of exactly why all these deaths made sense, would we feel happier or safer or more confident in God?" he wrote. "Wouldn't we feel something of a chill at the prospect of a God who deliberately plans a programme that involves a certain level of casualties?"[4] Such reflection did not sit well with all of William's fellow Christians. The Reverend Albert Mohler, president of the Southern Baptist Theological Seminary, for instance, said that Williams' essay was "how not to give a Christian answer."[5] Mohler preferred to see the tsunami as a warning of God's judgment.

Several striking reactions came from Muslims in regions that were affected by the tsunami. Mohamed Faizeen, manager of the Centre for Islamic Studies in Colombo, Sri Lanka, insisted that a satellite picture taken as the tsunami hit Sri Lanka's west coast showed that the shape of the waves spelled out "Allah" in Arabic. "Allah signed his name," Faizeen said. "He sent it as punishment. This comes from ignoring his laws."[6] Faizeen compared the tsunami to the great flood of the Old Testament, even though the Quran describes only a regional flood. Another story that received worldwide attention was about the 75,000 villagers living on the Indonesian island of Simeulue. The islanders had heard stories from their ancestors about great waves that followed earthquakes, so they ran to the hills after the quake, only 40 miles away, shook their island. Thirty-foot waves soon crashed down on the island, but only seven people died. "We were just thinking that God was doing this," said Suhardin, 33, an islander who uses one name and was told by his grandmother about the tsunami of 1907. "This is because God is angry."[7]

Through the weeks that followed, most religious figures in America preached about the need to provide relief for the survivors. It became not only the practical priority of most religious denominations but also a mission of faith. Raising money and awareness was framed as the correct theological response to the catastrophe. More and more, religious leaders could be heard saying that God was inspiring donations and that God was with the international relief workers who flocked to Indonesia and Sri Lanka. God's presence *during* the tsunami may have been unclear, but his presence in the relief camps was largely unquestioned. Sure enough, an unprecedented international relief effort raised several billion dollars during the first year after the tsunami.

As religious denominations promoted God's role in building temporary housing, several American commentators offered deeper reflections on the theological challenges posed by the tsunami. John Garvey, an Orthodox Christian priest who writes a sober, intelligent column for the Catholic magazine *Commonweal,* probably captured the feelings of many speechless people of faith when he offered that there is simply no explanation for the suffering in this world, which goes far beyond that caused by natural disasters. "God is finally unknowable, and, because of his infinite otherness we can only approach—but never fully arrive at—God," Garvey wrote.[8] The formidable and often cantankerous Leon Wieseltier, who writes for the *New Republic,* spoke for many angry skeptics when he railed against everyone who fell into line defending their benevolent God. "They should more candidly admit that they choose not to reflect upon the spiritual implications of natural destruction, because they wish to protect what they believe," Wieseltier sneered.[9] Then there was David Bentley Hart, an Orthodox Christian theologian who wrote a column for the *Wall Street Journal* about the tsunami, which provoked so much reaction that he expanded it into a 109-page book. In this book, he melded Garvey's impatience with simple explanations to Wieseltier's anger, slapping aside most rationalizations for the tsunami as "odious banalities and blasphemous flippancies." He concluded that this fallen, sinful world offers glimpses of both God's grace and the darkness of evil, and that Christians can look forward to salvation without having to explain the unexplainable suffering that people endure. "Our faith," he wrote, "is in a God who has come to rescue his creation from the absurdity of sin, the emptiness and waste of death, the forces—whether calculating malevolence or imbecile chance—that shatter living souls; and so we are permitted to hate these things with a perfect hatred."[10]

The reaction to Hurricane Katrina was something very different. Once the levees failed, New Orleans began to flood and it became apparent that many poor, black people were stranded in their own homes, the hurricane became a national *political* scandal. The debate was over which clueless politicians to blame. FEMA (Federal Emergency Management Agency) became an instant punch line. Commentators began asking why the preparation for Katrina was so poor at a time when the country could spend billions in Iraq. Theodicy did not disappear. But the raising of theological questions became itself a political statement. Conservative religious figures began to suggest that Katrina, like the tsunami, was punishment from God. New Orleans, they pointed out, was a city of drinking and sex. Liberal religious leaders belittled such arguments, placing the blame on President Bush and his cronies and hardly mentioning God's role at all.

Several weeks after Katrina, Franklin Graham, the evangelist son of Billy Graham, made Katrina sound like a good thing for New Orleans. "God is going to use that storm to bring a revival," he said. "God has a plan. God has a purpose."[11] Televangelist Pat Robertson suggested that Katrina and the tsunami could be signs that Jesus would soon be returning. "And before that good time comes there will be some difficult days," he said on CNN.[12] Around the same time, Rabbi Ovadia Yosef, one of Israeli's most prominent religious leaders, suggested that Katrina was "God's retribution" for America's support of the Israeli pullout from the Gaza Strip.[13] Still, the vast majority of American religious leaders had little to say about God's role in the hurricane, preferring to blame political ineptitude, societal racism, the destruction of the Gulf Coast by developers, and other man-made environmental mistakes. The lack of fingers pointed at God led Edward Rothstein, a *New York Times* critic-at-large, to cite a new theodicy that expects science and political power to control nature and blames public officials for moral failings when they don't get the job done. "Nature becomes something to be managed or mismanaged," he wrote. "It lies within the political order, not outside it."[14]

It's important that I explain what I was trying to do through the course of writing this book. I am not a theologian. Nor am I an expert on any individual religious tradition that I deal with here, although I am quite familiar with most of them. I am a journalist who specializes in religion. I believe I was well suited to take on this project as a journalistic enterprise. My goal was to pin down some of the country's leading religious thinkers and draw out their true feelings about God's role in natural disasters and, ultimately, about God's connection to human suffering. Academic culture grew more and more specialized through the second half of the twentieth century, forcing historians, philosophers, theologians, and others to focus on increasingly narrow specialties encased in their own jargon. This outlook has created an intellectual culture, I think, in which the big questions about life and death and God are often treated as unsophisticated, naive, and Old World, politically incorrect in an academic sense. Additionally, my experience has taught me that many within the religious world are adept at dancing around difficult questions by citing Scripture, quoting their own theological heroes, and inferring that people who pose such questions have antireligious motives. So my goal in conducting the interviews that make up the heart of this book was to ask clear, direct questions about God's presence, intentions, and influence when the tsunami and other disasters changed the world.

This is not to say that I pressured anyone to defend or accuse God. That would be a pointless exercise and would have backed each person into one of several predictable corners: *Have faith. We don't know. Don't ask.* Instead, I wanted each person I spoke with to focus on what was important to them. Of course, some went off on tangents, some became quickly repetitive, and some sounded as if they had been in this game of explaining the unexplainable for too long. But most rose to the challenge and tried to truly engage my questions (after two decades in journalism, I have a pretty sensitive radar for obfuscation). Some, I think, genuinely enjoyed the opportunity to address the big questions that they know ordinary people ask or wonder about. Many interviews started slowly, crawling along under weighty generalizations, before something sparked my interviewees to toss aside pat answers and just go with it. Some sounded relieved to reject even responsible answers as inadequate and to simply admit that they did not know.

I also have to say something about the format of this book. First off, the people who are interviewed and briefly profiled are not meant to represent their religious tradition in any kind of complete and thorough way. No five people could stand in for, say, mainline Protestantism, especially when it comes to the sweeping subject this book addresses. If there is anything I've learned covering religion, it is that the most emotional and heated disagreements take place within traditions, not between them. No one speaks for an entire tradition, with a few possible exceptions like the president of the Church of Jesus Christ of Latter-day Saints and—some would say—the pope. The people I have grouped together in each chapter are meant to give the reader *a sense* of the range of responses that one might find within that religious tradition. This is not to say that I have covered the entire range within each tradition or that I haven't left out important viewpoints. I have tried to include the broadest, most interesting range of credible ideas within each tradition, which five people or so can offer. It is the most I could do within this framework.

How did I choose the religions and religious traditions that are part of this book? The answer is obvious. I had to include the five primary world religions—Judaism, Christianity, Islam, Buddhism, and Hinduism. Because I am writing for an American audience, it simply made sense to break down Christianity into several traditions—Roman Catholicism, mainline Protestantism, evangelical Protestantism, and African American Protestantism (I figured that African Americans know enough about suffering to warrant their own chapter). Are other traditions, say Orthodox Christianity, Sikhism, or Bahaism, somehow not worthy of being included? Of course not. But I had to draw the line where I did.

How did I choose the people who make up the heart of this book? I had no formula. Some are people I had interviewed before. Some are people I had read or heard about over the years. Others were people I discovered as I did my research. I suppose that what they had in common was a demonstrated interest in the big questions. Some had written books about suffering. Some had weighed in about the tsunami or Hurricane Katrina or other *Acts of God*. Others were people who I had an inkling would be willing to tackle my questions with relish. Honestly, I did not have the time to interview people who were not likely to have something to say (although I did speak with a few, who are not included in this book). And, yes, I realize that there must be other deep thinkers out there who would have been perfect for this book, who have dedicated their lives to studying some of the questions I raise. If only I would have known about them.

A point about gender: Most of the people I interviewed were men. The fact is that most religious authorities in this country are men. Make that the world. I saw this clearly when I covered a gathering of the world's religious leaders at the United Nations several years ago. All ethnicities, all races, all colors. All manners and styles of religious garb. Virtually all men. I considered seeking out more women for this book, but decided that the imbalance of men and women in religious communities (which is changing ever so slowly) was not something I could or should address here.

A point about politics: All journalists know that whatever you write in America today will be seen through a political lens. On what side of the culture war are you? Each religious tradition I write about here has its own battlegrounds, where conservatives and liberals, the orthodox and progressives, wage theological war over revelation, belief, and how followers should live and act. Some of these battles are more prominent or familiar than others. But they are always there. I tried to keep these differences in mind when choosing people to interview for each chapter. I did not want to include only people who promote one type of thinking within a diverse tradition. At the same time, I did not want to get caught up in a numbers game: "I have two conservatives, one liberal and one moderate, so I better find someone who isn't right of moderate-liberal." Again, I tried to represent each tradition as fairly as I could, although I'm sure that some will say that I portrayed their tradition as being too *something* or not enough *something else*.

I chose to open this book with two self-contained chapters that I hope will add context and meaning to what follows. The first is about the tsunami itself. It is important for the reader to have a good handle on what took place that day—the science involved and the suffering that resulted—before encountering the explanations and anxieties of religious thinkers. So I do my best to explain what causes earthquakes and how, when particular forces align, quakes can set off tsunamis. And I describe the tsunami that rolled out of the Indian Ocean in 2004—how it came together, where it hit, and the damage that it wrought.

In Chapter 2, I take a look at how disasters were interpreted in the past— usually as God's will in a physical form. I spend most of the chapter examining the vast, if overlooked legacy of Noah's flood, the great flood of the Old Testament and the Quran. I contend that this story of God sending a flood to punish sinners, wipe out a stained human race, and give himself a fresh start still colors the way we interpret natural disasters today. To be a Jew or a Christian or a Muslim is to come from a tradition that says that, long before the tsunami, God was willing to drown the guilty. Also in this chapter, I'll explore the significance of the Lisbon earthquake and tsunami of 1755, which is widely considered the turning point for how humankind explains disasters. After that disaster (and some famous responses from Voltaire), God evolved from being the great executioner to having a more nuanced and unclear role in natural disasters. I conclude Chapter 2 with a look at the story of poor, old Job, who came up in many of my interviews. For people whose roots are in the three great monotheistic faiths, at least, his story is always relevant and perhaps the final word on the subject of this book.

The remainder of the book surveys the perspectives of religious thinkers— scholars, theologians, clergy—from different traditions on the question of natural disasters, focusing on the tsunami. I believe that a reading of all the musings, explanations, stories, and silences to come will give the reader the strongest possible sense of how our religions see and understand the cracking of God's earth, the rising of God's seas, the fury of God's storms and twisters.

Of course, my subjects—the interviewees—do not speak only of natural disasters. I learned early on that to talk about a tsunami or hurricane leads inevitably to larger questions: Why does God allow innocent people to suffer at all? What is the nature of evil in this world and why doesn't God overcome it? How involved is God in our day-to-day life? When you think about it, it's impossible to consider God's role in an earthquake without delving into God's role in other events and circumstances. Like when a loved one becomes ill. Or someone from your old neighborhood is hit by a drunk driver. Or when you read about peasants killed in some distant civil war. Even if one believes that God gives us free will—a gift that gives meaning to our lives—it's hard not to wonder why he didn't do something to prevent the Holocaust, the slaughter in Rwanda, and other genocides.

There have been no shortage of great minds wrestling with the meaning of suffering. After his wife died from cancer, C. S. Lewis wrote in his classic *A Grief Observed* that "If God's goodness is inconsistent with hurting us, then either God is not good or there is no God; for in the only life we know He hurts us beyond our worst fears and beyond all we can imagine."[15] In a 2005 interview, the Holocaust survivor and Nobel Peace Prize winner Elie Wiesel spoke of his enduring but wounded faith: "I would be within my rights to give up faith in God, and I could invoke 6 million reasons to justify such a decision. But I am incapable of straying from the path charted by my forefathers, who felt duty-bound to live for God."[16] In a PBS documentary about how faith was affected by the terrorist attacks of September 11, 2001, the Reverend Joseph Griesedieck, an Episcopal priest, said that staring into buckets of body parts at Ground Zero changed his understanding of God: "After Sept. 11, the face of God was a blank slate for me. God couldn't be counted on in the way that I thought God could be counted on."[17]

Terrible suffering is caused every day by illness, violence, accidents of every sort. But I don't know that any form of suffering in this world raises questions about God's presence, involvement, power, and goodness like that created by a natural disaster. Life is going on as expected one moment, and in the next, everything is different. The tsunami swept away everyone within striking distance—young and adult, good and bad, faithful and doubting. In a world filled with suffering that forces us to ask over and over the most difficult question of all—*Why?*—a natural disaster produces concentrated suffering. The laws of nature unleashed a tsunami that committed random mass murder. If God or some divine power set up those laws, how can he not be implicated?

As I worked on this book, many relatives, colleagues, and acquaintances asked me the same questions, tongue in cheek: Had I learned the truth? Did I have the answer? Did God command the tsunami forth, like a god of Greek mythology might? Well, now I'm finished, and I can confidently say it will be up to the reader to determine whether any answers—any truth—are contained in the pages to come. What I have concluded myself is that this book offers a tremendous amount of wisdom from many of the top religious minds in the United States. I appreciate their willingness to tell me what they believe, what they cannot believe, and what they can never know.

A final note: It is believed that the term *Act of God* was first used as a legal term during the mid-1800s to describe an unanticipated and uncontrollable event. It is normally used in contracts to protect a party from responsibility for some event they could not foresee. The courts have recognized many *Acts of God,* apparently without drawing the wrath of those who promote a strict separation of church and state (although can such protests be far off?). It just goes to show that when certain things happen in this world without explanation, even the courts will throw down their books and point their fingers at God. An organization called the Global Language Monitor, which tracks language trends, cited *Act of God* as the most significant label for 2005.

1 THE DAY AFTER CHRISTMAS 2004

The ground beneath our feet appears solid and ongoing, one great monolithic slab. It slopes down into vast tubs that hold the rivers and the oceans and rises in all the right places to give us rolling hills and mountain ranges. The earth looks and feels of one piece. Then again, the world looks flat to the naked eye.

The earth's crust is actually broken into pieces. Depending on how you count them, there are about a dozen major, ragged-edged chunks and numerous smaller fragments. They fit together, more or less, like a planetary jigsaw puzzle. Most of the time they do a fine job appearing as a single crust to the earth's tiny inhabitants. The pieces of the earth's surface are known as plates, which give us a nice image since they hold up the forests and seas and creatures that bring the surface to life.

As you read this, these vast chunks of rock are moving. They move slowly, from anywhere between half an inch a year to perhaps four inches a year. But that's fast enough to make the earth's crust an active place. The planetary shell is slowly but steadily reconfigured over thousands and millions of years. The plates float on the steamy and pliable insides of the planet. This soupy interior, known as the mantle, holds temperatures of up to 5400°F. The heat exerts tremendous, unyielding pressure on the plates above, prodding them to move. All the while, the mantle seeks weak spots in the crust to exploit.

Only over the last century has science learned that the movement of floating plates is slowly shifting the contours of the earth's surface. The theory of what is known as "plate tectonics" is now used to explain, for instance, that Saudi Arabia was once part of the African continent but was torn away as the Red Sea was born. Scientists also believe that three plates that now meet at the African continent may someday separate, isolating the Horn of Africa as an island and allowing the Indian Ocean to flood the area and perhaps create a new ocean.

So the plates that give the planet its famously global appearance are faced with the burden of holding up continents and oceans while under constant pressure from the steamy soup beneath. They react much like an extended family—butting heads and competing for position, rubbing each other the wrong way, moving together and moving apart.

Sometimes plates separate. They may leave behind chunks of land, new islands perhaps. Or they may create room for new bodies of water or for hot magma from inside the earth to rise, harden, and form a new land mass. Sometimes plates move together. They grind into one another like bumper cars, creating monstrous stalemates that may take centuries to be resolved.

During the course of such stalemates, one plate is often forced to slide ever so slowly beneath another. This process, which scientists call subduction, creates enormous pressures that build and build until they are finally released. It is along the boundaries where plates meet, pass one another, separate, butt heads, and overlap that mountains rise, volcanos erupt, oceans shrink and expand, and earthquakes shake and destroy.

Two of the largest jigsaw pieces making up the earth's crust have been at loggerheads for tens of millions of years. The Indo-Australian plate holds up the Australian continent and its surrounding ocean, extending northwest to India and China. The plate moves slowly and steadily north, a few inches a year. All the while, it grinds against the Eurasian plate on its northeastern shoulder. The Eurasian plate, which supports Europe and Asia, holds its ground like a patient sumo wrestler. The pressure created by this collision of behemoths is credited with forming the Himalayan Mountains between 70 and 25 million years ago. Over a vast period of time, the Eurasian plate buckled and folded upward. The grinding of the two plates pushed the fold higher and higher, producing the highest continental mountains in the world.

The seam between the Indo-Australian plate and the Eurasian plate lies partially beneath the Indian Ocean. Geologists call it a fault boundary. It is here that the Indo-Australian plate is subducted, that is, driven below the Eurasian plate. This is not a smooth project aided by engineering or lubrication but involves two masses of earth grinding against and tearing up one another. As the lower plate moves—this is important—it catches the lip of the Eurasian plate above it and forces it to curl downward. But the lip cannot warp indefinitely. The tension only builds over centuries as the lower plate moves deeper and deeper, pulling the lip along. At various points, the lip will snap back. Pop. Some releases will involve only a portion of the seam, setting off minor earthquakes. Others, far more infrequently, will rip the seam open.

That's what happened on December 26, 2004.

The previous day, of course, was Christmas.

Many of the world's more than 2 billion Christians celebrated the birth of their Savior, reveling yet again in God's willingness to send his son to walk among humankind. It is celebrated as a time of innocence and rebirth, of hope, even though the baby Jesus is destined to die a painful death to atone for the sins of men and women.

Pope John Paul II offered what would be his final Christmas wishes in St. Peter's Square. Despite his failing health, he managed the traditional holiday greetings and hoped for peace across the world, in Iraq, in the Holy Land, in Africa. He prayed: "Babe of Bethlehem, prophet of peace, encourage attempts to promote dialogue and reconciliation, sustain the efforts to build peace, which hesitantly, yet not without hope, are being made to bring about a more tranquil present and future for so many of our brothers and sisters of the world."[1]

Otherwise, the world went about its business. In the United States, disgruntled flight attendants and baggage handlers for US Airways didn't report to work, creating chaos in numerous East Coast airports during one of the busiest traveling weekends of the year. As piles of bags were lost, angry travelers who thought that the airlines had finally recovered from 9/11 felt betrayed and worse. "They ruined everybody's Christmas," said Shirley Malave of Toms River, New Jersey, who arrived in Tampa without any clothes.[2]

Some good news came from space, where a cargo ship reached the International Space Station manned by a desperate American–Russian crew. The crew had run low on food and supplies, putting the mission in danger. But all was now well, thanks to a delivery of 2.5 tons of food, water, fuel, equipment, and Christmas presents.

Surely many Americans smiled that day at reports of a surprise in Texas: a white Christmas. A surprising cold spell across the South dropped up to 13 inches of snow on parts of Texas and gave the town of Victoria its first white Christmas in 86 years.

As Christmas night became the early morning hours of December 26, Americans began to hear the first reports of a massive earthquake in the Indian Ocean, by northern Indonesia. At least hundreds had died, apparently washed away by tidal waves.

Most earthquakes last for a few seconds. A seam beneath the earth's crust ruptures and quickly settles. The size of the rupture determines the violence of the shock waves that follow, which do most of the damage.

But the epic tragedy that occurred on December 26 was set in motion by a force the likes of which has rarely been seen in modern history. It was a force that was beyond humankind's control, a force that had been building up for centuries and could not be predicted. It was the work, planned or random, of powers beyond our grasp.

The earthquake that struck under the Indian Ocean lasted for close to 10 minutes, an eternity in the world of seismology.[3] The tectonic plates finally adjusted themselves, with the Indo-Australian plate slipping further into the earth and the Eurasian plate snapping upward. But the seam between them continued to rupture for an hour. Picture a zipper bursting from pressure and the seam holding it in place just unraveling. The resulting gash ran for 800 miles, longer than the length of California and the longest tear in an ocean seabed that scientists have ever seen.

The earthquake would eventually be given a magnitude of 9.3 on the Richter scale, a number that most people would recognize as unusually high. But consider what it means. Each number you go up on the Richter scale translates into about 30 times more energy released. So a level 9 quake releases 30 times more energy than a level 8 quake and 900 times more energy than a level 7 quake.

The amount of energy that the Indian Ocean earthquake released was equal to that of 23,000 Hiroshima-size atom bombs. Or 100 gigaton bombs. That's as much energy as is used in the United States in six months.[4]

It took scientists using the newest instrumentation until the middle of 2005 to determine that the earthquake was the second largest in modern history—since quakes have been measured. The only one larger was a quake in Chile on May 22, 1960, which reached 9.5 on the Richter scale. The Indian Ocean quake caused the planet to wobble by about one inch. By making the planet spin faster, it shortened the day by about 3 millionths of a second.

The epicenter of the quake was located about 150 miles southeast from the province of Aceh on the Indonesian island of Sumatra, a region that had seen its share of trouble. Scientists have determined that two great earthquakes occurred along Sumatra in 1797 and 1861. Aceh had once been a prominent trading port and was visited by Marco Polo, the Venetian explorer, in 1292. It has been a devoutly Islamic place for more than 1,000 years and has long been known as the "doorway to Mecca" because of the many pilgrims who once stopped there while traveling by ship from the East to make the Hajj. The Dutch sought to colonize the island after taking control of it from the British in 1842, but they lost 10,000 men over the next century in an ongoing war with the Acehnese.

Nothing in this long and often difficult history could prepare the Acehnese for what was coming.

Every earthquake sets off shock waves. When quakes are deep within the ground, the energy released is more likely to dissipate within the earth's crust. This earthquake, though, was especially shallow, only about 18 miles deep. And it was beneath the sea.

After the quake began, the two sides of the ruptured seam in the earth moved up and down, shifting between 15 and 50 feet at different spots. Imagine a gash opening in the bottom of a pool, with one side of the split suddenly dropping and the other side whipping upward. What would happen to the water?

Only minutes after the earthquake, computers in Ewa Beach, Hawaii, began picking up signals. An operator at the Pacific Tsunami Warning Center there is supposed to page scientists whenever an earthquake scores at least a 6 on the Richter scale. It was clear that this one would. They would have to consider the possibility of a tsunami.

The Pacific Tsunami Warning Center was established in 1949, three years after the Hawaiian town of Hilo was practically washed away by a force of nature that its residents never saw coming. One resident, Kapua Heuer, remembered first encountering a real life sea monster:

> I looked out here and saw this great big black wall coming in like this...
> The noise was terrific, the rolling...And then you heard the screaming.
> You look and people were stomping, trying to reach earth, trying to get out.
> Dogs swimming around. Then came the crash...Well, it hit buildings, the
> lighthouse, and the railroad track, and everything...And I said, "Oh, that's
> good-bye to Hilo."[5]

By the time the monster pulled back and the waters subsided, 159 people had drowned or been crushed by floating debris. Among them were 16 students and 5 teachers at a school close to the shore, a location that in all likelihood had been considered idyllic.

Tsunami means "great harbor wave" in Japanese, although it is not born like an ordinary wave and does not act like one. Most people think of a wave and they think of a tall crest of white foam, flipped over at the top like a hair bob, with a bluish green underbelly. Maybe a surfer on top. A tsunami is a stealth killer, imperceptible to those outside the water, which is one reason that it is so dangerous. It drives through the sea without making visible waves, hardly even breaking the stillness of the water's surface. Then it sneaks up on a coastline in the form of an innocently looking but steadily rising and deadly flood.

So what would happen to the water in a pool if the bottom suddenly split and broke apart, with one section rocketing upward? The water would swish, jump, splatter. But there would be nowhere for it to go, other than harmlessly spilling over the sides. Not so an ocean.

The rapid displacement of water is the engine that drives a tsunami. There are four possible triggers for a tsunami, all major events in the life of the planet: meteorites, which are rare; underwater volcanic eruptions; landslides into bodies of water; and the most common trigger, shallow earthquakes beneath or beside an ocean.

When a shallow earthquake is set off by shifting plates, the crashing inside the earth's shell releases a torrent of energy that drives the ocean upward. What goes up, comes down. The gravity-induced movement of the ocean back toward the earth is what gives birth to a tsunami.

Waves are set off in several directions from the source. Depending on the size of the earthquake and the amount of water that is displaced, the waves can have enormous size and reach. But tsunamis do not rise into the skyline from deep in the ocean. They grow lengthwise and can stretch to more than 100 miles between the crest of one wave and the crest of the next. It is because tsunamis churn through the water horizontally that ships on the sea and planes in the air may notice nothing unusual about the waters below. And because the waves are so long, when one finally reaches shore, does its damage and recedes, it can be another hour before the next wave floods in on shell-shocked survivors who thought the worst was over.

The wave of a tsunami is practically an ocean onto itself, the length of up to 500 aircraft carriers. Yet it can propel at speeds faster than 500 miles per hour. That's fast enough to cross the Pacific Ocean in less than a day. A tsunami slows dramatically near shore, all the way down to 20 or 30 miles per hour. But by then it can be too late.

Tsunamis are impossible to predict. It is not understood why one earthquake will ignite powerful waves while another will not. In recent years, scientists have started to unearth evidence of tsunamis that took place hundreds of years ago, providing a much longer view of the gaps between tsunami-producing earthquakes in different regions. During the twentieth century alone, the world experienced 911 detectable tsunamis.[6] Only 96 were powerful enough to cause extensive damage to shorelines but even most of these were not mighty enough to capture the world's attention. Three-quarters of the century's tsunamis occurred in the Pacific Ocean, where a chain of faults in the earth's crust, known as "the ring of fire," has long set the stage for earthquakes, volcanic eruptions, and tsunamis. Otherwise, 10 percent occurred in the Mediterranean and 9 percent in the Atlantic Ocean. Only 5 percent of the century's tsunamis churned through the Indian Ocean.

While the Indian Ocean has been riled by relatively few tsunamis, one of the most powerful in history was unleashed there in 1883. The volcanic island of Krakatoa had long been said by the local population to be the home of a fire-breathing dragon. Several major eruptions had shaken the island in the distant past, but the volcano had been dormant for some 200 years. A mixture of congealed magma and rock held down the molten lava trying to burst out.

On August 27, 1883, the volcano gave way. The eruption sent out shock waves that reverberated around the planet seven times and blew up Krakatoa island. It also ignited a massive tsunami that set aim for the nearby islands of Indonesia. In little time, a train of violent waves flooded and destroyed 165 Indonesian towns and villages. More than 36,000 people died.

Why are tsunamis so deadly? It might seem that great waves and floods are escapable. When the ocean acts up, particularly after a ground-shaking earthquake, should coast dwellers not know to flee the beaches and seek high ground?

Perhaps the most ominous feature of a tsunami is its behavior when it reaches a shoreline. It practically sets up its victims, striving for the greatest possible death count. Something like evil seems to be at play as a tsunami reveals itself.

As a tsunami reaches land, its movement draws the ocean away from the shoreline. Up to a mile of the sea floor may be suddenly exposed like a drained fish tank. Facing such a bewildering scene, it is human nature for coast dwellers to move toward the dry seabed. Who wouldn't try to figure out what was happening? Imagine the day's low tide setting in all at once instead of gradually moving out over 12 hours.

But the instant exposure of the sea floor is a tsunami's calling card. As people walk among flopping fish, the first wave begins to rise and rush toward land. The front of the wave slows down at this point, but the back continues to surge and rise, creating a wall of seawater that might have red eyes and fangs if depicted by an artist. As volcanologist and tsunami expert Bill McGuire put it: "One of the big problems about trying to prevent deaths due to tsunami is trying to stop people from rushing down to the beach when the sea goes out."[7]

The only way to reduce a tsunami's destruction is to let people know that it may be on its way. Since an earthquake cannot be predicted, it is left to the scientists who watch for and measure quakes to act quickly when a quake has struck. Any time there is a sizeable quake in the Pacific Ocean, for instance, the Pacific Tsunami Warning Center goes into action. Pressure censors have been set up on the ocean floor to monitor the depth of the water above them. Any movement of the water up and down is relayed to buoys on the ocean's surface and then to a satellite, which sends the data to the warning center. This information, combined with data from coastal tide gauges, tells the warning center what the likelihood is that a tsunami will develop. In this way, the center has been able to warn communities around the Pacific of numerous tsunamis and to urge evacuations of vulnerable coastlines.

No such warning system was set up in the Indian Ocean when the second largest earthquake in modern history gave birth to a tsunami.

From the earthquake's epicenter, tsunami waves headed east and west.

It took only 15 minutes for the first eastbound wave to surge 150 miles and flood the northern shore of the Indonesian island of Sumatra. Each mile and a half of coastline was hit by 100,000 tons of water that likely washed away in an instant anyone's presumed understanding of the boundary between land and sea.[8] Video footage that was somehow taken only three blocks from what had been the shoreline showed cars and buses and trees being swept along like a child's pails and shovels. In the province of Aceh, the lower sections of industrial buildings were stripped of their facades. Concrete walls joined the rush of debris that washed over whatever got in its way. In short, the articles of everyday life became projectiles that could kill anyone who had not drowned. The eastbound train of waves surged onward to hit southern Thailand about 45 minutes later.

The first westbound waves did not hit Sri Lanka and India until some 2 hours after the quake. Hardly anyone knew that a tsunami was coming. In fact, because of the absence of a warning system in the Indian Ocean, the Pacific Tsunami Warning Center, which had been monitoring the earthquake from its first minutes, did not confirm that a tsunami had been formed until 3.5 hours after the quake. At that point, when many thousands had already been lost, the U.S. State Department began connecting the warning center to the embassies of countries that still had time to evacuate their people. The westward waves moved on to Maldives, an island nation southwest of Sri Lanka, and all the way to Africa, 4,000 miles from the earthquake's epicenter.

During the first 24 hours, the death count was estimated at tens of thousands. No one knew at that point how many were missing, how many had been swept from their homes or torn from the tree branches to which they had held. Every few weeks afterward, as the tsunami faded from the international news, the official death count climbed. Not until the following spring did the number become somewhat final, a milestone that might have been marked by a great memorial service but went essentially unnoticed.

The tsunami took about 230,000 lives, according to United Nations estimates. The vast majority, about 170,000, were lost in Indonesia, whose islands were hit first and hardest. Sri Lanka lost about 35,000 people, India 18,000, and Thailand about 8,200. An additional 51 countries lost from one to a few hundred citizens, most of whom were vacationing in or otherwise visiting the affected regions.

In addition, more than 1 million people were left homeless by the tsunami. Many of them were already poor and barely scratching by. It was initially feared that there might be 100,000 orphans whose parents were taken away by the waves. But the figure was quickly lowered to several thousands when it became apparent that most children in the raging sea's path were themselves killed. Children accounted for more than one-third of all victims.

The world's attention, of course, moved on to other things. There was the war in Iraq, terrorist attacks in Europe, another campaign to aid Africa. Hundreds of relief agencies set up shop in Indonesia and Sri Lanka. They started the laborious process of rebuilding communities that had hardly been part of the modern world before the tragedy. In the communities ravaged by the tsunami, the pain continued in numerous forms.

In Sri Lanka, for instance, civil society was ill prepared to deal with the worst disaster in the country's recorded history. Despite having perhaps the best medical services of the countries affected, there was no emergency system in place to identify the dead or dispose of bodies. Thousands of victims were buried in mass graves without being properly documented. In time, an international commission was formed to identify missing foreigners, and many bodies were exhumed with the assistance of foreign investigators. These shortcomings caused only greater suffering for Sri Lankan survivors who could not offer proper burial and religious services for their loved ones. The Human Rights Commission of Sri Lanka called into question whether the government was even interested in helping survivors and whether it could be counted on to fairly distribute foreign aid.

Survivors had to get by with little medical assistance. Doctors Without Borders sent a team of mental health professionals from Europe to Banda Aceh, the worst hit city in the province of Aceh on Sumatra, and found a near complete absence of services for devastated survivors. They discovered three psychiatrists in the entire Province of Aceh, home to 4.2 million people. All of Indonesia had only 500 clinical psychologists, about 1 for every 420,000 people. Most Indonesian people did not know what a psychologist does and associated mental health issues with shame. The medical team set up counseling for those most in need. The people of Aceh Province were used to difficult lives. Some had been involved in a violent, 40-year conflict with the Indonesian government over independence. Countless civilians had been caught in the middle, suffering intimidation at the hands of the Indonesian military. The tsunami was the latest and most severe blow to a people long under siege, most of whom turned only to Islam for solace.

"Our experience clearly shows that people know how to support each other when distressed but have no referral mechanisms when that support is not enough," the team concluded.

> The self-help and healing capacity of communities needs to be mobilized in conjunction with culturally adapted psychological interventions in which religion is acknowledged as an important coping mechanism....In Banda Aceh, many people expressed the hope that with the presence of Westerners the government will not forget them, and that the oppressive ongoing conflict will not resume as before. In other words, the mere presence of Westerners in the region is valued as important to their current sense of security.[9]

One of the many striking things about the violence delivered by the tsunami is that it could tear apart one community, ripping houses from their foundations and parents from their children, while sparing a neighboring village. The difference could be nothing more than the shape of the shoreline. Scientists who studied the damage along a coastal region of Tamil Nadu, India, determined that a naturally elevated shoreline or the simple presence of breakwaters could largely protect a village from destruction. Villages located by the mouths of rivers were hit harder.[10] The tsunami's havoc was delivered in an uneven and apparently random way.

It is sobering to grasp that the overall situation could have been much worse. The latter stages of the earthquake under the Indian Ocean unraveled much slower than the earlier stages. The northern portion of the seam between the two tectonic plates tore apart too slowly to generate additional tsunami waves. Had this portion ruptured faster, the overall size and reach of the tsunami would have been that much greater.

Only three months after the devastation, on March 28, 2005, a second massive earthquake struck off the west coast of Sumatra, a mere 100 miles from the December 26 quake. Changes in the earth's crust caused by the initial quake almost certainly created new pressure points on the fault. The stress quickly gave way and led to the second quake, itself an 8.7-grader that ranks with the great earthquakes of modern times. And there is no reason to believe that changes caused by the two quakes will not lead to a third at some point. "The 3-month delay between the two earthquakes has awakened fears that a domino-like failure of the already highly stressed plate boundary to the south and east may follow," scientist Roger Bilham wrote in a May 2005 edition of the journal *Science*.[11]

The second quake did not produce a tsunami. This may be because the quake was slightly deeper or because the fault zone ruptured differently. But the simple fact that science cannot explain why one huge quake set off a killer tsunami while a second in nearly the same spot did not shows how little we still know about the forces that shake the world. Bilham, in the same article, warned that the size and strength of the December 26 quake, followed so closely by the March 28 quake, appeared to show that science has utterly failed to grasp the dangers posed by faults in the earth's crust that have been quietly absorbing stress for a very long time.

Many seismologists are now wondering whether their assessments of future seismic hazards have been far too conservative.

Scientists—joined by a small community of passionate disaster mongers—have long predicted that a monstrous tsunami may one day strike American shores. For one thing, there's always the possibility of an asteroid hitting an ocean. Scientists are tracking 1950 DA, an asteroid two-thirds of a mile in diameter that is due to fly near the earth over the next few hundred years. Researchers at the University of California at Santa Cruz have estimated that if the asteroid hit the Atlantic Ocean at 38,000 miles per hour, it would open a cavity in the ocean about 11 miles across. The return of water toward the ocean floor would set off tsunamis that would deliver 200-foot waves to the entire East Coast of the United States in some 4 hours. Europe would be hit about 4 hours later.

It may sound farfetched, but researchers say there is evidence of past tsunamis caused by asteroids. They look for correlations between disturbed sediment on ocean floors, deposits of ocean flood sediment on land, and evidence of asteroids in the form of fragments and craters. "As these waves cross the ocean, they're going to stir up the seafloor, eroding sediments on the slopes of seamounts, and we may be able to identify more places where this has happened," said Steven Ward, one of the researchers.[12]

A more immediate threat could come from Cumbre Vieja, a volcano in the Canary Islands, which has not erupted since 1971. Scientists maintain that when it does blow, a 12-mile-long slab of rock that is slowly breaking off the volcano will finally snap and crash into the sea. The resulting tsunami could wash over Britain in 6 hours and unleash 165-foot waves over the eastern seaboard of the United States in about 10 hours. The rock is already slipping slowly from the volcano, preparing to dislodge when Cumbre Vieja erupts, maintains McGuire of the Benfield Hazard Research Centre in London, a reinsurance broker that specializes in predicting volcanic eruptions, earthquakes, landslides, tsunamis, and other forms of natural havoc. "It's happening right now and nothing can stop it," he said.[13]

Then there is Puget Sound region of Washington state, around the increasingly popular, Starbucks-rich city of Seattle. This is where the scientific record tells a scary tale and where the lessons of the Indian Ocean tsunami are being studied with urgency.

The written record of the region goes back only 200 years or so. But the record in the sediment of Puget Sound goes back further—as deep as researchers are willing to dig. In the sediment of former marshes, they look for a thin layer of sand from the ocean bed, covered over by many layers of mud and time. The evidence shows that a tsunami that may have been similar in impact to the Indian Ocean tsunami struck some 300 years ago.[14] Native Americans in the region tell multi-generation stories that seem to describe earthquakes and tsunamis. Unless the science is faulty, and these tales are myth, tsunamis have periodically hit the coast of Washington state. And one is due to hit again, as stress slowly builds along a major fault line in the Pacific Ocean. It could happen in 100 years. Or 10 years.

With little fanfare, the state of Washington is getting ready. A warning system is being put in place along the beaches to chase people inland. Sirens and loudspeakers are being mounted on poles. Because there may be no time to flee, officials are considering building tall, earthquake-proof buildings that could serve as destinations for so-called vertical evacuation. "Evacuation must be essentially complete within 30 minutes, possibly a little bit more, because you can see significant inundation begins even before that 30 minute mark," Tim Walsh, director of geological hazards for the state of Washington, said at a meeting of tsunami experts convened by *Smithsonian* magazine in February 2005. "Because this will have followed a major earthquake, the roadway is likely to at least be covered by soil slips, possibly a lot of damage to the roadway. Evacuation will have to take place on foot, and right away."

It is a scene out of a 1970s disaster flick. Chaos. People running for their lives. Children crying for their parents. Fear and prayers before death or a narrow escape. A community instantly and irrevocably transformed. Blame and guilt over what might have been done. A search for answers from above.

As I started working on this book, before I began speaking with clergy and religious leaders, I felt a need to speak with scientists who spend their lives studying the physical dimensions, the grit and dust, of natural disasters. I had just finished considerable research on the tsunami. A question was eating at me. Could scientists who study such great events that cause vast human suffering do so without wondering about the role of a higher power? I know that it is the scientist's job to focus on what is measurable and not on such existential matters. But how could anyone visiting a ravaged Indonesian community on a research project not throw down their tools and notebooks at some point? How could you not wonder about the role of God?

I reached out to a few scientists and failed miserably.

I contacted Charles McGreevy, director of the Pacific Tsunami Warning Center in Hawaii. His staff suspected that the Indian Ocean earthquake would produce a tsunami but had no access to data from the ocean and no efficient way to contact the countries in danger. I imagined that they were going through a difficult period, even if they had done nothing wrong. But McGreevy would not say whether his staff had discussed the larger meaning of the tsunami. It wasn't their business, he said.

I also reached out to Michael Rampino, a geologist at New York University with a very interesting job. He studies extinctions caused by the all-time great natural disasters of history. He concluded, for instance, that a volcanic eruption about 70,000 years ago near what is now Sumatra sent temperatures into a free-fall and led to the loss of three-quarters of plant species in the Northern Hemisphere. He is also an authority on the Krakatoa island eruption and tsunami in 1883 that devastated Indonesia. In an email to me, he dismissed my attempt to breach the science/religion boundary with one sweeping statement: "I feel these areas are not accessible to scientific discussion."

Finally, I contacted George Pararas-Carayannis, the retired director of the International Tsunami Information Center in Honolulu and one of the world's leading tsunami experts. I had higher hopes that he would take a broader view since he has been involved in many educational efforts, including an unlikely children's book about tsunamis. Instead, he focused on the human failings that allow natural disasters to cause maximum suffering. There would no need to worry about God's role in the tsunami if civil strife and political corruption in countries like Sri Lanka and Indonesia did not get in the way of preparing for disasters and taking care of people. He said:

Indeed, as a scientist I only evaluate the causes of natural disasters in terms of forces of nature on our planet—forces such as tectonic interactions and earthquakes, tsunamis or the effect of incoming solar radiation on weather disasters. I do not view the disastrous effects of natural disasters on innocent people as deliberate "Acts of God" but as manifestations of human failure by public officials in certain areas of the world to plan, prepare and adequately protect their people. Unfortunately, there is a high incidence of such disasters in underdeveloped countries around the globe where many innocent people, particularly children and women, lose their lives. The socioeconomic impact of disasters in such poor areas often exceeds their capacity to recover.[15]

People should focus on human factors rather than seeking to blame God, he said. I appreciated his willingness to add political dimensions to a scientific discussion. But it was apparent that I would have to leave the world of tectonic plates and cresting waves in order to address the elusive question of God's role in the tsunami.

2 THE FLOODS
OF THE PAST

When my wife and I were expecting our first child in 1998, she settled on a theme for the nursery. It would be Noah's Ark. I don't remember discussing it, and I'm sure that I hardly blinked at the time. I was about to become a dad, and the details of nursery preparation were not something I was inclined to care too much about. At the same time, it made sense. Who wouldn't support a roomful of wide-eyed animals marching in pairs onto a great, big boat? Our child would spend his first years surrounded by creatures great and small, from the land and the sea and the air, all teddy bear soft and innocent and perfectly at ease. The animals parading to the ark always look so secure, so comfortable, like they know exactly what they are doing. And why. And for whom. They are heading on a journey that can hardly be explained in illustrations for children. But the march of the animals is always depicted as implicitly hopeful. You can almost hear the animals walking and flapping in step, like a kindergarten class entering its classroom on the first day of school, all new and fresh and optimistic.

The story is so ingrained in our culture that it's easy to take for granted. Over time, it has evolved from a purely biblical story into something like a folk tale. The ark is everywhere in popular culture, especially that portion of pop culture that is aimed at young children. Noah is often absent from children's versions of his story. The stars are always the animals and the ark itself. The animals, of course, represent rebirth, a fresh start, a return to innocence. They are heading off to make a better world. The ark is home, a safe and secure oasis, removed from whatever might be outside. What better theme for a nursery? So when my first son, Raymond, was born, he slept on tiny sheets covered with drawings of the ark. As I write this, he is weeks from starting first grade and still sleeps most nights with a small blanket that shows elephants protruding from windows on the ark, giraffes raising their long necks above the top deck, and smiling seals in the waters right outside. A banner on the mast of the ark reads "Animal Crackers."

I recently went back to look at some popular children's books about Noah's Ark, which continue to introduce the story to new generations. I was immediately drawn to the velvety illustrations in Jan Brett's *On Noah's Ark,* which has Noah's granddaughter telling the tale. "Grandpa Noah says that the rains are coming," she says. "Soon the land will be covered with water."[1] The book shows small animals squeezing onto the boat and big animals thumping and bumping their way past. Even the blue-gray ocean looks calm, almost soothing, during the storms. Andrew Elborn and Ivan Gantschev's *Noah and the Ark and the Animals* represents those riskier books that attempt to tackle what happens *outside* the ark. Their story, told by a mother mare to her calf, explains that Noah was an exception to other men who lied and stole. "God told Noah that a great flood would come to wash away all the people who had forgotten how to be good, a flood that would clean up the whole earth." Most of the book shows the dreamy march of tigers, lizards, and insects onto the ark before the flood subsides and the animals are sent forth to replenish the world. "And God promised Noah and all the other living creatures that there would never be another great flood. Then He put a rainbow in the sky as a sign to remind all the earth of the promise and of His love for every living creature."[2]

I do not cite these books to critique the way they tell the story. Not at all. Nor do I think that children's books ought to scare their small readers with details about devastation and death. I believe, on the contrary, that pop culture's adaptation of the ark story is appropriate and meaningful. We want our children to believe in endless possibilities and the general hope that tomorrow can be better than today. Plus, every parent knows that anything involving animals, real or imagined, is your best hope of getting kids to pay attention, eat their breakfast, get dressed, practice their letters, and on and on.

But the popular emphasis on animals and rebirth is only one side of the story.

The other side of the story has to do with sin and punishment. It's about humankind's pitiful failure and God's ugly wrath. We all know God's charges to Noah, even if it seems that there is a social contract to talk about it only when necessary. We know why Noah had to build the ark. We know what must have happened to Noah's flawed neighbors after the rains began and the ark set off. But who wants to think about the implications of the story, of God's deep reserve of anger and violence (unless you practice a faith that focuses on mankind's sinfulness). For most people, it's safer to stick with the promise of rebirth, with pairs of animals starting new chains of life.

Then something like the tsunami happens. In trying to make sense of it, we remember that the story of the great flood is one of the central stories of Western culture, a tale that has been used to explain God's relationship with man for thousands of years. In the first days after the tsunami, the devastating flood was often called a tragedy of biblical proportion. Well, the great flood, Noah's flood, set that biblical standard of doom. And it was brought on by the creator of the universe, an inescapable part of the ark story that has colored the way half the world interprets natural disasters since long before we understood what makes the earth's surface rumble.

I could not see writing a book about the religious meaning of the tsunami without considering the impact of the ark story on our culture. For one thing, countless Jews, Christians, and Muslims (yes, Prophet Noah is in the Quran, although the flood is depicted as regional, not worldwide) have absorbed the message of the story that God may actively punish those who sin. The story is interpreted in many ways, of course. Many people may not even be aware that the story has touched their consciousness. But the great flood, in a sense, has washed over all of us.

If you have any doubts, don't forget that the story's meaning is still being fought over today. Evangelical Christian explorers are still trying to prove that a universal flood took place, hundreds of years after supposedly enlightened theologians dismissed the flood as myth. A book available at the Grand Canyon gift shop contends that the great flood *created* the canyon and that fossils found there are the remains of plants and animals that died in the flood. Big-budget journeys continue to search for the remains of the ark. The prize: proof of the Bible's authenticity as God's revealed word. The growing battle between those who support the theory of evolution and those who stand behind what is called creationism—in effect, a literal or semi-literal interpretation of the book of Genesis—ensures that the interest in Noah's journey and the meaning of the great flood will not subside any time soon.

This chapter will also consider flood stories and myths from other cultures. These stories seem to show that widely different cultures have shared a similar communal need to remember great floods that washed away sin and offered an opportunity for redemption. Many of these stories pose a challenge to creationists, fundamentalists, and other literal readers of Genesis, since they raise the possibility that the story of Noah was simply modeled on the myths of other cultures. Or, at least, that is one conclusion offered by scholars.

Then we will jump forward to 1755. This was the year that a great earth-quake, a tsunami, and a major fire destroyed the city of Lisbon, killing about 70,000 people. It was a disaster that took place at a significant time in history, when the fathers of the Enlightenment were breaking social traditions and challenging religious and other authorities in favor of a radical emphasis on human reason. For centuries prior, natural disasters were seen as messages from God, fire-breathing expressions of the Almighty's displeasure. Now for the first time, some were contending that Lisbon's misfortune was the result of unfeeling natural forces and that it was Portugal's responsibility to care for the people and rebuild, rather than to waste time blaming God. Russell Dynes, one of America's leading experts on the history of disasters, has described the Lisbon earthquake as "the first modern disaster." It relaxed Noah's hold on those trying to make sense of the world, at least for a time.

Finally, I will conclude this chapter with a short look at the lessons left to us by Job. It's true that Job was not the victim of a tsunami or an earthquake. But you can say that his individual suffering was a single, concentrated natu-ral disaster, an *Act of God* for the ages. The questions asked of him in the book of Job and the rich, timeless answers he gives will always be reexamined in times of great suffering, as they were after the tsunami of 2004.

In an age when the Internet and 24-hour television have opened a global window onto all sorts of day-to-day suffering, we can always turn to a weath-ered copy of the book of Genesis for some universal context. God told Noah that he was going to wipe out virtually the entire human race and most other living things. He would not limit the destruction to any particular class, not even to the most wicked. "I have decided to put an end to all flesh," he explained. The narrator of Genesis told what happened:

> And all flesh that stirred on earth perished—birds, cattle, beasts, and all the
> things that swarmed upon the earth, and all mankind. All in whose nostrils
> was the merest breath of life, all that was on dry land, died. All existence on
> earth was blotted out—man, cattle, creeping things, and birds of the sky; they
> were blotted out from the earth. Only Noah was left, and those with him in
> the ark.[3]

The flood comes only pages after God creates heaven and earth, only a few passages after we are introduced to the Garden of Eden, Adam and Eve, Cain and Abel. There are only enough words for Eve to bite the apple, for Cain to kill Abel, and for the narrator to outline Adam's descendants before God decides to blot out his creations. Only ten generations have passed since Adam when God describes his plans to 600-year-old Noah, who was either a righteous man or a relatively righteous man for a wicked age, depending on one's interpretation. It was a bad scene, on a metaphysical level as well as in purely human terms, as the Torah scholar Richard Elliott Friedman explains:

> One must have a picture of the structure of the universe that is described in Genesis 1 in order to comprehend the significance of the destruction that is narrated in the flood story. The creation account pictures a clear firmament or space holding back the waters that are above the firmament and those that are below. Now the narrator reports that "all the fountains of the great deep were split open, and the apertures of the skies were opened." The cosmic waters are able to spill in from above and below, filling the habitable bubble, thus: It is far more than an ordinary rain. It is a cosmic crisis in which the very structure of the universe is endangered.[4]

If you read Genesis word for word, without considering the centuries of published analysis by theologians and clergy, it's hard to walk away feeling that you understand the creator's actions. Genesis gives little explanation for God's wrath, other than to cite humankind's wickedness in the broadest of strokes. The Quran, too, leaves the faithful to assume that people chose to behave badly and were justly punished by Allah. After a chapter that describes the rewards of paradise vs. the ugliness of hell, a short chapter titled "Noah" (or *Nuh* in Arabic) begins simply: "We sent forth Noah to his people, saying 'Give warning to your people before a woeful scourge overtakes them.'"[5] Throughout the Quran, the story of the flood is repeatedly raised as a reminder to obey Allah and of what can happen if you do not.

The noted religion scholar Karen Armstrong writes that the flood, as described in Genesis, is nothing short of shocking. "Nothing has prepared us for this merciless divine violence. We have seen that human beings are sinful, but we have also seen that pathos of the human condition. Indeed, it has appeared that the conflict in the human heart is at least in part attributable to the Creator."[6] Armstrong writes that it is also hard to know what to make of Noah, who is portrayed in Genesis as little more than a dutiful soldier. He does not beg for God's mercy, as Abraham does when God announces his plans to destroy the cities of Sodom and Gomorrah because of their residents' sinful ways.

Interestingly, in the Quran, Noah not only fails to plead humankind's case, he begs God to destroy the evildoers. To be fair, he first calls on his people to turn away from sin and serve Allah. But they ignore him and commit the gravest sin of worshiping false gods. So Noah declares:

> Lord, do not leave a single unbeliever in the land. If You spare them they will mislead Your servants and beget none but sinners and unbelievers. Forgive

me, Lord, and forgive my parents and every true believer who seeks refuge in
my house. Forgive all the faithful, men and women, and hasten the destruction
of the wrongdoers.[7]

The Islamic scholar Muhammad Shaykh Sarwar writes that the Noah of
the Quran is a prophet, not simply a messenger.

> The Old Testament's Noah is portrayed as simply carrying out the orders of
> his God. The Koran's Noah takes a more active role, praying to Allah not to
> allow the unrepentant, sinful people of his era to survive the flood. Noah's
> prayer parallels the earlier (Koranic) Prophetic mission of Abraham. Both
> missions explicitly condemn not just the sinfulness of unbelievers, but also their
> strong attraction to the sin of idolatry.[8]

According to the most orthodox traditions of Judaism and Christianity, the
book of Genesis was dictated to Moses by God. More liberal Jewish and
Christian traditions offer a wide range of interpretations on the origins of
Scripture. Regardless, Armstrong feels that the God of Genesis is difficult to
forgive:

> The twentieth century has been long holocaust. We have seen too much
> massacre and genocide to condone such behavior in our God. Believers who
> rush to God's defense here should reflect that if we excuse a deity who almost
> destroys the entire human race, it is all too easy to justify earthly rulers who
> have undertaken similar purges.[9]

The flood story, Armstrong says, maintains a hold over us because it
demonstrates God's power. But Genesis offers few easy answers or even a
consistent image of God, even as people facing modern-day suffering turn
to it for explanation:

> When we contemplate the tragedy of a world convulsed repeatedly by natural
> catastrophes which wipe out thousands of innocent people, to say nothing of
> the atrocities committed by human beings, it is very hard to believe that there
> is a benevolent deity in charge of the world. The authors of Genesis do not
> attempt to deny the theological differences inherent in monotheism. We should
> not construct a theology that is so facile that it enables us to blunt our sense of
> life's horror and cruelty; rather we should admit that, like Jacob, we have to wres-
> tle painfully in the dark before we can discern the divine in such circumstances.[10]

For centuries, Jewish and Christian scholars scrambled to explain, analyze,
interpret, and spin the story of the flood, not to mention the entirety of

creation as outlined in Genesis (I would imagine that much has been written about the Quran's version, but most English-language studies of Islam's holy book only describe what the Quran says without delving into what it means or how interpretations of the flood have changed). I have neither the space nor the knowledge to outline the long, complex evolution of thinking regarding God's punishment of the first ten generations—God's curious desire to start over after being seemingly surprised by the failings of his all-too-human creations. But suffice it to say that no damp stone in the post-flood world was left unturned by believers seeking to explain God's actions. As the British scholar Norman Cohn put it:

> What could be more enthralling than to treat the story of the Flood as a realistic but incomplete historical narrative—to enquire after all those points of detail which Genesis failed to consider, to solve all those problems which it failed to tackle? Jews as well as Christians addressed these tasks with enthusiasm.[11]

Cohn, for instance, looks at some of the myriad issues studied by the rabbis who wrote the *Genesis Rabbah,* a Midrash or commentary that includes analysis through about the year 400 and considers Genesis verse by verse. Among other things, the rabbis argued (often without consensus): that the generations before the flood showed no gratitude toward God and lived immoral lives; that people ignored Noah's warnings of a flood for 120 years or believed that they could escape the waters and God's anger; that there were between 330 and 900 compartments on the ark but no clear accommodations for unclean animals; that the flood waters were boiling hot to further punish sinners; and that Noah did not sleep for a year because he was so busy tending to the animals.

Cohn also surveys some influential Christian thinkers, who accept the truth of the flood story while finding clues and predictions of the coming of Christ. No less a figure than Augustine looked to the ark for clear and powerful messianic meaning. In his epic *The City of God,* Augustine writes that every aspect of the ark's construction is symbolic of something to come in the Christian church. The door on the ark's side, for instance, "certainly signified the wound which was made when the side of the Crucified was pierced with the spear." He offers that the three stories of the ark may stand for the three virtues praised by the apostles: faith, hope, and charity. "Or even more suitably they may be supposed to represent those three harvests in the gospel, thirtyfold, sixtyfold, and hundredfold— chaste marriage dwelling in the ground floor, chaste widowhood in the upper, and chaste virginity in the top storey."[12] Non-Christians and even many Christians may scoff at the theologian's leap. But Augustine's thirst to find meaning in every corner of the ark shows the flood story's power.

The context for reading the Genesis story of the flood changed dramatically during the mid-1800s. A rich period of Middle Eastern archeology yielded several history-changing tales from the ancient civilization of Mesopotamia, where maps now show Iraq. These tales were written as poems and preserved mostly on clay tablets in the Akkadian language. Several of them include stories of a great flood, a flood that scholars believe may have hit an ancient Sumerian city. The stories date back to 2000 BC and some scholars believe they predate the book of Genesis.

The earliest of the flood tales concerns the Sumerian king Ziusudra, who builds a boat to survive a flood sent by the gods and is eventually rewarded by them for preserving humankind. A more fully intact story is known as the Atrahasis Epic and is believed to date from around 1700 BC. It fleshes out the earlier story, explaining that the ornery gods created humankind to take over some of their labors, but that people multiplied too quickly and became too noisy. The gods try to reduce the population through plague and drought, but eventually decide on a flood and tell a wise and devout king, Atrahasis, to build a boat: "Reject possessions, and save living things...Roof it like the Apsu/So that the Sun cannot see inside it!/Make upper decks and lower decks./The tackle must be very strong,/The bitumen strong, to give strength./I shall make rain fall on you here."[13]

The Atrahasis Epic, finally, is folded into the Epic of Gilgamesh, the most famous of the Mesopotamian myths. This long poem, believed to tell the story of another king/conqueror who lived between 2800 and 2500 BC, describes a flood that even the gods feared and that some regretted. A "Mistress of the Gods" says she should have ordered a battle to destroy her people because it would have been more humane than watching them drown:

> I myself gave birth (to them), they are my own people,
> Yet they fill the sea like fish spawn![14]

Scholars agree that these Mesopotamian myths had incredible reach for the time, crossing all kinds of geographic and cultural boundaries to give birth to regional myths. Stephanie Dalley, who participated in Middle Eastern excavations and translated numerous works from Mesopotamia, wrote that the myths were universally known in antiquity and were translated into the major languages of the day, Sumerian, Hittite, Hurrian, and Hebrew:

> This happened partly because Akkadian was the language of diplomacy throughout the ancient Near East from the mid-second to mid-first millennium BC, even in Egypt, Anatolia, and Iran, and trainee scribes in those far-flung countries practiced their skills on Akkadian literary texts; also because strong nomadic and mercantile elements in the population traveled enormous distances, because national boundaries frequently changed, and because trading colonies abroad were ubiquitous. Therefore Akkadian stories share common ground with tales in the Old Testament, the *Iliad,* the *Odyssey,* the works of Hesiod, and the *Arabian Nights;* they were popular with an international audience at the dawn of history.[15]

A family of flood myths spread around the world, a diaspora that may have descended from the "genesis" of flood stories in Mesopotamia. Maybe the stories survived because different cultures needed context to explain their own local or regional floods. Many flood myths have tried to spin the moral of the stories away from divine punishment and toward a future filled with hope, just as our popular culture does with Noah and the ark today. David Leeming, a scholar of myth, writes that many flood stories are connected to stories about the creation of the world (like in Genesis). After humankind falls short of God's plan, a cleansing flood gives both God and humankind a second chance—and reminds future generations that rebirth as well as punishment remains forever possible. The flood hero

> represents the positive seed of the original creation, which we hope lies in all of us. Whether he is called Ziusudra (Sumerian), Utnapishtim (Babylonian), Noah (Hebrew), Manu (Indian), or Deucalion (Greek), he is the representative of the craving for life that makes it possible for us to face the worst adversities...The persistence of this archetype, expressed so universally in deluge myths, suggests an important aspect of humanity's vision of both its own imperfections and of the possibility of redemption in a new beginning.[16]

Such myths may have noble and hope-filled reasons to be. But if they all have their roots in Mesopotamia and survive because of a shared need across cultures for explanation in times of crises, what does this mean for Jews and Christians who read the book of Genesis literally or for Muslims who only know how to read the Quran as the angel Gabriel's dictation to the prophet Mohammed? There are no easy answers. In the West, at least, tradition-minded Christians and Jews have had to defend their beliefs from academic deconstruction for more than a century. By the early twentieth century, secular scholars of religion were dismissing the flood story as an unusually hearty myth, propped up by stubborn religious traditions intent on holding up both the story's example of punishment for sin and its promise of rebirth for believers. In a section on the deluge, for instance, in the *Encyclopedia of Religion and Ethics,* a monumental, eleven-volume series compiled between 1908 and 1927, the story of the flood is swatted away as a relic of the prescientific age. Its writers maintained, in the most high-minded language, that a basic knowledge of geology and of flood myths leads anyone to conclude that Noah was no more than a colorful hero of folklore, Johnny Appleseed in a boat. "It need hardly be added that the religious value of the Bible story does not lie in its improbabilities, which sometimes amount, as has been shown, to absurdities, but rather in the religious and moral lessons...that Jahweh hated and would punish sin, but would save those who were faithful and obedient."[17]

Each religious tradition has dealt in its own way with academic and scientific arguments that question the flood story. Many traditions have loosened their interpretations of the story, and of other narratives from Genesis, to conclude that the flood is somewhere between pure myth and representative of a single or even several actual events. Others maintain that the story in Genesis (or the Quran) is God's revealed truth and took place as described, even if we cannot explain how or where Noah and the animals did their duty. Still others hold to a middle ground, seeking to find truth even if the details of the flood story cannot be defended. A Torah commentary released by the Conservative movement of Judaism in 2001, for instance, deals directly with the potential meaning of the Mesopotamian flood stories. An essay by Rabbi Robert Wexler offers:

> The most likely assumption we can make is that both Genesis and Gilgamesh drew their material from a common tradition about the flood that existed in Mesopotamia. These stories then diverged in the retelling. Each account was shaped and refined by a specific religious message and embellished by the imagination of those who transmitted it through the generations.[18]

The Catholic Encyclopedia does not address specific historical challenges to the story in Genesis but acknowledges that the story faces difficulties that call into question its literal meaning:

> The opinion that these chapters are mere legendary tales, Eastern folklore, is held by some non-Catholic scholars; according to others, with whom several Catholics side, they preserve, under the embroidery of poetical parlance, the memory of a fact handed down by a very old tradition. This view, were it

supported by good arguments, could be readily accepted by a Catholic; it has, over the age-long opinion that every detail of the narration should be literally interpreted and trusted in by the historian, the advantage of suppressing as meaningless some difficulties once deemed unanswerable.[19]

The search for Noah's Ark has only intensified in recent decades. This is true whether talking about actual expeditions for the boat, spiritual journeys in search of the meaning of the story, or scientific queries to identify actual floods that may have been—or fed into stories about—the Great Flood. A centuries-old battle over the flood, over what it was and what it means, only seems to be heating up, stoked by the larger culture wars between orthodox, Bible-quoting religionists and the more secular or modernist crowd.

No one knows how many explorers have visited Mount Ararat in northern Turkey, long believed to be the landing spot of Noah's Ark. There are stories of monks ascending the almost 17,000-foot peak, which date back as far as the fourth century. The first modern expedition is believed to have taken place in 1829. French explorer Fernand Navarra made several journeys during the 1950s and the 1960s and claimed to bring back a piece of wood from the ark, but scientists later discredited his discovery. Numerous Americans joined the club during the 1970s and the 1980s, often producing books or videos that revealed "dramatic" if wholly unclear evidence of boat-shaped sections of Ararat or nearby mountains.

For many scholars, what we know, or think we know, about the great flood was radically changed during the 1990s by two prominent geologists. William Ryan and Walter Pitman offered a wide range of evidence that 7,600 years ago vast amounts of water from the Mediterranean Sea had blasted through a narrow valley and inundated a fresh water lake that is now the Black Sea. The lake became a salt sea and its coast was destroyed, washed away, by unimaginable floods. Their theory, compiled in a 1998 book and a National Geographic television special, became that the survivors of this flood scattered far and wide, telling a tale that would over time evolve and spawn new sagas. The story may have influenced Mesopotamian mythology and, the theory goes, could well have provided a framework for the writers of the book of Genesis to introduce a single, all-powerful God who does not take lightly the moral indiscretions of his human creations. Ryan and Pitman described it this way:

The flood myth lives for a number of reasons. First, it is surely a true story of the permanent destruction of a land and its people and a culture suddenly and catastrophically inundated, of farmers uprooted from their hard-won fields, their villages permanently destroyed. . . So the tragedy was indelibly implanted in their oral history. Over the thousands of years since, with war, invasion, migrations, and other calamities, the legend disappeared from the folk memory of many. However, to those who fled to Mesopotamia and whose progeny are still there, the flood lived on.[20]

Of course, many readers of Genesis have rejected Ryan and Pitman's theory, just as they have rejected academic arguments that other flood myths may have influenced the writers of Genesis. There is no shortage of Christian apologists anxious to defend the Bible's historical accuracy from all scientific or man-made theories. There are certainly Orthodox Jews who are ready and able to do the same, if less interested in debating the wider culture. And, without a doubt, much of the Muslim world would find it strange and insulting to have to defend the Quran's description of the great flood and how Noah's boat protected the species as Allah desired.

For a good sense of the forces aligned to defend the story of the flood, consider the international evangelical group "Answers in Genesis." Organized to help Christians protect the book of Genesis from attack, the group runs a sophisticated Web site that offers detailed comebacks to the common positions of scientists and other doubters. "How did Noah's family dispose of the waste of thousands of animals every day? The amount of labor could be minimized in many ways. Possibly they had sloped floors and/or slatted cages, where the manure could fall away from the animals and be flushed away." And how did animals get to the ark? "If there was only one continent at that time, then questions of getting animals from remote regions to the ark are not relevant." Could there have been dinosaurs on the ark? "The largest animals were probably represented by 'teenage' or even younger specimens. It may seem surprising, but the median size of all animals on the Ark would most likely have been that of a small rat."[21]

And the debate continues. In fact, a slightly broader debate over the depiction of creation in Genesis has evolved into one of the defining battles of the culture wars. In growing numbers of states, creationists—or those promoting the pseudo-scientific idea of intelligent design—are challenging the teaching of evolution in public schools.

Whatever camp you're in, whether you see Scripture as God's inerrant word, as divinely inspired, as meaningful mythology, or simply as a collection of stories, the saga of Noah's Ark and the great flood has likely touched you in some way. If you are a Jew, a Christian, or a Muslim, purely orthodox or divorced from traditional belief, you have probably grown up surrounded by images of pairs of animals marching toward rebirth—and away from torturous punishment. Whether you believe it happened or not, the flood is part of the foundation of Western thinking about sin, natural disasters, and the relationship between God and humankind.

In a sense, the great flood rushed on for centuries, refusing to subside. Its story continued to help define the way people reacted to natural disasters, to the unexplainable forces that could cause vast human suffering in an instant and leave survivors shattered. When the ground shook, it was punishment from God. What else could it be?

Everything changed on the morning of November 1, 1755, All Saints' Day, when a massive earthquake hit Lisbon, the fourth largest city in Europe. Many city dwellers were in church and were likely saying their prayers when they were buried in rubble. A tsunami washed over the ports. A fire swept through many of the buildings that had withstood the quake. Tens of thousands died.

This disaster might have been explained like those before it, as another *Act of God,* had it not fallen in the middle of the Enlightenment. Old modes of thought were already being questioned. The institutions of church and state were facing polite skepticism from some intellectuals and artists and open rebellion from others. The time was right for a new kind of public debate, especially over the meaning of something as overwhelmingly as an earthquake. Many of the positions taken and questions raised, considered radical at the time, continue to resonate today when disaster strikes. This was never so clear as during the weeks after the 2004 tsunami, when numerous writers, at a loss for ways to make sense of a mind-numbing disaster in a mysterious part of the world, retreated for the words of Voltaire and Rousseau.

The early reactions to the Lisbon quake had been predictable. Numerous clerics announced that God had lost patience with the sinful ways of a city where traders had built great wealth. In addition, Protestants pointed out that Lisbon was predominantly Catholic, implying God's disapproval. Catholics who had problems with the Jesuits made use of the fact that Lisbon was the Jesuits' capital. And on and on.

Into the fray stepped Voltaire, the philosopher-king of Enlightenment thinkers, who would define much of his legacy by reacting to the earthquake. Voltaire was already known as an intellectual rebel-rouser who loved to tangle with government officials, church leaders, and more mainstream thinkers. He had big problems with the so-called "optimists" of the day, philosophers who believed in a wise, rational creator and insisted that humankind lived in the best of all possible worlds. Voltaire wanted to believe that and certainly agreed on the presence of a creator. One of his most famous lines remains: "If God did not exist, it would be necessary to invent him, but all nature cries out to us that he does exist." Still, Voltaire could not hop on the optimism bandwagon. He saw too many contradictions.

Then came the earthquake. Within weeks, he wrote one of his most lasting poems, *Poem on the Lisbon Disaster, or An Examination of the Axiom "All is Well."* He offered no solace, no attempt at explanation, but mocked both those who saw the earthquake as God's punishment and those who insisted that this world was the best we could hope for. He asked the questions that people still ask when natural acts kill the innocent and God must be a participant or a bystander:

> Cannot then God direct all nature's course?
> Can power almighty be without resource?[22]

In their epic *The Story of Civilization,* Will Durant and Ariel Durant tried to describe Voltaire's mind set:

> The poet looks upon the world of life, and sees everywhere, in a thousand forms, a struggle for existence, in which every organism, sooner or later, is slain...How does this scene of universal strife and ignominious, agonizing death comport with the belief in a good God? He exists, but he is a baffling mystery. He sent his son to redeem mankind, yet the earth and man remain the same despite his sacrifice.[23]

Rousseau stepped forward to challenge Voltaire's dark words, writing in a letter to Voltaire that he remained consoled by the knowledge of God's good intentions. "I do not see how one can search for the source of moral evil anywhere but in man," he wrote. Rousseau insisted that far fewer people would have died if they did not live in large, densely populated dwellings close to the shore. And he raised the larger question—asked by clergy and others after the tsunami—of whether it was truly worse to die suddenly in an earthquake than from a slow disease or other natural causes. People die every day, he said, and we do not question God's intentions. What makes the earthquake different?

Voltaire would respond in kind through perhaps his most famous work, the scathing and satirical *Candide,* which became a best-selling book of 1759. The story tells of the main character, Candide, traveling the world and encountering both suffering and self-satisfied explanations for suffering. The story mentions the Lisbon quake but goes far beyond it to argue that people are sitting ducks in a world that makes little sense.

The exchange between Voltaire and Rousseau was far more meaningful than they and their contemporaries might have imagined. Not only did they break from centuries of simple, black-and-white explanations for natural disasters, modeled on the lessons of the great flood, but their arguments and counterarguments set up a rich, human framework for trying to understand natural evil, one that is still used today. This is not to say that Voltaire and Rousseau offered answers that satisfy or allow us to move on from catastrophe without pangs of doubt, anger, fear, and hopelessness. But they settled on what might be the meaningful perspectives we have—not answers, really—when there is otherwise nothing to say.

Rousseau offered two arguments that still resonate and were especially popular after the tsunami, Hurricane Katrina, and the Pakistani quake. In regard to faith, he reemphasized his belief in God and in a world in which good and evil live side by side. The suffering of innocents is no reason to disavow God's work in the universe, much of which is good. Nothing about the Lisbon quake made him think any different. This basic statement of faith is uttered time and again by modern clergy and the faithful.

In regard to humankind's own culpability when natural disasters lead to great loss of life, Rousseau took a truly original turn. His contention that the people of Lisbon made themselves especially vulnerable to an earthquake and tsunami by living in tall dwellings, crammed together, right by the water, is now echoed after each major natural disaster. Activists, politicians, and the media all blame government for poor planning and for not looking out for the public good. They blame businesspeople and developers for greedily planning homes and industry too close to shorelines, in disaster's way. Disaster-historian Dynes has credited Rousseau with offering the first social science view of natural disasters, a philosophy that would not be tapped again for almost two centuries. "It was Rousseau's argument that to understand the meaning of Lisbon depended not just on the overarching philosophical assumptions but on an understanding of the social structure and culture in a specific community."[24]

Voltaire, too, left behind a sophisticated, challenging philosophical outlook for those who believe in God and see order in the universe but cannot come to terms with wanton suffering. He did not simply blame humankind's sinful ways or give a pass to God. Instead, he railed at God, questioned the meaning of it all, but held onto a desperate, but ultimately hopeful, faith. This outlook has been widely adopted by Americans who believe in God but refuse to accept simplistic explanations for our often troubled existence. It is a defining characteristic of mainline Protestantism, much of Judaism, and other mainstream religious movements with a modernist bent.

One Voltaire biographer, Alfred Noyes, has noted that Voltaire is often seen as antireligious because he was pitted against religious optimists after the Lisbon quake. "Voltaire's Poem on the Lisbon Earthquake is, by tradition, among those who do not read it, a bitter and despairing rejection of the idea that the universe has a beneficent Ruler." But Voltaire mocked shallow paeans to God, insisting instead on an honest grappling with life's meaning and God's role in the world.

> No new principle was involved; but Voltaire seized the occasion to elucidate his own philosophy; and this philosophy, properly examined, is about as near to the true philosophy of Christendom as any man, in any literature, has ever expressed without availing himself of Christian dogma. He arrives at it, by the honesty of his own questioning, and as a philosopher.[25]

Job. A synonym for suffering. Everyone knows Job the sufferer, whose limitless ability to absorb punishment is evoked in the face of every kind of challenge, great and small. But Job's universal renown, his leading role in the human drama, is not due merely to his unyielding faith or his superhuman patience. It is due to his willingness to point his finger at God, to ask the questions of God that everyone ask when blind sided by suffering that cannot be explained. Job represents all of humankind when he admits that he is not up to the task of remaining docile in his faith as his world crumbles around him. He stands in for every man and woman when he admits that he has lost his place in the universe, that nothing makes sense any longer. He asks "Why? Why me?" for everyone who lost their loved ones, their homes, or their hope in Sumatra or New Orleans or Kashmir. Job's example will be cited, as a last resort by some, for as long as hurting people seek consolation.

As the Orthodox Christian theologian John Garvey wrote weeks after the tsunami: "The Book of Job, in which a good man is afflicted by a seemingly capricious God, provides us with the best answer to the problem of evil, and it isn't an answer."[26]

The outlines of Job's confrontation with God are well known. He had it all, a large family, great wealth, and greater integrity. A good man. But God, in what comes across as a cosmic bet, allows Satan to test Job's faith by taking away his family and wealth and attacking his body with ailments. Job loses everything—like the distraught survivor of a natural disaster. Then he has to listen to his friends tell him to accept God's will and the fact that he was probably guilty in some way.

But Job knows that, while he is not perfect, he has tried to do good. So he lashes out at God:

> I cry out to You, but You do not answer me;
> I wait, but You do not consider me.
> You have become cruel to me;
> With Your powerful hand You harass me.
> You lift me up and mount me on the wind;
> You make my courage melt.[27]

Job's long, emotional plea strikes a divine nerve. God speaks to him. But rather than addressing Job's complaints, God condemns Job's—and human-kind's—right and ability to question his creator.

> Would you impugn My justice?
> Would you condemn Me that you may be right?
> Have you an arm like God's?
> Can you thunder with a voice like His?[28]

Job relents and apologizes. He says that he spoke without understanding. That's good enough for God, who gives Job a new family and greater riches than before. So Job says his piece, gets no answers, but dies "old and con-tented," according to the last line of the book.

So what kind of piece of mind do we get? The religious scholar J. David Pleins, speaking on a panel about the tsunami at Santa Clara University in California, said that Job makes us feel less alone by asking our questions and getting a "no comment" from God.

> This is the crux of the book: By challenging God and rejecting the received wisdom about suffering, Job went to a deeper theological level than his friends...Rather than giving us the answers about God's justice and the meaning of life, the Book of Job teaches us how to live as people with faith in the question "why?" Perhaps that's the only answer we can hope for.[29]

Perhaps. But that still does not mean it's enough. Elie Wiesel writes that he was offended by Job's submission. Job appeared more human when he was cursed and grief-stricken, Wiesel says, than when he simply rebuilt his life by having more children and tending to his land and animals.

> He should not have given in so easily. He should have continued to protest, to refuse the handouts. He should have said to God: Very well, I forgive You, I forgive You to the extent of my sorrow, my anguish. But what about my dead children, do they forgive You?...I demand that justice be done to them, if not to me, and that the trial continue.

Wiesel is so dissatisfied with the ending of the book of Job that he sees a deeper, almost hidden, meaning. Job relented so quickly as a sign to us—a wink-wink—that he was continuing to interrogate God.

> By repenting sins he did not commit, by justifying a sorrow he did not deserve, he communicates to us that he did not believe in his own confessions; they were

nothing but decoys. Job personified man's eternal quest for justice and truth—he did not choose resignation. Thus he did not suffer in vain; thanks to him, we know that it is given to man to transform divine justice into human justice and compassion.[30]

3 THE JEWISH PERSPECTIVE

There is an old joke that if you put twenty-five Jews in a room, you'll get at least twenty-five opinions. It may well be true when it comes to understanding God's role in human suffering. The Torah introduces a God who is intimately involved in our lives. The Jewish people, who are presented as the people chosen by God to deliver monotheism to the world, have always focused on their relationship with God. The God of the Torah is right there, acting as a shepherd to the Jewish people—guiding them, warning them, making promises to them, judging them, protecting them. But Judaism is also known for raising questions above answers (or at least to an equal plane). There is hardly a Jew who will seriously confront the nature of suffering without raising the story of Job, who rails at God without forgetting that he is God's creation. The story remains so powerful not because of the incredible suffering that Job must endure, but because he is able to strike that balance.

RABBI HAROLD KUSHNER/FACING THE UNDENIABLE

Anytime I told someone I was working on this project, the chances were good that they would say something along the lines of "Are you going to talk to that rabbi, you know, the one who wrote the book?" Often, they would think for a second and then recall the supposed name of the book, "Why Bad Things Happen to Good People." Yes, yes, I would tell them. I'm going to talk to Harold Kushner—or I already have. And then I would feel obligated to correct them. The title of the book is *When Bad Things Happen to Good People*. When, not why. One of the main points of the book is that we have no answers for "Why?" But Kushner had a lot to say, and still does, about what happens when bad things happen to good people.

I was little intimidated to speak with Kushner. This is a man who has endured tremendous suffering and channeled his experiences in such a way that he has been able to help countless others. *When Bad Things Happen to Good People,* first published in 1981, has sold more than 4 million copies. And it paved the way for him to write other books like *The Lord Is My Shepherd* and *Living a Life That Matters* that, while they are not cultural touchstones, have become best-sellers that have also brought solace and wisdom to those in need. What could I ask him about natural disasters— about any source of suffering—that he hasn't been asked 10,000 times?

Kushner's story is well known. He was the young rabbi at a Conservative synagogue in a suburb of Boston when his 3-year-old son, Aaron, was diagnosed with progeria. This is the "rapid aging" disease that makes a child look like an old person while still in his or her teens and takes the person's life soon after. Aaron died two days before his fourteenth birthday, and his father would set out to write *When Bad Things Happen to Good People.* Anyone who has read it has surely been struck by the opening line: "This is not an abstract book about God and theology."

The night I called Kushner, he was busy and said to call back quite late. I suggested waiting for another day. "You never know what the future holds," he said. "We better do it tonight."

I had decided what my first question would be. It was a question I would regularly ask people for this project: Is the mystery of God's role in the tsunami any different than the mystery of God's role when one innocent person suffers? Kushner is an expert, from experience and from study, on individual suffering. I wanted to know if there is any distinction to be made when considering the deaths of 230,000 people in the tsunami. He answered:

> Theologically, the unfair life of one child is as much a challenge to God's goodness as the unfair lives of the entire population of Bangladesh. Theologically, they must have been asking the same questions when the first retarded child was born. Functionally, we can somehow learn to live with the individual disaster, but something on the scale of the tsunami or the hurricanes in the Gulf Coast or anything like that overwhelm us. They make us take notice in a different way.

When Bad Things Happen to Good People became famous for helping people through crises. But it was also highly controversial because of Kushner's conclusion about God. In the book, Kushner swatted away the most common explanations for suffering—that it is punishment for sin, that it is part of God's larger plan, that things even out in the long run, that victims are somehow prepared by God to die, that tragedy can be a lesson from God, and others. Then he reached a radical conclusion for a rabbi: that God cannot be all-loving and all-powerful. Not both. Kushner sided with an all-loving God who, when faced with the suffering of innocents, is simply unable to stop it.

He was quite comfortable using the same line of reasoning to explain a natural disaster. "I solve the problem in my book by compromising God's power in order to maintain God's goodness," he told me. "What I do in this case is separate God from nature. God is kind, fair, loving and moral. Nature is not."

For a long time, Kushner was criticized by religious figures, including Orthodox Jews, who were revolted by his conclusion. One of the foundations of Judeo-Christian belief and tradition is that God is all-powerful. Kushner was more than willing to debate some of his detractors over the years and has not backed down an inch.

My answer is that if I have to choose between an all-powerful God who is not fair and kind, and a fair and kind and loving God who is awesomely powerful but not totally powerful, I think I'm more in line with Jewish values if I affirm God's goodness at the expense of his power rather than vice versa. I am describing a God for adults, not the God of our childhoods. Unless you want to deny the undeniable—the world's randomness—I just don't think we can affirm a God who controls everything. You would have to compromise God's goodness in order to affirm his power, and I'm not prepared to do that. When my book came out, I got into some very interesting discussions with people. I'm almost disappointed that they have not responded with the same vehemence to my other books. I hope it's not because I have become tame.

Kushner is a soft-spoken man with a calming voice, much the same as his voice on the page. It's a good thing he has such a soothing presence about him, as his message is direct and potentially disconcerting. I asked him about the widespread belief in this country that God is intimately involved in our lives. I outlined some of the ways that people explain God's presence in a natural disaster, all of which were quite familiar to him. Kushner had no interest in criticizing the many people who feel differently than he does, but he also offered a harsh explanation for the common belief that God is somehow with us.

People would like to believe somebody is in charge. We are more comfortable that way. You see this even with young children. It is easier to believe that we deserve what we get than to believe that the world is random. The idea of randomness terrifies us. Elaine Pagels, a fine scholar at Princeton, says that people would rather feel guilty and blame themselves than feel helpless. They would rather say that their own behavior caused something terrible than to say it just happened. By the way, people would rather say, if they can get away with it, that somebody else's behavior caused something terrible. We see a lot of that.

Let's say that God is all-loving and not all-powerful. Does that mean, I asked Kushner, that during the tsunami God was sitting on some kind of divine sideline, weeping for us. Not exactly, he said. Kushner explained that God is present in other ways, even if he cannot stop the tsunami from happening. Here, he offered much more common ideas about the good that God does in the midst of human suffering. He said, for instance, that God provided the compassion with which people responded to the tragedy. "That's not natural," he said. "That's the intervention of God working through people. The willingness of people to take in refugees, to build, to give money and blood, that is an act of God." He suggested that God even fueled the outrage that human beings expressed after the tsunami, whether at nature or God. Kushner also told me that God is in the laws of physics that make the world go round, make life possible, and produce natural disasters.

"Randomness may explain why the tsunami struck at a particular place on a particular day," he said. "There was no purpose to it. But it's not as if the laws of nature were being capricious. And God, I believe, does not have the power to prevent the laws of nature from operating. He does have the power to move people to be charitable and brave."

I'm certain that Kushner's understanding of God would fall quite short for many people. Some, if they read his book, would be deeply offended. Kushner is aware, but he doesn't mind. After reading his words and speaking with him, I get the sense that he believes his own experience—the loss of his son to a terrible disease that seems to mock our expectations of what it means to be human—gives him the authority to go where others might not. "People would like to believe that somebody is in control of the world," he said. "My response is that if there is, he is not doing a very good job."

Is he as convinced, I asked him, about God's limitations as he was when he wrote *When Bad Things Happen to Good People,* soon after his son's death?

"I'm more convinced I am right," he said. "Because my answer helps people. If I come out with a book that is theologically open to challenge but enables people to feel better, to cope with the challenges of life, then it's true. That is all the truth I'm looking for."

Rabbi Benjamin Blech/Searching for an Aha Moment

Benjamin Blech has made a second career of trying to explain the unexplainable. Well, that's not really fair. In his first career, Blech—a tenth-generation rabbi—served for decades as the pulpit rabbi of an Orthodox Jewish congregation in Brooklyn. In this role, he not only taught Jewish law and philosophy and led services in shul but counseled people going through all sorts of hard times in their day-to-day lives. Any clergyperson who leads a religious congregation knows what it means to hold hands with people in grief and pain and spiritual crisis.

What I might refer to as a second career began during the 1980s, when Blech left the pulpit and began delivering lectures around the world about one of the fundamental questions facing humankind: If God is good, why is the world so bad? He did so, he told me and others, in order to rebut Kushner's best-seller. He couldn't abide by Kushner's book leading people to believe that Judaism accepts the idea that God is less than all-powerful. So Blech wrote his own book in 2003—*If God Is Good, Why Is the World So Bad?*—based on an 11-hour lecture series that he had crafted on the subject. In a remarkable coincidence, his book was translated and published in Indonesia only two months before the tsunami. "There's God at work," Blech said. "The book was available to help people struggle through this. I hope Muslims are able to find some benefit from Jewish insights."

I went to Blech knowing he is a master handler of the questions we ask about suffering and catastrophe. He's heard them all. He's written about the tsunami and Katrina, measuring what Americans were thinking at the time of each. And he's adept at turning to Jewish tradition for his philosophic arsenal. He gleans bits of rabbinic wisdom, of Hasidic folk tales, of his people's perpetually challenging history, of the whole thing, to try to bring perspective and hope to a broad audience. After the tsunami, he spoke on the Dennis Prager radio show about how God could allow it to happen. He's been talking about it ever since.

Every time something goes wrong, it's as if people are asking these questions for the first time. We're a generation removed from the Holocaust, so it's pretty remarkable that any disaster is seen as unique or new. The first distinction to make, which some people intuitively understand, is that when human agency is involved in the perpetration of evil, you can't really blame God. God gave us free will and that can lead to things God is opposed to. When something like the tsunami involves no human agency and is an act of nature, an act of God, whatever you want to call it, you have a different problem, a serious problem, but not a new problem.

As an Orthodox rabbi who teaches Talmud at Yeshiva University in New York City, Blech starts his writings and lectures with some pretty orthodox assumptions: that God is good and that God is all-powerful. He doesn't allow any wiggle room on these fundamental points when dissecting catastrophes that might appear to challenge the existence of such a God. Instead, he offers the best of what Jewish tradition has to say in times of crisis, turning to a variety of sometimes unrelated stories and lessons. He moves from one to the next and hopes that something will stick. Even when he was a pulpit rabbi, he told me, he would offer congregants a variety of explanations for their challenges and pains. Eventually, something would connect with the person to ease their burden. He would often see in someone's eyes an "Aha" moment, when a given explanation or answer turned out to be true for them. He told me right off that there simply are no pat answers that work for each person or each situation, particularly in the case of a natural disaster.

> First off, Jewish tradition holds that God is involved in the world. This means many things. For example, Jewish tradition, in the main, following Maimonides, offers this remarkable concept: the closer people are to God, the closer and more direct is his relationship to people. If you choose to separate yourself from God, to live apart from God, to not live a godly life, to not give a damn about what God says—if you're saying that God is a stranger to you—then God is more removed from your life. There is no formula, but if God is more removed from you, you may be more vulnerable to natural forces. You are not being punished by God, but are simply apart from him. The closer you are to him, the tradition holds, the more God will see to it that you won't be in the wrong place at the wrong time. That's one way of thinking.

One way of thinking that left me unconvinced. Certainly among the victims of the tsunami were those who tried to be close to God and those who did not. But they all died, just the same. Still, Blech insisted that this philosophy may affect the world in ways we do not understand, since only God knows who has sought to be close to him. Then he moved to another concept that presents God as a bit more generous.

> There may be times when God creates or allows moments like these, natural disasters, in order to test people or allow people to express heroism, kindness, compassion, the kinds of things they would never get the opportunity to demonstrate, vis a vis their character, in the normal course of events.

This was the emphasis that so many people chose in the weeks and months after the tsunami, and again after Katrina: that the meaning of a catastrophe is in how we react, how we go to bat for our fallen brothers and sisters.

There's no doubt that this is an important component of the human response to any tragedy. Religious leaders, again and again, call on people to rise to the occasion in times of crisis, to think of others before themselves. Yet, at the same time, the greatest relief efforts do not address the question of why innocents had to suffer. Could it be worth it to God to see tens of thousands drown so that relief workers could show their stuff and the well-to-do could feel good about writing checks to the Red Cross? Blech seemed to realize that this point was limited in its power and talked for a time about the human responsibility to prepare for disaster. In many interviews I did, this argument became an oasis of sorts when even learned people of faith found themselves grasping for explanations for God's inaction (or action) during the tsunami or the hurricane.

> Natural events based on scientific principles are rooted in God, but they're rooted in the way the universe works, like the sun rising and the sun setting at fixed times. Earthquakes and tsunamis must be from God. But God asks us to be smart enough—just like we can figure out sunrise/sunset—to figure out water and fire and to protect ourselves by building what we need to keep us safe. We have a responsibility, in other words, to work with God. Every aspect of nature has the positive and negative, has the potential for tremendous good or tremendous evil. We have to make sure we are the recipients of good. Without water, the world would not survive. But we have to make sure we deal with water and how it's accumulated, so we can continue to live. Another example: If you build a city that is basically under water and you don't build levees that will properly take care of it, and when the time comes to vote on it, you choose to build casinos instead of protecting your city, you can't blame God. A hurricane is a natural event, but this wasn't nature. This was people not dealing with nature properly.

As I worked on this project, I grew to understand the necessity of blaming human failure for much of the suffering that stems from natural disasters. If God gives us free will and we fail to use it to prepare for catastrophes we know might strike, how can we blame God afterward? The failure of the levees around New Orleans is the perfect example, especially when considering that scientists—including those at FEMA—had long said that a hurricane could wipe out the city. But human failure still does not address why God would allow a tsunami, an underwater killer wave, to strike so near the populated coastline of Indonesia.

When I asked Blech about this, the author of the enlightening and funny *The Complete Idiot's Guide to Jewish History and Culture* spoke of God's mysterious ways. He said that the Midrash, a first-century collection of rabbinic insight and commentary, warns that "once the destroyer is out of the box, he no longer differentiates between the righteous and the wicked." In other words, everyone—good and bad, pious and non-pious—are subject to the same forces. Blech finally returned to the power of faith. Without it, he said, no answer is likely to satisfy.

> If you have faith, you can live through almost anything. Faith doesn't mean to suspend judgment. It means to say that If I really and truly believe that someone smarter than me is running this thing, I can be comforted in knowing that what is happening makes sense to a higher intelligence. I've found that simple faith is very helpful to people. There is so much in the literature, people who have endured suffering, like an Hasidic Jew who has nine children perish in a fire and says "God knows what he is doing. I will suffer knowing that he is still my father in Heaven and he has a plan. If he has a test, I hope to pass the test. If this is punishment, I hope to be a better person. If this has meaning historically, for what we have to go through in order to bring the messiah, I am willing to do my sacrifice just as Abraham was ready to sacrifice his son. If, God, that is what you want from me, I will do it." There is a story of a man who goes through all these horrible experiences and says to God, "God, you can deprive me of everything, but one thing you can never take away from me is my faith in you."

RABBI IRVING GREENBERG/THE MATURATION OF FAITH

On the day I called Rabbi Irving "Yitz" Greenberg, I knew he was under the weather. I asked him whether he would be able to talk. "I'll be fine," he said. "In the long run, we'll all be dead. But in the short run, I'll be fine." We both laughed, he sounding rather hoarse.

Not many distinguished thinkers are known almost universally by a nickname. But this one is. Yitz. Yitz Greenberg is a unique figure in the Jewish world. He's a liberal Orthodox rabbi who has dedicated much of his career to broad educational missions, to improving relations among Jews from different backgrounds, and to developing understanding among different religions. He is a big picture guy who will modestly and gently consider any legitimate religious question and isn't afraid to cross boundaries of understanding that others will eagerly avoid. For several years, Greenberg has partnered with Jewish mega-philanthropist (and avowed atheist) Michael Steinhardt to create new ways of enriching American Jewish life. In his 2004 book, *For the Sake of Heaven and Earth,* Greenberg argued that Judaism and Christianity, rather than being contradictory, were meant by God to stand side by side.

Greenberg is well known for dissecting the lessons of the Holocaust. From 2000 to 2002, he was chairman of the U.S. Holocaust Memorial Council, which runs the Holocaust Museum in Washington. I knew that he would be eager to tackle the hard questions raised by the tsunami. Sure enough, he got right to the heart of the matter:

> When good people, innocent people, get washed away, if you are a believer in God, it is very troublesome. A good religion is a positive one, with a loving God, a God who cares about the world. If you think that the world is run by God, it puts the problem in spades. How is this compatible with a belief in a kind, loving God? When a blind force of nature wipes out so many innocent people, it challenges the central religious beliefs about God. It also suggests all kinds of terrible, negative possibilities. It seems we live in a world where we are like flies being killed by kids for sport, like Shakespeare said. Are we humans the victims of cosmic forces that don't care about us? That's the core, central question.

I knew that Greenberg had special reason to wonder whether we really are no different than flies when it comes to meeting our fates. In 2002, his 37-year-old son, J.J., was hit by a car and killed while bike riding with his brother and a friend in Jerusalem. J.J. was known for his vibrancy and generosity, for rollerblading to Ground Zero on September 11 to help rescue workers. His organs were transplanted into five people, including a Palestinian, as his parents knew he would have wanted. Yitz Greenberg didn't mention J.J. to me when we spoke, but I knew that his son's death informed much of what he said. He insisted that it is proper, even necessary, to question God and argue with God when our rational, ordered lives are upended by tragedy. "There are passages in Psalms, in Jeremiah, where they argue with God, where they say...'This is wrong,'" he told me. "A religion that is authentic should say that people should protest—to other people and to God—when innocent people suffer and when bad guys win. You should protest. But should you lose your faith? That's another question."

Greenberg turned to the Talmud, telling me that it is full of passages where the rabbis question God:

> There is a very famous Talmudic story of Rabbi Kiva, who was probably the greatest rabbi of his time, just after the destruction of the Temple. He was caught by the Romans. He was one of the Jews who revolted against Rome. The Romans crushed the revolution and caught him and tortured him to death. Here was a great teacher, a good man and kind man, and they tortured him to death. So, the story goes that the angels scream in protest. "How can this be? Look at what they're doing." And God answers: "Be silent." That's the way it is. So the Talmud says you have to protest, but there is no answer. You live with

it. There is a level at which, for the religious person, it shakes your faith. On the other hand, you live with that reality. That's part of a mature faith.

Of course, Greenberg turned to the book of Job, citing Job's willingness to call out God—and Job's decidedly mixed results.

You can argue about what the book is saying, but I think, in the end, the book says that the cosmos are so vast, that God is so vast, individual human suffering is dwarfed. Job accepts this, saying "At least I have God with me, even if I don't understand it and it's all beyond me." Part of it is growing up and saying the world is not built around me, to guarantee that I won't suffer, that I won't be in pain. As long as I know that I'm not alone and that God is with me, and that I'm still loved and I'm still precious, I can live with that suffering.

We live in a time, Greenberg said, when there is a clash between premodern religious thinking (God causes illness and earthquakes) and postmodern thinking (it's hard to know where science ends and God begins). The more we know about science, the less many people need to ask about God. Even liberal religious traditions, though they may believe that God created the universe, may quietly accept that God is no longer intervening. But many fundamentalist traditions, Greenberg said, are trying to compartmentalize scientific knowledge and return to a simpler, premodern focus on an intervening God. This voice rose up after the tsunami and Katrina, when clergy of numerous faiths announced God's dissatisfaction with human ways.

Greenberg told me that his position on God's presence might play out like this:

God created the universe and sustains the universe, but its expression is *in* the natural law. It's permanent, it doesn't flip every two minutes. It's part of the divine, eternal, permanent, creative, nurturing sustaining of the world. God doesn't intervene Monday or Thursday or every time you pray. Sometimes natural law operates in very devastating ways. Earthquakes and tsunamis. When an innocent person is pushed off a cliff or falls off. God is present, God is consistent, but is not the interventionist God who gets insulted if you don't pray and punishes you.

He talked at length about the maturation of faith, a complicated process that involves prayer, study, daily living, and probably benefits from experiencing sorrow. Greenberg noted that the famed Lutheran theologian Dietrich Bonhoeffer talked of a "God of the gaps," a God who people turned to explain what they didn't understand. As people know more about the world around them, the gaps disappear. What's left is a purer, more intimate, complicated relationship with God. "He's not just a guy you turn to when you're in trouble, a Don Corleone with a cigar, but a God who sustains you."

Even if you develop a mature faith, Greenberg said, it may be impossible to make peace with God in a world where tsunamis crash down and individuals are struck down in the prime of life. He told me that the prophets said that people may only truly know God during the messianic age:

> The prophets said that as long as there is evil, suffering, you don't really know God. To really know God—like you know someone biblically, to make love to somebody, you know it, you feel it, you experience it emotionally, intellectually, physically—we can't know God that way because all these things interfere, interrupt. So you believe in God, but knowing God is clouded by all these experiences—and should be clouded. It's a challenge to us to improve the world. For example, if you had an early warning system, a lot of lives could be saved. So the correct religious response, you might say, is to argue with God and then say "What can I do to improve the world?"

Rabbi Adin Steinsaltz/Don't Ask Me

As I was preparing to meet with this famed Talmudic scholar, I had a feeling it would be no ordinary interview. Rabbi Adin Steinsaltz is no mere teacher or interpreter of Scripture. He is regarded as a sage, as a mystic. Others speak of him as they do the great rabbis of yore, whose wisdom was so vast that it can be reexamined again and again for new meaning. So when I sat down with Steinsaltz at a small shul, where he was about to speak on a complex Hasidic text, I expected some brilliant explanation for God's role in the tsunami. When I started to frame my first questions, though, I felt a bit leery.

Sure enough, his initial response stumped me: "People don't ask me such things," he said in a heavy Yiddish accent. "They know I have the ability to say...I don't know. I know the local rabbi and the priest and the pastor and the mullah, they may have all the answers. I don't have all the answers." Then he stared at me.

Now what? How would I pursue the question with such a formidable adversary when he wasn't ready to bite? I was not in for a standard interview. Steinsaltz is responsible for what seems like more than one lifetime of scholarship. He has produced a monumental translation and commentary of the Talmud, from Aramaic to Hebrew, that is more than thirty volumes and counting. Most of the volumes have been translated into English and other languages. One of his commentaries has even been translated into Chinese. He has also written numerous other works, particularly on Kabbalah or Jewish mysticism.

An Orthodox Jew who grew up in a secular home, Steinsaltz runs a chain of Jewish day schools in Israel. He is also responsible, through the founding of colleges and publishing houses, for Jewish instruction to thousands in the former Soviet Union.

He is probably as familiar as anyone with the "repository of thousands of years of Jewish wisdom" that is the Talmud, as he defines it. So what does all that wisdom have to say about a force of nature, of God, that kills thousands for no apparent reason?

"I am not trying to avoid the question," he finally said, after several, long minutes of dismissing my question with a volley of rhetorical swats.

> I am trying to define it. These things, you see, happen everyday, but not in such an enormous way. People ask these questions when you have a tsunami because it is so dramatic. People die every day. But it is not so dramatic. The people who die are usually not of one kind, in one place. Someone dies in a traffic accident, it is the same thing. When the dramatics are bigger, the question is not bigger. It is the same question.

At this point, I thought that Steinsaltz felt bad for me, perhaps for not understanding the enormity of what I was asking. Or maybe he was so used to dealing with the minutia of complex texts and Jewish ethics that he did not have any patience for such a vast query, a pop culture type question, disconnected from the world of scholarship. Steinsaltz slowly moved forward, speaking softly, at times almost in a whisper, through his long white beard:

> The life of every individual is incredibly complex and interwoven with thousands of others, people, friends. All these others. And I demand an answer: Why did something happen? I don't know anything. I don't know about the future. I don't know about the interconnectedness of things. And I want an answer. If the Almighty would give me a good answer, about anything, not only the tsunami—not only why thousands died, but about the suffering yesterday of one person—that answer would be far greater than my ability to comprehend it. Anything I can't comprehend, I cannot really use.

He continued:

> The death of somebody I don't know, you see, should not make such an impression on me. The death of my goldfish that dies in my fishbowl might make an impression on me. What does that mean? Things happen. Everything happens. Everything is connected. And we expect that the Good Lord will report to me,

will tell his business to me? He doesn't want to. I ask for a full report, like asking the mayor. But this is not asking the mayor.

We focus on something like the tsunami or a hurricane, he seemed to be saying, by separating it from everything else. But you can't. You cannot forget the accidents and illness and civil wars that cause suffering, great and small, each day in every corner of the world. To focus on all that suffering would paralyze us—and stop us from seeing all the good in the world. We can't do that. But it is pointless to call God to account on only the tsunami, as great a tragedy as it was. Somehow, the meaning of Steinsaltz's words were getting through to me, even though he said little. "When the dramatics are bigger, the question is not bigger," he told me. "It is the same question."

He stared at me some more. "So people are asking, are *asking,* like they're reading a good detective story," he said. "When you have a good detective story, you have six, seven, eight threads leading to different possibilities. But when you have real life . . ."

He looked at me as if he had just noticed that I was there. "I don't know anything about you," he said.

He asked me if I was married. Yes. Did I have children? Two sons. He nodded and continued:

So you have a wife, two boys. There are people that you work for, people that you meet in the street, people that you encounter. All these people are connected to you. If anything happens to you, it has meaning to them, more so for those closest to you. So how do I get all the information (from God) for this case, if anything happens to you? For *why* it happens? Just this case? The simple, clear-cut answer is . . . shut up. That is a good answer.

So that was it. Don't ask God. Just shut up. I laughed. He smiled. But he did not want to let the matter go just like that. So Steinsaltz turned to the Ground Zero of questioning God: the book of Job:

In the Bible, in the Book of Job, God tells Job, in different words, "Look at nature, look at the animals. And you want me to do a reporting of why I do these things?" There is a beautiful description of nature and all these things: How does an eagle fly? How does a doe give birth? How does a crocodile move in the water? "Do you understand any of these things?" God asks him. "And you want me to give a report?" My answer to you just now wasn't very nice, but here you have it in 10 chapters of very beautiful language. It says that it would be far better if you did not ask for an answer. Job, at the end, says "I keep quiet."

Steinsaltz squinted at me, with a bit more satisfaction, as if he might have gotten a point across. "I keep quiet," he said.

RABBI SHIRA MILGROM AND DAVID ELCOTT/WITNESSES TO TRAGEDY

When I started this project, I knew I had to speak with Rabbi Shira Milgrom and her husband, David Elcott. Because they were there.

They were visiting their daughter, Liore Milgrom-Elcott, a recent graduate of Cornell who was doing volunteer work in India for American Jewish World Service. They joined her in December 2004 and traveled together to the beach resorts of Mamallapuram, a city on the Bay of Bengal. On the morning of December 26, Elcott and his daughter went for a jog on the beach and then sat down to breakfast at a restaurant overlooking the bay. The tsunami had hit Indonesia hours before. Tens of thousands were already dead. But word had not reached the coast of India. So the tsunami, inexplicably, arrived unannounced.

What happened next, Milgrom and Elcott described in emails that they sent to friends back home, emails that quickly spread through Jewish and other circles and gave many Americans their first or only taste of what it was like to be there. Milgrom's email reached me after about 24 hours. "As we were running, the main path that was just below us filled with rushing water," she wrote. The family got into a car and picked up as many older people as they could fit as they drove to higher ground. After the tide appeared to wane, Liore and her father returned to the hotel to gather their belongings. They looked over a first floor that was destroyed and they left. Minutes later, the second wave of the tsunami hit. They narrowly avoided death. Twice.

When I visited the family at their home in White Plains, eight months had gone by. They had retold the story many times, of course, and had received countless hugs and blessings and "Thank Gods." And they had moved on with their incredibly busy lives. But it was clear that the tsunami was still with them. As I listened to them, it was obvious that they had been changed in ways they were still trying to understand. There were struggles going on just beneath the surface.

Milgrom is co-rabbi of Congregation Kol Ami in White Plains, a large, thriving Reform temple. Elcott, when we spoke, was U.S. director of interreligious affairs for the American Jewish Committee, but has since moved on. He has long worked as a Jewish educator and as a consultant to religious and social justice agencies. As a couple, they represent well the progressive, tolerant, intellectual wing of American Judaism and are extremely well suited to try to make sense of the senseless by tapping Jewish tradition and modern thinking.

Neither Milgrom nor Elcott was really interested, though, in providing explanations, or at least the types of explanations I would receive elsewhere. They all but conceded that God's role in the tsunami is impossible to understand. They did not even want to hear that God saved them. "So we're alive," Elcott said. "We won't say that God saved us—and not the person next to us." He explained:

> In the email I sent out after it happened, I said that there is a blessing one says when living through a catastrophe, a near-death experience. But you can't say that in this case. You can say it in case of car accident or if you have a heart attack and you're saved. Those things make sense. But in the face of such great random loss, to say that blessing. . .you can't say it. In Judaism, if you see a fire in your town, you're forbidden to say "I pray to God it's not my house." It is *somebody's* house.

After seeing so many homes and businesses and lives ruined, Milgrom was disappointed, offended, and angered by much of the response to the tsunami. In India, lower castes were brought in to clean up the bodies. Hindu authorities offered little solace, other than to conclude, rather coldly to Western ears, that the victims had simply run out of time, as determined by karma. There was no real communal grieving of any kind. Then, as the weeks went by, she had to listen to and read the comments of religious leaders—Muslim, evangelical, Jewish—who suggested that the victims had paid for their sins. She heard comparatively little talk about the scientific reasons for the earthquake or why there was no warning system in the Indian Ocean that could have saved lives in India and elsewhere.

For Milgrom, the vapid religious response—placing blame and offering little compassion—was symptomatic of the growing worldwide influence of fundamentalists on most major religious traditions. "I'm in a very angry place right now," she said. She explained, coolly:

> There is a long liturgical tradition in Judaism to try to give meaning to catastrophe, to suffering. The rabbis teach "The sun shines on the wicked and the righteous alike." So the flood water floods the wicked and the righteous alike.
>
> But there has to be a balance between the essential human endeavor to assign meaning to what happens in life—and thinking you understand these things in such a way that it becomes, well, oppressive. There is a fundamental human sense that life makes sense, that things have meaning, that life has meaning, intrinsically. There is certainly a powerful Jewish sense that life is imbued with meaning. But if it's taken to a point where virtually nothing is meaningless, where we are making up explanations because we have none, it can be dangerous.

Milgrom was deadly serious. Her whole point seemed to be that before anyone questions God, they should focus on the many human failings that were exposed by the tsunami. *People* should be held accountable for their lack of responsibility and compassion.

> When people say that God was involved in the tsunami, it is a question of transferring responsibility. It is said by people who don't want to assume any responsibility or connection. God becomes this horrible excuse for disconnection, at best, or horrible inaction. The poor are expendable in India. The part that was agonizing for us is that no one in India needed to have died. There were three hours after the tsunami hit Indonesia before it hit the coast of India. There was more than enough time to sound an alarm and evacuate everybody, but no one was prepared or cared. Now, no one is begrudging Hindus or anyone else the right to live as they wish. But this wasn't about karma. It was about a lack of human initiative, of caring. Then they waited for the lowest caste, the untouchables, to do the dirty work, deal with the bodies.

Elcott listened intently to his wife but was clearly eager to speak. He had many of the same impulses to express disgust with what he saw and heard in India. But he was very reluctant to force the values of educated, suburban Americans on a foreign culture and a different belief system. Particularly in a place where poverty and suffering are common, he said, there may be a need to explain a great tragedy in a simple, efficient way. Attributing tragedy to karma may appear heartless to Westerners, but Hindus in India have very different reference points. He said:

> I think Shira was in some ways radicalized by the experience. The first time I ever saw her spiritually angry was in India. There were dead bodies all over the place and no one attended to them. Their religious reactions might seem so horrendous to us. But in a world that is overwhelmingly frightening for those experiencing it, we need to be modest before we judge too negatively beliefs that allow people to live their lives and not experience complete chaos in the face of unredeemable suffering. We all want to believe that goodness should prevail. When my mother asked "Where was God" in the Holocaust, after her family was wiped out, there was a sense of wanting a moral equivalence to "The sun rises in the East and sets in the west." There was a sense that goodness should prevail, that "The righteous shall flourish like the palm tree," and that catastrophes, whether natural or human, are not right. This shouldn't be happening.

Elcott described his wife's unwillingness to accept the religious answers of others as a more extreme response:

It is the modern response, the enlightenment response: "We can take care of these things. We can make sure there will be no starvation, there will be no hunger, there will be no suffering. We can change the physical world. We can stop bacteria from killing. We can build dykes that will prevent flooding. We can do all these things." I think that belief spawned incredible discoveries, but it also spawned Communism and Nazism and other secular rubrics that did terrible things. At the end of the 20th century, one of the things we're dealing with is a deep disappointment in modernity. It didn't answer all the questions. That may be why we're seeing extremism in all religious communities, particularly over the last 15 years. Attributing everything to God may be a reaction to the idea that God is not in any of these places where bad things are happening and that man can fix everything. We can't.

Milgrom sat impassively, picking at her toast. I spoke with them a few days after Hurricane Katrina hit. The *New York Times* was resting on the counter, its lead headline stating that the dykes around New Orleans had failed the day before. We knew that things looked bad down south, but we did not yet understand *how* bad. It's hard to remember now, but there was a brief period of time after Katrina hit when the news media and the rest of the country did not grasp the seriousness of what was taking place. Elcott, glancing at the *Times,* briefly wondered about the failure of the dykes, but our conversation about the tsunami was hardly touched by Katrina. Of course, everything that Milgrom said about human failings in India would apply many times over to what happened in New Orleans.

When Elcott finished, his wife gave little ground:

India is a place where 700 million people live below the poverty line. I think there is a connection between things people believe and the structures a society creates that allow poverty to continue. I don't think it's so benign. You say it's personal, the way they interpret the world. But there is huge suffering, and they are not unrelated.

Elcott continued to seek a moderate voice, sidestepping any opportunity to condemn a foreign culture or belief system. But he agreed with Milgrom that it is a desecration of God's name to invoke God's name as an excuse for inaction or to maintain religious authority. "The air we breath is of God's blessings, but it is possible for God's presence to be blocked by human indifference or evil," he said.

We live because of the oceans, because of water, and all it would have taken was a warning system that may have required some corrupt government officials to have a little bit less. This wasn't Indonesia, where it hit in seconds. We live with the blessings, but they can be blocked by human evil.

After directing unforgiving blame at Indian officials and Indian culture, Milgrom said that she did not believe that God was in the tsunami. She praised her co-rabbi at Kol Ami, Tom Weiner, for turning to a passage in the books of Kings on the first Shabbat after the tsunami:

> In the text, Elijah is despairing that he wants to kill himself and wants to experience God's presence. There is a huge shattering wind and God is not in the wind. And there is a tremendous earthquake and God is not in the earthquake. And there is a huge fire and God is not in the fire. And then there is silence. And out of the silence God speaks to Elijah. You can see God in the voice of conscience that emerges from the stillness. Judaism has songs about God being in the thunder. They're part of the liturgical canon. They're part of our consciousness as a people. But there is also that beautiful text from Elijah, which is really a rebellion against that view. God is in the stillness.

THOUGHTS

I knew going in that the right assortment of Jewish thinkers would give me *anything* but a unified Jewish view. On the question of challenging God over the suffering of innocent people in a natural disaster, I would break down the answers I heard this way: (1) Don't ask because we can't know (Steinsaltz); (2) You can ask—but must arrive at a faithful answer (Blech); (3) You should challenge God, even loudly, but the end result will likely be a stronger faith (Greenberg); (4) You must challenge God and rethink who God is (Kushner); and (5) Don't ask because we have earthly problems to contend with first (Milgrom). That's Judaism. In the Torah, there are numerous stories of people questioning God, losing faith, and falling victim to their own hubris—before returning to God (sometimes on their own, sometimes because of God's insistence). The Jewish perspective on suffering is bound to come from many angles.

I found something to admire in each of their philosophies. I liked Greenberg's soulful yet grounded appraisal that facing suffering will lead one to a more mature faith, rich in solace if not answers. Steinsaltz' unwillingness to obsess over a single instance of suffering, small or vast, in a world so full of mystery struck me as the prerogative of a true sage. But can an ordinary working stiff who doesn't have the time to study Talmudic philosophy be expected to follow his lead? None of Blech's particular explanations for natural evil made me up sit and take notice, but I respect his desire to keep throwing out ideas and parables until something jives with an individual's sense of God.

There you have the clergyperson as teacher, philosopher, and friend. Listening to Milgrom and Elcott debate the appropriateness of criticizing a foreign culture and religion was like having an internal struggle. I mean, in my own head. I agreed with both of their positions and wanted to defend whoever was speaking: "Tell the Indian government to wake up and act civilized. No, wait. We have to strive to understand a very different culture with different needs. No, wait."

Kushner's voice would stay with me for the duration of this project. He told me that the world's randomness is undeniable. God can't be calling the shots. When studying the tsunami, it sure seemed that way. But few people I interviewed for this book would agree. Most would say that the world isn't random, but we're not privy to the details. Those I interviewed for the next four chapters of this book would say that we know this much: that God sent his only son to die for humankind's sins. Jesus suffered for us because this is a broken world and humankind needs to be saved. I think it's safe to say that Christians agree that suffering is unavoidable, but they have very different ways of coming to terms with it.

4 THE ROMAN CATHOLIC PERSPECTIVE

The story of Galileo is often pointed to as proof that the Roman Catholic Church has some sort of antipathy toward science. While Galileo certainly suffered for being ahead of his time, the modern Catholic Church has a record of supporting scientific endeavors. Many church leaders, for instance, are open to the theory of evolution even as they maintain that God created the universe and that the scientific pursuit cannot be separated from church teachings. Catholicism avoids neither science nor questions of suffering. The meaning of suffering is central to Catholicism. Catholics prefer crucifixes that show Christ in the midst of suffering to lone crosses that symbolize the resurrection. They often refer to the Christlike qualities of those who endure suffering and are able to maintain their faith.

THE REVEREND BENEDICT GROESCHEL/THE MYSTERY REMAINS

I had known Benedict Groeschel for several years when I got word in January 2004 that he had been hit by a car and was near death.

Groeschel was, and remains, one of the best-known Catholic priests in the country. He is something of a hero to conservative or orthodox Catholics for defending church teachings from the challenges put forth by reformist Catholics. He's written many books about the meaning of the Eucharist, how to deal with suffering, and other subjects that speak to his dedicated audience. For decades, he's been worldwide lecturer and leader of retreats, often for other priests, and has been able to make use of his background in psychology in hundreds of small-group settings.

Groeschel is also noted for his cofounding of a religious community, the Franciscan Friars of the Renewal, which aims to return to what its members see as the original, pure goal of Francis of Assisi: to serve the poor. Groeschel and the community's other founders left the Capuchin Franciscan Order after concluding that it had lost its vision. Finally, Groeschel's visibility owes much to his regular appearances on EWTN, the national Catholic television network founded by his friend, Mother Angelica. Devout Catholics, and others who watch EWTN, have long been familiar with Father Benedict's scraggly beard and gray, hooded robe, trademarks of the community that he helped create.

I wrote about his accident, how he was hit by a car while in Florida to give a retreat. And I wrote about his slow, difficult recovery, visiting him at a rehabilitation center when he returned to New York. We talked a bit about his well-regarded book on suffering, *Arise from Darkness*. He made a small confession that stayed with me. He said that he had underestimated what it takes to rebound from tragedy. His painful recovery had taught him that. The depression that one faces when weak and broken, he said, is a dark and difficult challenge.

I had this confession in mind when I went to talk with Groeschel about the tsunami. I also knew that he does not shy away from difficult questions and that his quick, often self-deprecating, sense of humor would come into play. He did not disappoint.

> It's incredibly interesting to me that human nature is built not to quit, even when we don't understand what is happening to us. Look at me. I got belted and should be dead. Within eight days, I went to the door of death three times. I am permanently incapacitated. It's been hard. But I could not wish right now that it didn't happen. So many good things have occurred because of this accident. So many people have written to me, of every religious denomination, to say they were praying for me. I can't say I'm glad it happened. But I've heard from so many people, everywhere I go. You pick up the pieces and you go on. It's amazing what people can do.

He was still figuring out the lessons of his accident and recovery. Groeschel stared at me with tired eyes. He always looked worn out, even before his accident. He is one of the busiest people I've ever known, his days scheduled and booked weeks and sometimes months in advance. I could see in his eyes that he wanted to address the real questions at hand. Why was he hit at all? Why did the tsunami hit thousands with an even more unforgiving strike? Was God involved in either? Only a few days before we spoke, in November 2005, the *New York Times Magazine* ran a magnificent, startling piece that reconstructed the tsunami from the vantage points of six men and women in Banda Aceh. The article, the longest ever printed by the magazine, showed that whether one lived or died seemed to be determined by pure chance. Did one grab onto a tree or a piece of floating roof? Did one run to the left or the right? Groeschel, no fan of the media, had read the piece and remarked on its power. Could it be, I asked him, that our fates are completely random?

"This is something I've been interested in my whole life," he finally said. "Nobody has the bright, sparkling answer. Anybody who thinks they have the answer to evil, just reply to them . . . Wait." Groeschel even conceded that if someone were to lose faith after something like the tsunami, he could not chastise them. "I would have to say, I can understand. I mean, why did the assassination attempts on Hitler miss? Why didn't the heavens open to help? I don't know. And no one else does."

Groeschel felt a need to briefly survey for me how the five major world religions explain the presence of evil, as if to hammer home that no one has a satisfying answer. He said he could understand the Hindu view that God creates everything in the world, good and evil. He respected the Buddhist concept that evil is simply one way that people perceive and interpret reality. He had a problem with the Muslim idea that Islamic law and culture can produce an ideal society in this world. "Many people who have tried to set up a perfect society have failed miserably," he said. "Muslims have usually been moderated by the kind of realism that comes when you stick around a while." Groeschel had great admiration for the traditional Jewish reliance on the book of Job. He spoke several times of how the Jewish people have survived the Holocaust, maintaining Job's ultimate faith in the face of horror. "When death occurs, the Jews say the Kaddish, which people who don't know think is a prayer for the dead. It's actually a prayer of thanksgiving. Let's pick up the pieces and do the best we can." Finally, he got around to the Christian response:

> The Christian answer, put succinctly, is that God comes and accepts the worst of the human condition. That's what Mel Gibson's movie was about. In Christianity, you have the only religion where God suffers. In Judaism, God rejoices and God gets annoyed, but he doesn't suffer. The next step is that God suffers—with us and for us. This has to get a Christian through. That doesn't mean there isn't mystery. As we read the accounts of the tsunami or the World Trade Center, there is the mystery of evil, different kinds of evil. Thomas Aquinas, the great theologian, says the reason most people who believe in God believe in him, is the problem of evil, and the reason that most people who don't believe in God don't believe in him, is the

problem of evil. It depends where you want to go with it. St. Augustine, who was very concerned about this, says that God does not cause evil, but he causes that evil does not become the worst. Is this enough for us? No.

Groeschel turned from the great theologians to the Gospels. He opened to the story in Luke of a water tower that collapses and kills eighteen people. "When the tower collapsed, everybody asked Jesus whether these people who died were worse than everybody else," Groeschel said.

They saw it as a punishment. He said they were no worse than anybody else, but that you have to be ready. That may be the message of catastrophe. Be ready. Jesus says be ready because he comes like a thief in the night. So it's right there, an important message of the Gospel. But it still doesn't explain the mystery of evil or why the tidal wave happened.

We are forced to conclude that suffering is part of life, he said. The death of a single elderly person from illness, while awful and tragic for the person's loved ones, is inevitable. "The tsunami is one person—250,000 times over," he said. For a Christian, Christ died on the cross to redeem the world. Suffering is part of a world that needs to be redeemed.

Interestingly, Groeschel came alive, his pale blue eyes suddenly twinkling, when he remembered the words not of a theologian, but of Albert Einstein. He had me reach for a file that contained a quotation from the Jewish physicist, in which Einstein wrote of the mystical nature of the world and of the importance of believing in what we can't see. "My religion consists of a humble admiration of the illimitable superior spirit who reveals himself in the slight details we are able to perceive with our frail and feeble minds," Einstein said. "That deeply emotional conviction of the presence of a superior reasoning power, which is revealed in the incomprehensible universe, forms my idea of God."

Even a man who understood the physical world like no other, despite that world's imperfections and natural disasters, still believed in God. Groeschel read the quote out loud—twice—but didn't try to expand on it. Instead, this old Franciscan started to speak like a scientist himself.

When you think about it, the tsunami did not violate any laws of physics. There was some order to it. But who thinks of that? When you think about it, with the size of the earth and the size of the universe, these waves were small. Cosmic events of incredible magnitude go on, galaxies crash, but there is no life there—as far as we know. What does it mean?

THE REVEREND GEORGE COYNE/SCIENCE AS PRAYER

I was intrigued by Groeschel's closing comments about the vastness of the cosmos and how, in the universal scheme of things, the tsunami was a blip. Still, I never would have thought of contacting the director of the Vatican Observatory. I was vaguely aware that the Vatican had an observatory and probably had the same reaction as countless others: "The Vatican has an observatory? How odd is that?" But it would not have occurred to me to contact George Coyne because he is, after all, an astronomer. His interest is supposed to be in what's "out there," not in what is bubbling up beneath the earth's surface. There's some seventh-grade level scientific reasoning for you.

So I was fortunate to come across an article that Coyne wrote in August 2005 for England's the *Tablet*. Without mincing words, he ridiculed an assertion by a prominent cardinal that the theory of evolution is incompatible with Catholic belief. Coyne stated plainly that natural selection is beyond dispute and therefore must be under God's dominion. Coyne described a "fertile" universe that is always evolving, fueled by necessary processes and chance processes. As I read this, I wondered where a tsunami would fit in. Is it a chance process that somehow feeds the fertility of the universe? Coyne's article was written from a scientist's point of view and could just as easily have been written by a volcanologist as an astronomer. I had a strong feeling that he would have something to say about God's role in natural disasters. I should note at this point that Coyne is not only a decorated astronomer but a Catholic priest. He joined the Jesuits as a teenager and was ordained in 1965 (the same year he was a visiting professor at the University of Arizona Lunar and Planetary Laboratory).

He gave me a lot to think about, taking my search for answers to places I hadn't expected to go:

> The tsunami was a terrible physical evil, especially for thousands of people who died. But if it did not happen, we would not be here. The surface of the earth would not be habitable. That tsunami was required, as hurricanes are required, as a lot of earthquakes are required, in order to have energy exchange over the surface of the earth. Otherwise, too much energy would build up in one place. We need to have circulation of this energy. The only way we can have it is through these big natural events, which are terrible from the point of view of human beings. But again, they're necessary in order for us to be here at all.

I will come back in a moment to what Coyne means by all this. But first, since his statement might seem cold and callous, too scientific for a priest, I want to share what he said when I asked him how he first responds to news of a natural disaster. As a scientist? Does he zero in on the natural forces that built up over many years and finally gave way as the laws of nature say they must? "Oh no," he said.

> My first reaction is to imagine the human suffering. It brings you to your knees. I understand why people wonder how God can allow this. As a priest, I've counseled mothers whose small children were dying. What do you say to a mother whose 2-year-old is dying. "Sorry 'bout that ma'am, but that's the nature of the universe?" That doesn't go very far. You say that it's all in God's hands.

Coyne became director of the Vatican Observatory in 1978 and held the job until August 2006, months after we spoke. He was retired at that point by Pope Benedict XVI (who replaced him with another Jesuit), fueling speculation that Coyne the scientist had been too outspoken. Anyway, at the time we spoke, he was researching the "polarization produced in cataclysmic variables, or interacting binary star systems that give off sudden bursts of intense energy." This meant nothing to me, but sure had the ring of astronomical natural disasters. At least that's what I assumed when I called Coyne in Rome.

Coyne was eager to address the idea that an earthquake and the resulting tsunami are somehow beyond the cosmic pale, an unreasonable attack on the ordered lives of human beings who, after all, are made in God's image. He wanted me to glimpse the scientist's perspective that we play a much smaller role than we think in a much larger universe than most of us can image.

> The scientific end of this requires a distinction about what we mean about order and disorder. We experience disorder. But the world itself is ordered. My life is pretty ordered. I get up at the same time, I have breakfast, I go teach class, I come home. But, say, one morning I'm walking to teach my class and a meteorite comes down from heaven and hits me on the head. I say that is out of order, and yet, if I look at the universe at large, that meteorite is obeying physical laws of gravity, of its orbit. It was time for it to fall out of orbit. That meteorite did not intend to hit me. It was all ordered as far as the universe at large goes.

Again, this line of reasoning is not particularly satisfying on a spiritual level. You couldn't use it to console Coyne's loved ones if he was obliterated by a meteorite. But the more Coyne talked science, the less interested I became in pursuing questions about God's role in disasters. He was changing my perspective, little by little, and I began to wonder if my questioning of other religious figures would be somehow different in the future.

Coyne may be an astronomer, but he emphasized again and again the centrality of natural selection. Human beings are the products of an evolving universe, he said. This is easy to lose sight of because the human brain represents such a large jump in the evolutionary process. We feel separated from it all, above it. But we are part of a process nonetheless. And part of a larger universe. A tsunami doesn't strike because people are in the way. It strikes and we happen to be in the way. That's science. "We could not be here without stars dying off, giving us the chemical abundance that we need," he said. "It is the nature of the universe, that life requires death. It fits in well with Scripture, which says that a grain of wheat must fall into the ground and die or you won't have a crop the following year."

The universe itself has a life span and will eventually reach old age, Coyne told me. The amount of energy being introduced into the universe is finite and is destined to run down. This is what's known as entropy, the big batteries running down. The very concept makes a single natural disaster seem quite small, if you can temporarily block out all the suffering and stick to the science. The universe still has some time, though. Coyne figures the sun will live for another 5 billion years, converting energy through a thermonuclear furnace, before the whole operation shuts down.

But human beings will be long gone by then. Something like 95 percent of the species that have appeared on the earth are extinct and we'll join them, Coyne figures. "We are here for a very short period of time," he said. "This is a 14 billion-year-old universe, and human civilization has been around for a few million years at best. That's a small fraction and it will end. We will die off. As extremely complex products of an evolving universe, we are not very stable."

So the obvious question becomes where is God in all this? Did he set the evolution of the universe in motion and step out of the way? That might make a tsunami easier to understand. It would simply represent one tiny step in the distribution of the world's energy—and an even smaller step toward the dissipation of that energy. The people of Sumatra would mean little more than the grains of sand that were washed off the beach. Is there room for God in this picture? Yes, Coyne says. "I believe God created the universe, so I ask myself: What does the nature of the universe, known scientifically, say about God?"

First off, God does not *cause* things in the simplistic way we understand causes, Coyne told me. "God is the creator and creation is not a cause," he said. "There was nothing on which God could bring about effects. God does not bring about effects." So what is God's role?

The best image of God I can reach is that God created the universe out of love. Love, by its very nature, is a reciprocal process. We know that to love someone, you expect to be loved in return. To me, God was that way with respect to the universe he created. He wanted a universe that would have within itself the creativity to love him. To have that kind of universe, it required that the universe evolve, that it be dynamic and creative. But this requires the presence of physical evil. We could not come to be without death, without stars dying off. Big, physical events are necessary for us to be here and return God's love.

Coyne told me that the more he understands about the physical world, the stronger his faith becomes. After 50 years of research, he feels that his work itself has become a form of prayer. "The more I know about the world, the more I can glorify God," he said. He also believes that human beings, despite being part of the evolutionary process, must be special to God. God's given us extraordinary power, scientifically through the human brain and theologically through our souls. "Catholic theology holds that God intervenes by creating our soul," he said.

As a scientist, it's a little difficult to grasp because we see continuity in the evolutionary process rather than God intervening. I don't doubt that God can do it, and it doesn't contradict science. But I wonder where it fits in with my knowledge of the universe. If I didn't wonder, I'd be schizophrenic.

Ultimately, Coyne believes that God must be present in the universe but does not dominate it. He sees God as a parent nurturing a child. The parent lets go at some point, but is still involved, and loves the whole time.

Maybe God emptied himself in order to create the universe. He shared his love and emptied himself. This has been a big theme in theology since the time of St. Paul. But all of this finally is mystery. I haven't explained a whole lot. I have tried by science to get some hold on it. I don't propose an ultimate explanation of the mystery of evil. But I don't think we can even approach all this without a theological point of view, a belief in God. I don't know how people handle it, who don't believe in God, and simply accept the nature of the universe as it is. Entropy will win out in the end, scientifically speaking. But God created this universe and did so for a specific and important reason. That is love.

SISTER MARGARET GUIDER/HELPING TO REBUILD FAITH

I was carrying a big pile of mail back to my desk at work when I noticed a magazine sticking out from between the press releases. On the cover was a picture of a church steeple lying in ruins in front of a white clapboard Methodist church in Mississippi. Under the picture was this headline: "Finding God in Catastrophe/Groundbreaking course spotlights ministry in the midst of chaos." I rushed the magazine home, planning to read it when I could carve out a half hour of solitude. By the time that half hour came, 10 days or so later, I could not find the magazine. I could not recall what it looked like or who published it. I began to wonder if I dreamed up the whole thing: A magazine article that fell into my lap about a course dealing with the very subject I'm obsessed with. Who could the teacher be?

I wasn't losing it. My wife found the magazine in one of her files. It was published by the Weston Jesuit School of Theology in Cambridge, Massachusetts, an intellectual and pastoral capital of progressive Catholicism in the United States. And the teacher of the groundbreaking course was Sister Margaret Guider, a professor of missiology at the school. Without further delay, I blew through the article. This was someone I had to speak with. I was immediately drawn to her idea that ministers who work with victims of disaster must develop an "apocalyptic sensibility." An apocalyptic sensibility? Sounds like quite a burden to carry, even for the most sober among us. When we spoke, I asked Guider what this means.

> In Christian tradition, the liturgy for the first Sunday of Advent tells us: Stay awake, be watchful, you don't know the date, you don't know the hour, anything can happen. That is what I mean by an apocalyptic sensibility. The more that ministers can cultivate that sensibility in themselves, the more they are ready to receive the unexpected. The idea is that people *expect* the unexpected and that we live in a posture that tomorrow is going to be different from today—and I don't know how. I could win the jackpot or my school could burn down. People in our middle-class existence in the U.S. aren't living close to the edge, and you can feel cut off from the forces of nature. We don't focus on how tenuous our earthly existence is, which you have to do to minister to people whose world has fallen apart.

The idea for her course first germinated after 9/11, when Guider thought about the challenges facing former students who were ministering at Ground Zero. She thought about the stories told by students who had come back from Rwanda, Sudan, and other sites of catastrophe. Then came the tsunami and a pilgrimage of ministers and counselors from around the world to South Asia. Perhaps Guider could design a course to help students prepare for ministering in the worst possible circumstances.

Seventeen students signed up for the first class in the fall of 2005, just before Hurricane Katrina. They would talk about how to serve people whose lives had been turned upside down. On the one hand, this means dealing with practical issues like finding loved ones, food, and shelter. On the other hand, it means dealing with faith—faith that is shaken, faith that is being tested, and faith that is in danger of being lost. Guider wanted to help her students prepare to answer some of the same questions that I ask of well-trained theologians. Where was God? Why do catastrophes take some lives and not others? Her students will have to confront these questions when face-to-face with people who are bruised and battered, physically and spiritually, not with deep thinkers ensconced in their studies.

I asked Guider how one begins. She started from the top:

> First thing you need to know is what kind of a theological stance and background is the person asking the questions coming from. Are they asking why God allows the innocent to suffer? Or have they done certain things in their life and have somehow internalized suffering as punishment for them? Or do they have a theology where they believe life is suffering and everybody has to suffer in some way at some time. You have to know how to listen and how to ask questions that will help you to know what the person needs from you. Have they lost their faith? Do they need from you some kind of inspiration to help them recompose their faith? Some people are able to recompose their faith. Some don't. Some people recompose their faith in isolation. But I think most people recompose their faith—at ever greater degrees of complexity—in community. That's why I think it is so important in these times for communities to gather together, to be in solidarity with those who are suffering and to resist what we might call evil. Of course, when it comes to natural disasters, there is a diversity of opinion on whether they are evil or just a part of life.

I could not see, and still can't, how even the most empathetic minister can figure out so much about a survivor who is still trying to find his or her loved ones. You can't ask them to fill out a survey or sit through an interview. Still, I wanted to know more about how a minister can understand what has happened to someone's faith. After all, faith can be hard to talk about in the best of times. Guider told me that it is important to grasp what a victim believes about his or her relationship with God or a divine power. It's not simply a question of whether the person believes in God, but whether they feel God's presence in this world. Someone who believes that God created the world but is not involved day-to-day will react differently from someone who feels God's abiding presence. Someone who believed in God's abiding presence *before* a disaster may still trust that God is with them through devastation—or may feel suddenly abandoned. "The same theology can have very different outcomes," Guider said.

Of course, when you talk about ministering to people with different conceptions of God, you are also talking about ministering to people from different religious backgrounds. How does a Roman Catholic trained at a Jesuit school connect with a Muslim or a Hindu or even a Bible-quoting evangelical Christian? It's not easy, Guider said. But in today's world, it's essential. "From a Christian perspective, all I can say is that we need to have at least a solid, impressionistic understanding of what other world religions believe with regard to God's action. I know that's a lot," she told me.

> But if you're going to live in an urban setting in the United States and you're a Christian minister, you better be prepared. You can't even speak to an Italian Roman Catholic the way you would a Dutch Calvinist about original sin, how God treats us, what our destiny is. And Hinduism is every bit as complex as Christianity.

This explanation, I realized, would come across as very generous and charitable, very Christian, to many. But others might say that she is going too far to meet non-Christians where they live religiously, instead of bringing them the *Good News* of Jesus Christ when they need it most.

Once a Christian minister gets a handle on someone who has been through hell on earth—their image of the divine and of the hereafter, their definition of evil and of deliverance—then what? Things get mighty tricky. Guider told me that in times of disaster, many people, including survivors, want to know what God might be teaching us. The idea that there are lessons to learn can be consoling and comforting. The tsunami, some might say, brought the world together. Hurricane Katrina exposed the depths of American poverty. But this line of reasoning, which I have heard time and time again, leaves me cold. Must the victims of disasters be sacrificed in order for God to teach those who are left behind? Guider knew what I meant. "There are always victims," she said. "Different theologies have different victims. Somebody is always expendable for someone else's learning."

Guider talked often about helping people to recompose their faith. I thought her choice of verb was a bit clunky, but what better word can you use for such a task. Recomposing faith. It does not necessarily involve helping someone to become recommitted to Catholicism or to Judaism, Guider explained. It is a much more basic, open-ended task:

> I am talking about creating an environment where the human person can again have a capacity for faith. There are things you don't understand, but you basically take on trust. When I think of the capacity for faith, for hope, for love—in Christian terms, we talk about these as virtues—I look at them as the centers of gravity that enable human persons to make meaning of what's happening to them. Part of recomposing one's faith has to do with making meaning out of what is, in the eyes of some, a totally meaningless experience. The whole thing is so absurd, so horrendous, that you would have to be a crazy person to make meaning out of it.

Meaning, I began to see, was the key. Help a victim of disaster find meaning—in their life, in the world, in what happened to them—and they are on the way to recomposing their faith, their ability to see the world and their place in it. "When people say there is no meaning to be found, we have to really pay attention," Guider told me. "Part of the human condition is to make meaning. When you say you can't make meaning, that's like saying 'I don't want to eat anymore.' There are things we have to do everyday. We have to eat. We have to breathe. We have to make meaning."

FATHER MICHAEL SCANLAN/FROM DESPERATION TO SALVATION

I had a feeling that the chancellor of Franciscan University would not tell me that the meaning of the tsunami was to be found in the vast relief effort. It's not that Michael Scanlan doesn't think that the effort was important or that people of God aren't obligated to help their brothers and sisters in time of need. When we spoke, he did talk about God's goodness coming through in the work of so many. But this was not something he emphasized, not in the way that others did. Scanlan, I knew, would have a much more spiritual focus.

"God allows evil, devastations, disappointments, troubles, all those things, to draw us closer to him and to create more desperation in us so that we can find the savior and the kingdom of God that lasts forever and that can't be interfered with," he told me. "It also allows us to see there is evil in the world. There is the existence of Satan and demons. God ultimately draws good out of these terrible, evil situations."

He was once a man of this world. He graduated from Harvard Law School in 1956, and that is as "of this world" as you get. He served as a staff judge advocate for the U.S. Air Force. But he heard a call that would set him on a new path and in 1957 entered the Franciscan Third Order Regular, a community of priests and brothers. He was ordained a priest in 1964 and took his first job with the College of Steubenville in Steubenville, Ohio.

The social upheaval of the late 1960s and the early 1970s rocked Catholic colleges in different ways than it did the great secular universities. The questioning of old ways and orders produced a rethinking of what it meant to be a Catholic college. Many of these colleges began to focus first on academic excellence—encouraging an atmosphere of moderation, pluralism, and open-ended inquiry—and less on Catholic teachings and tradition. The fallout continues today, with many conservative Catholic leaders calling for a recommitment to Catholic identity at Catholic colleges.

Not at the renamed Franciscan University of Steubenville. Scanlan became president in 1974, at a time of declining enrollment, and took the school in a different direction. Toward orthodoxy. Over three decades, he would build what would become the educational center of orthodox Catholicism in the United States. Today, the university has 2,370 students from all 50 states and brings thousands of others to campus for 23 annual adult and youth conferences. And Scanlan is regarded as the hero of Franciscan University. There was grave concern in the orthodox Catholic community when he stepped down as president in 2000, but relief came when he became Franciscan's first chancellor.

It was early in our talk that Scanlan told me that God doesn't cause natural disasters, but allows them, in order to create desperation within us. This idea rattled around in my head until, at the first possible chance, I asked him to expound. This is what he said:

> We live in a society of presumption. We presume we can control things, we are in control. If we are not quite in control, we just have to get a little more education, a little more science, a little more something, and then we will be in control. That is simply false. We are basically creatures who live by the providence and mercy of God. God has to allow the truth to come home to us and break through. There are times that the only thing that can break through is something big enough to knock us off our feet. It takes humiliation. A tsunami is very humiliating. What do you mean we cannot control these things? What do you mean we are not masters of the waters, the seas? What do you mean? In New Orleans, what do you mean our precautions and levees weren't enough? It creates a humbling situation. Out of humility comes an openness to new truths. Out of new truths come a openness to salvation.

Scanlan's insistence that God needs to shock us out of thinking that we run the world brought to mind David Elcott's debate with his wife, when he said that the modern worship of progress had failed us. Whenever people believe they can control events through science, reason, or a new theory of government, Elcott had said, they're heading for trouble. Scanlan agreed but went further by suggesting that disasters are a reminder from God of who is in control.

Any time someone suggested to me that the tsunami, or any other tragedy, is a message from God—even if God is simply allowing the message to break through—it was important to me to ask about the victims. They are not around to experience the humiliation and humility that Scanlan spoke of. He understood my concern, but had no blanket answer to justify the suffering of individuals as part of a larger message to the world. "It's very difficult," he said, in the weary voice of someone who has tackled the question of suffering too many times. "We're dealing with mystery. You look at the tsunami, the statistics, the misery, the broken families, it has a humbling effect and a bonding effect, but it's overwhelming to our heads and hearts. It stirs the question of how God can allow this when he is all-powerful, supposedly."

Scanlan would never talk of the darkness of unexplainable tragedy very long without returning to the light of God and the need for salvation. He is a leader of the growing movement of charismatic Catholics, who believe that prayer can draw the power of the Holy Spirit and produce physical effects, such as healing of the sick and speaking in tongues. Wherever our talk led, he returned to the power of prayer and the saving grace of Jesus. He seemed to take comfort in telling me this story:

We had one of our students die in an automobile accident. Very innocent. Tragic. We had the funeral here on campus in the field house. At the end of the funeral, the father of the dead boy stood up on the stage and said "I don't have the answers. I can't explain why this happened. But all I know is where my son is now, he wants to stay and he doesn't want to come back here." That had a powerful effect on the whole student body. Yes, when someone goes to heaven, no matter how tragic the circumstances, he isn't saying that he wishes he were alive and could go back to earth. He is with God. This is a perspective we must have when dealing with death: Who are we more concerned about, the people who died or ourselves with our sense of loss and shock?

He also told me a story about visiting the Holy Land and standing where Jesus was when he got word that Lazarus was sick and that he needed to come quickly. "It was a short distance," Scanlan told me. "You could see from one place to the other." But Jesus waited two days before he went. And it was too late.

Jesus was confronted—"If you had been here, you could have saved him." But Jesus said that for the glory of God, raising Lazarus from the dead was the greater good. I use that a lot in my mind to hold on to and trust that God's grace is working.

The message of both stories was that salvation through Christ awaits and offers the ultimate and complete answer to any suffering in this world. Still, I wanted to know more about the idea that God allows disasters that cause desperation and serve to wake us up. Scanlan explained to me that God has active and passive wills. His active will initiates, determines, and acts. His passive will allows us to live with the consequences of our sins. "There is our inherited sin, from Adam and Eve, and the sinful condition of this world," he said.

Could a natural disaster be a result of sinfulness, I asked him. "Yes," he said. "I believe that. It's part of the disorder in our world. I don't believe there ever would have been a tsunami in the Garden of Eden."

Scanlan was talking in a universal, almost cosmic sense, but from a very Christian point of view. He believes there are links between original sin, disorder in the world, God's need to keep us alert, and the various calamities that might result. But we can't see the direct connections. He stops short of blaming the victims or saying that God's wrath is directed at any group in particular.

But what about those people who say that God aimed Hurricane Katrina at New Orleans or that he delivered the tsunami as one of a long list of possible messages?

> We don't have God's mind. We certainly know that there is a history, from Scripture, of God allowing punishment, both for correction and for the greater good. How much is punishment after a given disaster? We don't know. People who speak out that way better be speaking out based on a sense of what God is telling them. I don't see how we can make any definitive conclusions.

I asked Scanlan what his first reaction would be when he hears that the earth beneath our feet or the elements have created human suffering on a scale that we can hardly comprehend. His answer didn't surprise me. "Pray. Pray. Pray immediately," he said.

> It drives me to the chapel. I urge others, let's join together and pray. Do that first and then we have a chance with enlightened minds to see the situation more as God sees it. Ask for God's greater glory, greater mercy, to come down and care for all those suffering, and for his mercy to be on all those who died, so they may go into eternal glory.

For Christians, he said, there is one path to final understanding:

> Jesus. He's the savior, the way, the truth and the light. He's the one you cling to. His Holy Spirit gives you wisdom you don't have, gives you knowledge you don't have and enables you stand with Jesus as a faithful disciple, trusting him and knowing that he is the source of all good.

THE REVEREND THOMAS WEINANDY/SUFFERING MAKES US HOLY

Coyne would hold that hurricanes, tornadoes, and tsunamis are not intrinsically evil. On paper, they represent some sort of atmospheric correction or a sharp shift in energy. That's it. If one such event was to occur someplace where there are no people, who would think of it as a disaster? Father Thomas Weinandy laughed as he raised the question, as he did often during our conversation. "The problem is," he said, "if you happen to get in the way of these things." So, I thought, he's saying that if an earthquake occurs in a vast forest and no one hears or feels it, did it really happen? It was an interesting point posed by a priest who is used to making them.

Weinandy, a member of the Capuchin Franciscan Order, has spent his entire adult life engaged in intellectual pursuits and is considered one of the leading Catholic scholars in the United States. He's taught at numerous universities, including, from 1991 to 2004, at Oxford. His areas of specialty do not make for light reading: the history of Christology (more or less, the study of the person and nature of Jesus), the history of soteriology (the study of salvation), the history of Trinitarian theology, and the philosophical notions of God. But I contacted Weinandy because of his current position. Since 2004, he's been serving as a chief advisor on doctrine to America's Catholic bishops. Needless to say, it's not a post they give to any old priest. As executive director of the Secretariat for Doctrine and Pastoral Practices for the United States Conference of Catholic Bishops, Weinandy is a counselor on issues great and small. A committee of bishops could ask him, in theory, what Catholic doctrine has to say about natural disasters. So I asked him. Weinandy first posited that natural disasters are only as disastrous as their proximity to people, a point that I don't remember anyone else making. Then he continued:

> Let's say that people *are* in the way. From a Christian perspective, could God stop something like this? Could he say "We've got an earthquake in the middle of the sea. I could have stopped it then, but it's already happened. But we have a tsunami coming now, so should I step in now..." On one level, yes he could, if he wanted to. He's the God who created the whole thing. The Psalms talked about how even the seas and the wind obey. So he could do it if he wanted. But normally he doesn't. I mean, he does do miracles and there are probably more out there than we think. But normally, the laws of nature, he put them in place and they do the things they are supposed to do. But then you ask, if he's a good God, why would he let these natural disasters happen? If he has the ability to stop them? In one sense, we don't know.

Weinandy, who wears a brown, hooded robe as a Capuchin, laughed again. For someone who deals with heavy theological stuff, he's pretty blunt and has a good sense of humor. He likes to mix it up. He told me right away, for instance, that the mainstream media's sudden and brief interest in God after a disaster is little more than a business decision. "They never raise the God question unless they figure they can give God a bad name," he said. "I take other people seriously when they raise these questions, but I never take the media seriously."

I asked Weinandy how the Catholic Church interprets natural disaster these days. The Vatican, after all, is now very respectful of science, and Catholics are not prone to read the Bible as God's word-for-word lesson plans. "From the Catholic perspective, back in the Middle Ages, a lot of people said the plague was a punishment from God," Weinandy told me. "Well, maybe it was, maybe it wasn't. Today the church, the official church, is very, very cautious about making any kinds of statements that a given act is a punishment from God. It may be, but how do you discern that?" He said that there are probably messages from God in all kinds of events, but that they are unlikely to be niche messages aimed at a particular market. "Any time something bad happens, God may be telling people that you can't depend on your big car and big house for happiness," he said. "There's more to life than that. But let individual people make their individual judgments for what God is telling them. I would be hesitant to make a blanket statement."

Catholics generally don't read Scripture in a literal way, as evangelicals do. But Weinandy did want to make sure that I understand that the church believes in original sin and the fall of humankind. There is no way for a Christian—Catholic or otherwise—to look at natural disasters without taking into account the sinful, fallen nature of the world. "I'm not sure how to figure this out philosophically or scientifically, but I suppose that if sin never entered the world, the world would be a little more user-friendly than it is," he told me. "Somehow or other, our human sin has affected not only our relationships with one another, our free human actions through which we do evil deeds, but has brought on the brunt of natural disasters as well." He said that after Christ's return and the redemption of humankind, not only will people rise from the dead and live in heaven "in a manner we cannot even imagine," but the physical universe will be transformed. "Without earthquakes," he said. Then Weinandy started to laugh, truly amused by what he was about to say: "Or there will be even bigger earthquakes, but they'll be fun to watch and won't be hurtful. I've often wanted to see a tornado, not having come from the Midwest."

Until then, we will remain confounded about human suffering, about why one person is struck down by a tornado while his next-door neighbor is saved, about why one person recovers from a critical disease while another tries every available treatment but still succumbs.

I know people who have been healed of cancer. I know tons of other people who have died of cancer. There is no medical reason for why one person's cancer disappeared. Maybe they went to Lourdes and got healed. I don't know. But God knows for some reason it was for the betterment of this person that he got healed, but maybe not for the betterment of the other person who died.

Maybe if the other person was healed, he would end up committing mortal sins and going to hell. So he's better off dying, in one sense. Saint Paul says that for those who love God, God works out everything for the better. We may not fully appreciate or understand that. None of us go through a day without some kind of suffering. You might wonder "Why did God let that happen?" or "Why am I struggling as I get older with my prostate?" I think it's all part of God trying to make us holy. In a world in which we are fallen, these sorts of things help us to become holy. If we put our trust and faith in God a little bit more, if we're not so self-assured and cocky.

I asked Weinandy about those who died in the tsunami or the Pakistani quake, and who aren't around to learn from these events or from the smaller struggles that can make us holy. But he didn't hesitate to answer that the victims are already taken care of.

If you're a Christian, you figure that we don't know who gets to heaven or who doesn't, but you know that death isn't the worst thing that can happen. If they got to heaven, they're perfectly happy. They don't look back and say "Heck, too bad I got mowed over by a tsunami." We all want to live as long as we can, but the whole point is to get to somewhere that's even better.

We talked about whether America's religious leaders spend enough time unraveling natural disasters, at least in terms of God's role in this world and the meaning of suffering. Many people must ask these questions of themselves. But the Catholic Church, like other traditions, tends to concentrate on funneling money to relief organizations. Weinandy agreed that this is the case but said that parish priests are in a tough spot when Sunday Mass follows a mysterious and devastating event.

What gets preached from the pulpit and by the bishops is "Let's support these people, take up a collection and do what we can to help them get back on their feet,"—rather than addressing the theological issues that may be raised. Part of the problem is that there is no simple answer. You can't get on a pulpit and say this is why this happened, other than to say that God has his purposes and ways and hopefully it will all become clear in heaven. What is there to say other than that we have to know that God loves us, that we have to trust in him, that he's on our side in the end? Other than that, what can you say?

THOUGHTS

I often get the feeling when talking to ordinary Roman Catholics that they believe their church is overly rigid in its thinking—a "religious right" with the Eucharist. The Vatican is certainly unbending on high-profile moral issues of the day (abortion, stem cell research, etc.). But I've found that many Catholic scholars are very open to confronting the challenges posed by secular thinking, as long as they aren't expected to abandon their faith when doing so. This open-mindedness came through during my conversations for this chapter. None of my interviewees tried to avoid the thorny questions raised by the tsunami or other examples of terrible tragedy inflicted on the innocent. Groeschel, an orthodox Catholic by any measure, told me that anyone who thinks they have a handle on evil will be taught otherwise by the dark realities of life.

Catholicism does not look away from the mysteries of life that we can't unravel. In fact, it focuses on the mysteries, as if they are the missing pieces to a jigsaw puzzle that God held back from this life so that we won't become complacent and will keep searching. Scanlan said that God needs to create desperation within us but that the Holy Spirit will give us wisdom if we listen. Guider said that we must live with an apocalyptic sensibility because of the uncertainty that we face at all times but that faith can be somehow restored in the face of any tragedy.

I thought that Weinandy illustrated the Catholic sensibility well. We must accept that we live in a broken world, he said. We must assume that God knows what's best for each of us, that suffering makes us more holy, and that the next life is better than this one. That's what the Catholic faith offers. Beyond that, we can try to laugh at the mysteries before us.

Then there's Coyne, the Jesuit astronomer. He is understandably fixated on the magnificence of the universe, on its evolution over billions of years, and on its inevitable loss of energy. He can't see the tsunami as anything more than one event connected to so many others (not unlike Adin Steinsaltz, who draws the same conclusion from Talmud). Coyne said that his scientific explorations only increase his faith, even if he doesn't believe that God *causes* actions in the common sense. He prefers to think that God created a fluid, unpredictable world out of love, so that we can actively return God's love. It's a concept built on faith and open to mystery.

5 THE MAINLINE PROTESTANT PERSPECTIVE

If Catholics approach suffering by looking to Christ on the cross while embracing the mysteries of this life, mainline Protestants are prone to emphasize God's enduring love and how this love must power human compassion and action. Mainline Protestants come from traditions that were once puritanical and fundamentalist, traditions that demanded strict adherence to Scripture and moral codes. Over the last half-century, though, mainline traditions have developed a very different vision of Christian witness. They emphasize Jesus' love for the oppressed and the absolute need to act on behalf of the marginalized. They preach tolerance and inclusion and seek not to be judgmental. They present an image of God that is all-embracing and decidedly unthreatening, an image that can be difficult to reconcile with the aftermath of a natural disaster.

THE REVEREND SHANTA PREMAWARDHANA/THE SEARCH FOR COMMON GROUND

Almost from the time the tsunami struck, certain religious leaders were destined to play key roles in organizing the American response. One would be Shanta Premawardhana.

He is associate general secretary for interfaith relations for the NCC (National Council of Churches), the most visible ecumenical organization in the country. Clearly, the NCC's influence has been on the decline for years due to an assortment of reasons. Its uniformly liberal agenda has not exactly captured the public imagination, even though there is widespread support for many of the individual peace and justice issues that the council promotes. Interest in ecumenism or improved relations among Christian traditions, the NCC's reason for being, has also been ebbing for some time. It's impossible to ignore the fact that the mainline denominations that make up the NCC have watched their cultural prestige slide for decades, as evangelicals and Catholics have become the dominant Christian voices in America. Predicting the NCC's demise has been a popular sport for some time. But the council still has 36 member denominations—Protestant, Anglican, and Orthodox—that claim 140,000 congregations. And the NCC remains effective at speaking out on certain kinds of social justice issues. The council may be at its best when there is a disaster, and it can give voice to the voiceless, organize relief efforts, and work with other faiths with a high degree of sensitivity.

This is where Premawardhana comes in. As the NCC's chief interfaith officer, it became his job to represent the council's Christian membership before Muslims in Indonesia, Hindus in India, and Buddhists in Sri Lanka. A native of Sri Lanka himself, he also understood the culture of the bludgeoned region, particularly the complex, often difficult relationships among Christians, Hindus, and Buddhists. As a veteran Baptist pastor and hospital chaplain, he understood the pastoral side of ministering to those whose bodies and spirits are broken. So Premawardhana set out for Indonesia and Sri Lanka one week after the tsunami and again three months later. He returned to Sri Lanka just after the one-year anniversary. After each trip, he faced the same assortment of questions that I would turn on him and everyone else in this book.

> Everywhere I went, people wanted to know how to help. They asked what was my theological reflection about where was God in the tsunami or where was not God. They wanted to know what are people thinking and feeling and doing. And people wanted to know how Buddhists in Sri Lanka and Muslims in Indonesia processed this. I would have to tell them that there are people there of all religious traditions—Buddhist, Muslim and Christian—who would say that this was God's will. Some would say that "God is punishing *those* kinds of people." Some Christians said God was punishing the Buddhist people in Sri Lanka. Some said God was punishing Muslims. And some Muslims said— this gets interesting—"We are not living out our faith properly. We are not fulfilling God's law properly. That is why this happened to us." So people responded in a variety of ways that I am still trying to explain to people.

The idea that God was punishing anyone with the tsunami, or that one religion somehow brought it on everyone, is about as contrary as possible to the mainline Protestant way of thinking. These Protestants were once America's Puritans, evangelicals, and fundamentalists, the original fire and brimstone preachers who warned that sinful behavior would lead to eternal damnation. But their traditions came to form the nation's religious establishment, the mainstream or the mainline. Today they are the preachers of tolerance, pluralism, and inclusiveness, bedrock American values to be sure but hardly religious priorities to more conservative Christians who focus on prayer, individual repentance, and traditional "moral values."

Mainliners are not known for judging others, especially people of other cultures. Premawardhana strongly disagreed with the theories of God's punishment that seemed to be "mainline" in Indonesia and Sri Lanka. But he avoided all opportunities to condemn such views. Premawardhana has spent much of his life seeking reconciliation between Christians and others. In Chicago, where he pastored a Baptist church, he led people of different faiths in fighting for economic justice and immigrant rights, took the lead in combating historical anti-Judaism in churches, and led a group that lobbied to reform education funding. No matter how much he may have disliked what he heard at the scenes of the tsunami, he preferred to tell me how he dealt with the tragedy. He described how during his first visit to Sri Lanka he visited the site where a close friend had perished. He prayed and reflected. Then he walked a short distance to the beach.

> A beautiful beach. Beautiful ocean. I sat on a rock. I thought what a beautiful place this is. Look at the rhythmic lapping of the waves. So rhythmic. So predictable. So safe. Except on *that* day. I thought it was too soon, much too soon, to reflect on God, where was God. Even now, more than a year later, I'm afraid we should stay in silence. We need to stand in awe and in silence at the mystery of what happened. I know there are lots of people who will jump in and say "This is why it happened." My faith perspective says to me that I can never fathom what God is or what God does with absolute certainty about anything. In fact, my faith perspective is to be in silence, to absorb the pathos and pain and the tragedy of it and to incorporate it into my own response of love and caring for people.

Premawardhana is something of a one-man clearinghouse of information on the tsunami. He knows the cultures. He's worked with the different faiths. He's familiar with many of the relief agencies involved. He's comfortable with the pastoral responsibilities of a clergyman. Despite all this and his visible leadership role with the NCC, his personal response to the tsunami is silence. Prayer, contemplation, and silence. I pushed him a bit to consider God's role or presence, but he did so more out of politeness than any personal inclination. He talked about seeing God in the rhythmic lapping of the waves, in the natural processes of life, and in the commitment of American volunteers wearing blue "USA" T-shirts who went to work clearing rubble. These were familiar answers and not particularly enlightening. At one point in our conversation, Premawardhana said that questions about God's role in tragedy and suffering are important and should be asked. He even joked that my questions would help him organize his thoughts for an upcoming return to Sri Lanka. But for him, silence remained the best possible answer. "As a Christian and a pastor, I would say that it is right and appropriate for people to seek God's guidance in our day to day life," he told me. "But we need to be sensitive to how we interpret events. To put it simply, if a student does not study for a test and prays to God to help pass the test, does failing the test mean that God is not there? God is there. God was crying with us during the tsunami."

Premawardhana faced similar questions when he worked as a hospital chaplain. Patients asked why they got cancer, especially when they did not smoke and tried to eat well. He would tell them that getting cancer is part of being human. "That is how we are created," he tells them. "My faith response is to be silent and absorb the mystery." He knows this answer does not always satisfy. He recalled preaching on the first Sunday morning after a gunman killed several people at a Baptist church in Texas. His congregation was deeply hurt and looked to their pastor for sustenance.

> Many people were really touched. They were asking why God let this happen. The victims were praying to and praising God when this happened. Why didn't he stop it? I said that God was very angry that day. Young people were killed and God wanted us to go out and do something, to deal with violence and make things better. I think of God as being much more involved in our day to day lives, but not in the sense of swooping down and stopping the gunman from doing this or stopping the tsunami from happening. God says "I am involved in the pain of this." To me, that is what Jesus on the cross is about. God is involved in human suffering and pain and is urging us to engage with that pain so that we might bring healing, we might be agents of healing. That is a Christian response, a biblically supportable response. There will be people who will disagree with me, but that's okay.

Of all the issues that came up in the aftermath of the tsunami, one that particularly concerned Premawardhana had to do with Christian evangelizing in the devastated communities. This came as no surprise, considering his longtime focus on cross-cultural respect. As a Christian, he has no problem with bringing word of Christ and the Bible to non-Christian cultures. But he is very aware of a tricky situation that has arisen over the past 30 years or so when American evangelical groups send English teachers, computer programmers, and others to Sri Lanka, India, Indonesia, and elsewhere. It has to do with money. "They go and start Bible study and prayer meetings in rural villages, which is fine," he told me.

The problem arises when you've gathered a group of village folks who are pretty poor by any standard. You're praying together and somebody says "My roof blew off" or "My son is in difficulty." You are the American with dollars in your pocket. Out of good Christian charity, you give out some money. The person keeps coming back and pretty soon you have a convert. Now, is that an ethical conversion?

These conversions are seen as bought or forced by the local communities. As a result, governments are trying to ban what they call unethical conversions. Communities that feel taken advantage of are sometimes unleashing violence on local churches and even native-born Christian pastors. The situation worsened after the tsunami when numerous American evangelical agencies set up shop among Muslims, Hindus, and Buddhists, mixing relief work with proselytizing.

It is a situation that Premawardhana finds to be quite disturbing. As he sees it, Christians should first work to provide shelter, food, and medical care to those whose day-to-day existence is uncertain. This example is evangelizing in a pure sense. There will be time and opportunity for Bible study. To use the tsunami as an opportunity to proselytize is decidedly un-Christian. "Ultimately what happens is that churches get burned and pastors get killed," he told me.

Some of these relief efforts are very clear about wanting to get people converted. Is that right? I think this is not only inappropriate for Christians, to mix evangelism and aid, but it breaks down a very intricate interfaith balance that has been set in these countries. We need to speak out and to revisit this issue again and again.

The Reverend Charles Henderson/Uniting Faith and Intellect

Believing in a God who is powerful and good in the face of the bad things that happen in the world is really tough. It's not easy. There's no way of rationally explaining it. But I don't believe that God sends hurricanes and tsunamis at people. It's not his *judgment*. I know there are people who say this, but they're unhinged.

Charles Henderson likes to speak and write frankly about the connection between religious faith and ways of thinking that he believes are not unhinged. That's why I contacted him. Henderson is executive director of something called the Association for Religion and Intellectual Life, which publishes an always interesting and provocative journal, *Crosscurrents.* He is very much in touch with the many trends firing up the religious world, the interaction between what's in the news and what's being said in churches, and the growing roles that technology and the media are playing in many spiritual and intellectual pursuits. I knew he would be in a good position to judge the many religious reactions to the tsunami, Katrina, and whatever else. His reactions are rock-solid mainline Protestant reactions: worldly, thoughtful, liberal, and impatient with ideas he sees as small-minded, close-minded, and no-minded. He is a Presbyterian minister who has led churches in New York, New Jersey, and Connecticut, served as a chaplain at Princeton University, and lectured on most Ivy League campuses. His wife is an official at Auburn Theological Seminary in New York, one of the bricks in the mainline foundation.

Conservative Christians would likely describe Henderson as part of the Eastern liberal elite. He would not care.

"Do we worship a God who micromanages the natural order? I don't think so," he told me.

> Do we worship a god who directs hurricanes to hit certain cities at certain times for certain reasons? There is a persistent group within our population that says that God has reasons for everything that happens. Not only that, these people, like Pat Robertson, know what those reasons are. They can read the mind of God, so to speak.

Henderson told me that many Americans are not well prepared to deal with complicated theological questions. Even children who regularly attend houses of worship receive only an hour a week or so of religious instruction each week. Most adults cling to childlike understandings of God and Scripture and have no real understanding of competing theologies. "Therefore the public generally is less knowledgeable about religion than about other things, even though there is high level of church attendance," he said. "This shows up in the lack of informed opinion on these topics." The mainstream media then make things worse by treating religious questions superficially and by highlighting the polarizing views of people like Pat Robertson and Jerry Falwell. "My own little conspiracy theory is that a lot of people in the news media have a pretty negative view of religion and Robertson and Falwell reinforce their negative view," Henderson told me, sounding pretty proud of his idea, a quirky liberal Christian take on the common criticism that the media are devoutly secular. "They're saying 'We think religion is pretty stupid, so let's bring on people who confirm how bad it is.' The truth is that people like myself, who try to have nuanced viewpoints, with complexity and subtlety, have not exactly mastered soundbites for the media world."

I asked Henderson why God's role in the tsunami captured the attention of so many people with underdeveloped religious views (aided as they were by the secularist media, which perhaps pumped up the tsunami as a strike against religion, following Henderson's theory). He explained:

> I'm not sure the tsunami made people ask the question any more intensely than other things. If a person in your own family gets cancer, the same questions will certainly arise. But this was a massive disaster and everyone asked the question at once. This created a public forum. It happened during the holiday season, which was big. And there were pictures of the waves coming in that dramatized it in a powerful way. Contrast it with the earthquake in Pakistan, which didn't get anywhere near the publicity. We didn't see pictures of the earthquake. It wasn't like it was happening before your very eyes, so Pakistan got short shrift in terms of the attention of the world. The thrust of the concern after Katrina had to do with seeing the poor suffering disproportionately. In the tsunami, there were a lot of poor people suffering, but it didn't expose the kind of contradictions we saw in our own country. With the tsunami, those people were just helpless. No one expected the government to help them. So the theological questions came to the forefront. The response to Katrina was more of a moral response. We saw a failure of the local, state and especially federal authorities to deal with it, so there was a scapegoat. The most powerful nation on earth can't get basic relief to the people. This is ridiculous.

Henderson is quite comfortable swatting aside what he sees as the divisive, theologically vulgar views of many conservative Christians. But he was more eager to offer his own view of God's role in suffering. It is a view that I would imagine would connect with most Christians on some level, even if Henderson has little to say about God's intent or the sinfulness of those who suffer. It is important to ask where God was during the tsunami, he told me, and to wrestle with the implications.

> The crucifixion of Jesus is not all that extraordinary. My general take is that God is within nature, as well as beyond nature. When people are suffering, that is God suffering. The crucifixion is powerful because it is so typical. It is an experience that many, many people have in life—not being crucified for crimes they didn't commit, but suffering for no apparent reason. Senseless suffering is a part of human life. I think that God, being all encompassing, omnipresent, is suffering right there with us. That is part of the message of Jesus. God isn't up there like a king on a throne who sends warriors into battle to die but remains safe in a command center. God is right here. We are created in the image of God. So when a human is put in a situation that violates the dignity of a person, like the tsunami, that is the image of God being violated. It is blasphemy.

Henderson believes that by refusing to blame the victims of suffering, he is in the minority, in the United States and around the world. But he said that there has always been a strong current through the great world religions, of the East and West, that holds that the just and unjust suffer alike and that the religious response to suffering is compassion. He believes and hopes that this view is slowly building momentum, in part because different faiths are coming into contact all over the world. "One religion will not predominate, so we have to be respectful of different points of view," he said. "It is harder to stick with the idea that my God is the only God, my truth is the only truth."

Support for such views will only whip up fundamentalists of all faiths, Henderson concedes. So he doesn't see the popular image of God—"throwing down lightening bolts, hurricanes and tsunamis to punish people and lottery tickets to reward other people"—fading away any time soon. People still have a need to find God's will in everything and a closely related need to blame the victims of suffering. The alternative is still too much for many people to bear.

> After Katrina, what did we hear?: "The people were told to get out, but they didn't get out. If only they had been sensible enough to get out, it wouldn't have happened." When people get sick, there is often an attempt to explain it. In the case of a smoker, it's a quick explanation, but even when there is no obvious connection, people will say "She should have had a check-up more frequently" or "His lifestyle was a problem." People tend to blame the victim because we want to think that things occur for a reason. We are reluctant to accept the fact that life is a crap-shoot and that random behavior is a very important part of the events in the world around us.

In the last chapter, Benedict Groeschel lavished praise on the words of Albert Einstein, who needed room for divine mystery in the universe. Henderson also remembered one of Einstein's most famous sayings but told me that he found him to be overreaching:

> Einstein is famous for saying "God doesn't play dice with the world." He wanted to see a world of order that could be explained more or less through natural laws. But it turns out that God does play dice with the world. The building blocks of life are to some degree random events, mutations. There is a huge element of chance built into it all.

PAUL CHANG-HA LIM/THEOLOGY ON THE GROUND

If Paul Chang-Ha Lim thought that his new faculty post, as an assistant professor of historical and systematic theology, was going to be, well, systematic, he had another thing coming. During his very first week at Gordon-Conwell Theological Seminary, his syllabus was interrupted by the 9/11 terrorist attacks. It was a stinging lesson that theology cannot be confined to classrooms, textbooks, and the timeless wisdom of the church fathers, not when there is a world outside that all too often leaves people groping for any semblance of security. So Lim stood before his students and grappled with the theological implications of terrorism, of moral evil, of a potential clash between religions. He would have to confront the unknown again and teach real-world, blood-and-guts theology after the tsunami and yet again after Hurricane Katrina.

> For me, when the tsunami occurred, there was no way to avoid the philosophical and theological questions in class. To what extent can we speak of God being in the tsunami? This was the question. I went right to New Testament Scripture, Romans 8: 17–25, which deals with the whole creative order. St. Paul sets the whole story. According to this Christian narrative, St. Paul says that creation is groaning right now. He says that something isn't right, that it's not meant to be the way it is. But it's not because of its own choice, but because of someone else's choice, namely the primordial parents, Adam and Eve. They brought about this cursed ground, the ecological imbalance. Even so, the Christian theologian still has to grapple with whether God has abandoned this world. Is that why these things are happening? If my wife and I leave my 15-month-old son, even for a few hours, we could get arrested, right? So do we have a celestial absentee parent?

Although Lim was an accomplished theologian before 40, specializing in Puritan thinking and teaching at a prominent evangelical seminary (more about that soon), he is by no means a fragile academic who wants to stay in the distant and unthreatening past. He is a Presbyterian minister who has faced his own difficulties and is eager to apply the lessons of Scripture to life as it's led. He wanted to wrestle with the questions posed by 9/11 and the tsunami. He feels that his academic credentials, not to mention his faith, will be strengthened by facing the hard questions. "There is nothing worse than an armchair theologian," he told me.

That means leaving campus. Lim spent part of the summer before the tsunami in Sri Lanka, right by the ocean, teaching a group of local pastors. During the summer of 2005, he visited Geneva, Switzerland, to give lectures about the problem of evil to Christian humanitarian aid workers who had spent time in some of the world's worst trouble spots. It was his job to remind them why it was a Christian mission to return to Sudan or Afghanistan, where they would meet victims of unspeakable suffering. "It was a humbling and sobering thing," Lim told me. "I can talk about the problem of evil all I want in this nice suburban school. It's a different ballgame when you have to hang out with these people who face grim reapers everyday." After Katrina, Lim took five students to Biloxi, Mississippi, to work with a Presbyterian relief agency. "They said it was the highlight of their theological education," he said with some pride.

Lim knows something about how faith, Christianity in particular, can serve as an antidote to many forms of uncertainty. He grew up in Seoul, Korea, where his father—who had escaped North Korea during the war—was jailed for having a lack of allegiance to the government. "When you're a 9-year-old boy, that throws you for a real existential loop," he said. His father was released on the condition that the family would leave the country, so they moved to suburban Cherry Hill, New Jersey, when Lim was 15. He was a teenage political refugee without a culture, friends, or a purpose. Friday nights of Bible study, Burger King and bowling were miserable. Only after he enrolled at Yale and was dragged along on a church retreat was he struck by a line from a praise song: "I don't need your money, I want your life." "As strange as it might sound, I felt like someone other than the praise band was addressing me," he told me.

> At that moment, things that were repressed for years opened up. I kind of broke down and began my spiritual journey. I instinctively knew that the Christian God wasn't distant. I had suffered with my father's incarceration and our coming to America. As I understood the Christian gospel, here was a God who would accept me as I am. It was liberating and overwhelming.

After college, Lim worked for two years as an analyst at a New York investment firm. He was ready to go to law school. But he began attending a Korean Presbyterian church in Queens and working with troubled kids. A minister advised him to avoid talking about the Bible because he knew little about it. That realization led to seminary and a whole different career path. When we spoke, Lim was serving as an associate pastor at a Presbyterian church and teaching at a respected evangelical seminary (he would soon leave for Vanderbilt University). His friends say he talks, walks, and thinks like an evangelical, but Lim won't take the tag. "My core beliefs are evangelical, but I serve a mainline church," he said.

> I have an allergic reaction to the triumphalism of evangelicalism. American evangelicals do not have a theology of suffering. I would never say the tsunami happened because they're not Christians or that Katrina happened because New Orleans has so many gays. The best thing we can do is weep with those who weep and roll up our sleeves and get on with it.

Lim teaches theology with a personal bent. He tells his own story. And he isn't afraid to confess that he doesn't have answers, at least the kind of answers that students want when the natural order rises up to swallow innocents or when some people inflict suffering on others without any opposition.

> When you hear stories of those who have given up on faith, more often than not it is horrific suffering that precipitates a torpor of doubt and eventual denial. The more I study theology, and I just told my class this, these eager theology students, the less I think I know. When I was a second year student in seminary, I knew a lot more than I do now. I don't have that cocksureness. While I hold on to more things, I hold them a little less tightly. Certain things are non-negotiable if I'm going to continue on my journey as a Christian. One of them is the involvement of God. However mysterious and perplexing it is, I cannot give up on the idea that God is present with and in the world. But it is the suffering presence of God that has been most clearly revealed, through the event of Jesus and the cross and the empty tomb. It still doesn't solve all the subsequent problems of evil and suffering, but there it is.

So what does Lim tell his students about the tsunami? For one thing, he splices together bits of Scripture that offer wisdom and perhaps consolation. But he doesn't pretend to have answers and doesn't try to avoid Scripture's niggling soft spots.

> When Jesus and his followers encounter this man born blind, they ask him, "Rabbi, who sinned that this man was born blind, his parents or himself?" But Jesus says neither, that it wasn't some kind of karmic debt that rendered this man blind. He says that the man was born blind so that the work of God might be displayed. The man receives his sight. But he doesn't complain. He doesn't say "Hey man, why did I have to be blind for the last 30 years?" That's what I might say.

On the day I spoke with Lim, he had been talking about the problem of evil with a seminary student, a very conservative evangelical who was a graduate of the Air Force Academy. The student, Lim told me, was committed to accepting authority and could not see how it was right to question God. Lim told him that God is mightier than anyone's doubts, but he suspected that the student probably dismissed him as a flaky liberal. Lim laughed as he told me this story. He said that he tries to teach his students that they can be true Christians without looking away from a world that is rife with maddening inconsistencies and unexplainable pain.

> I encourage my students to shake off some naivety and look afresh at Scripture, strip it down to the bare essentials of this cross of Jesus Christ. What does it tell me about God's power? If we say that God's most powerful display of might was on the cross, that seems ironic. God's power was most clearly displayed in the

helpless death of God's son. I tell my students, when you think of God, you're probably thinking of some celestial Arnold Schwarzenegger, so many degrees stronger and taller and buffer. Maybe Zeus was like that. But is it the Christian portrait of God? I encourage my students, when looking at the question of theodicy, to reframe it as Christodicy. We're not talking about some generic deity, but the specific deity of Jesus the Christ who presents both the problem *and a solution* to the whole question of human suffering in this world. It is this God who, alongside fallen humanity, came and suffered. The historic reality is that after two millennia, God is still on the dock. Where are you, God? Where were you at 9:30 a.m. on Sept. 11, 2001? Where were you when the earthquake occurred in Pakistan? Where were you when these torrential waves drowned unsuspecting people? Is the cross of Christ a sufficient answer? If a Christian thinks her faith will never be tested, she better give up on Christianity right now. There will be severe trials, tribulations and temptations along the way. There will be counter evidence. There will be ground-shaking faith busters. Count on it.

THE REVEREND JAMES ROWE ADAMS/A DIFFERENT UNDERSTANDING OF GOD

At some stage while working on each chapter of this book, I wrestled with which points of view I needed to include. As I said in the Introduction, it would be impossible to represent the range of views within a given religious tradition through the words of only five individuals. But for each tradition, I wanted to cover certain bases. A problem arose when I couldn't make up my mind what those bases should be. Take mainline Protestants. There's a big mainline world out there, a landscape dotted with hundreds of denominations that have family trees whose branches extend back to the Old World. There are countless subtle differences among them, even if those differences are usually more important to denominational leaders than they are to the people in the pews. One of the more interesting trends that I've observed, though, has been the spread of extremely liberal theologies—some would say radical—in mainline churches. This kind of thinking, characterized by liberal understandings of God, the incarnation of Jesus and the stories of the Bible, has long been around, for sure. But it isn't widely recognized in the culture at large and is not shared (or at least spoken of) in many mainline churches across the heartland.

I was trying to decide whether I should include a truly "different" way of thinking in my mainline Protestant chapter, a theological point of view that is common but hardly acknowledged, when an editor sent me a copy of the October 2005 newsletter of the Center for Progressive Christianity. It included an article about religious reactions to Hurricane Katrina by

James Rowe Adams, an Episcopal priest who founded the center in 1994. Adams, predictably for a self-proclaimed progressive, dismissed the explanations of "fundamentalist Christians" and "Muslim extremists." But then he went further: "I think if we are to hold out the promise of discovering God's love and justice, we must abandon all notions of an interventionist God."

I had to speak with Adams.

Why? Through the course of working on this book, I spoke with many liberals and progressives who refused to accept that God delivers natural disasters like lightning bolts but who fumbled for words when trying to explain what God *is* doing when innocent children are being drowned by a tsunami. They wouldn't give up the notion of an interventionist God but simply focused on God's positive interventions (inspiring people to help, contribute money, etc.). Adams, though, would circumvent the problem of believing in an interventionist God in a world filled with sorrow by telling me that God does not intervene in our physical world, at least in any way that we can understand. That would not be the most radical thing he would say.

"Many in the progressive Christian movement have abandoned the idea of an interventionist God," he told me. "It simply doesn't work for us. You end up trying to make excuses for God or you have a God who is unworthy of worship—arbitrary, capricious or cruel. We have put that aside as no longer a workable concept."

Right off the bat, I understand, these words would cause many traditional Christians, and others, to shudder. If you believe in a God who does intervene in our lives, Adams is saying, you worship a God who is far, far short of all-loving. "It's the hardest thing for some people to do, to accept that life is filled with random tragedy," he said. "If God did indeed set things up to happen that way, then I don't think God deserves our worship or praise. To me, the God people discuss in these matters turns out to be a monster."

So what does he believe? Adams was for three decades the rector of St. Mark's Church on Capitol Hill in Washington, D.C., where he saved a dying parish by attracting educated skeptics. He still takes great pride in the *Washington Post* calling his parish "the citadel of enlightened Christianity." "I *love* that phrase," he said. He started the Center for Progressive Christianity in order to build a network of support for like-minded congregations. Adams stepped aside as president in 2006 after more than a decade. His group has about 270 member congregations, mostly from the Episcopal Church and the United Church of Christ, with others coming from Lutheran, Methodist, Presbyterian, Baptist, and "independent Catholic" traditions. In 2005, Adams released a book, *From Literal to Literary*, which explores the stories of the Bible as metaphors as opposed to actual events.

Here is his explanation of religion:

Religion is the business that nearly everybody is up to of trying to make sense out of existence—which is nonsense. Existence itself is nonsense. We all have to come to terms with it one way or another. Progressive Christians say they look to God for the capacity to face the nonsense, not to explain it. I think it's something we can't know. I would never say, except in a metaphorical or poetic sense, that God created the universe. We use creation metaphorically as a way of expressing our sense of awe and wonder at our surroundings, not to make a statement about a being who did something.

So who is God, I asked him.

"Our understanding of God is that which we encounter when we find ourselves connected to one another, connected to nature, connected to our inner selves," he answered. "We think it can be part of a traditional Christian understanding of God. That is how we operate. We take the bible as myth and metaphor to help us understand the nature of these basic connections."

Adams' explanations of God and faith would clearly leave many Christians and other monotheists unfulfilled. A good many would say that Adams can't possibly be a Christian, not under any common definition, and that what he preaches is nothing short of heresy. Adams, of course, is not put out by this, as he is not terribly concerned about what conservative thinkers have to say. In fact, he is equally offended by liberal Christians who think they know what God wants (even if they think God has a different agenda).

"The idea that somebody understands what God wants is a mistaken conception and dangerous to the society as a whole," he told me. "People who think they know what God wants think they have a right to make the decisions. That's the problem with theocracy, whether you're talking about Iran today or Switzerland under Calvin."

There is one question that I asked of just about everyone who is part of this book: What was your very first reaction when you heard about the devastation caused by the tsunami? I want to know whether they prayed or cried or sat glued to CNN. Did they appeal to God or scream at God? Did they focus on the science involved or on the failings of humankind? On this point, Adams' answer was similar to that of clergy with much more traditional views:

Random tragedy I find one of the most difficult sort of events to deal with. What we cannot explain in a satisfactory manner is deeply disturbing. I'm always deeply disturbed because it makes no sense. You can explain scientifically how a tsunami happened. You can even see that a tsunami, from a scientific point of view, has a regenerative aspect. It may even be necessary for the ongoing function of this planet. But that doesn't help me feel better about the incredible loss of life.

Adams broke from the mainstream religious pack, though, when I asked him to try and describe God's role in the physical universe, including when cracks open in the earth.

> I don't think we can describe God in any way. Humans saying that God exists is to me a nonsense statement. That would mean that God is somehow confined within our intellectual capacities. The only thing we can do is say we have experiences and talk about some of those experiences by using God language. It is the only way we have to talk about such wonders as how we find ourselves at one with each other and the universe.

Adams insists that there are large numbers of progressive Christians across the country, although he concedes that most can be found on the coasts and along the Great Lakes. I would argue that "progressive" is far too vague a term to describe his kind of thinking, which is truly radical in many ways and probably needs its own catchy tag. Adams told me that like-minded thinkers have been slow to organize and reach out to the uninitiated because they are not even recognized by church hierarchies or the media. Like Henderson, he believes that the secularist media focus on conservatives in order to lampoon all faith. I suggested to Adams that his kind of theology may also be difficult for the mainstream media to absorb and explain, a point he conceded. He does have hope that his movement will grow and gain a voice in the national religious dialogue, largely because he thinks that conservative Christians are scaring people away from faith. "I think they see, through the media, the only option as being of the extreme conservative sort in any tradition, and they don't want any part of it. I don't blame them. Many people are quite surprised to find that Christianity has another face."

I had to ask Adams about the understandable Christian reflex to focus on the crucifixion and resurrection of Jesus when trying to come to terms with the suffering of innocents. At this point, I knew that his answer would not be something you're likely to hear preached in most churches on Sunday mornings. But who knows how many mainline Protestants might share some of his views, even in an unformed sort of way, or at least be willing to listen with interest.

> Christ's suffering obviously makes some people feel better. It doesn't make me feel better. I think the emphasis on Jesus' suffering is quite misplaced. I put the emphasis on new life. The metaphor that his early followers used was sacrifice, and it is greatly misunderstood. It didn't have to do with the

suffering of the animal in order to make the animal feel pain. It was about release of the animal's life force. They chose that metaphor to try to make some sense of what they experienced. This contact with the Jesus story and teachings gave them a new sense of energy and enthusiasm and power. They felt a life force had been released, had been made available to them through Jesus' death. I think it's a beautiful metaphor. But when you emphasize the suffering instead of the new life and energy, you probably have missed the point. When it comes to suffering, I think you can't say anything good about it. You get the capacity to endure through your understanding of the Jesus story. That is the way I understand God.

THE REVEREND LARRY HOLLON/CHRISTIAN RELIEF AS PRAYER

While working on this book, it became clear to me in a new way just busy and distracted people are by the demands of our hyperactive, media-driven culture. The tsunami, Hurricane Katrina, and the earthquake in Pakistan were still current events in every sense. Many of the victims remained homeless. Massive rebuilding efforts were underway. But often, when I contacted clergy and scholars to talk about these natural disasters, I felt like I had to shake them free from their more current distractions and obsessions and gently guide them back to the feelings and thoughts they experienced after each of the disasters. Often, I sensed that these feelings were buried under layers of day-to-day problems and anxieties. I had to help people get back to a particular time and place, even if it wasn't that long ago.

So it was like a gift when I received in the mail at work a DVD entitled *God, Why?: Teachings from the Tsunamis.* The makers of this DVD would not have to have their memories jogged. They had set out to deal with the theological questions raised by the tsunami in a way that would stand the test of time. The text on the back cover offered this description: "Feelings of grief and a loss of spiritual compass are common when natural disasters strike. We ask questions that we all struggle to answer: Why would God allow such a terrible thing? Is this a sign of God's wrath?"

It made perfect sense to me that UMC (United Methodist Communications) would produce such a DVD. The communications arm of the United Methodist Church, the largest mainline Protestant denomination with some 8.5 million members, had impressed me over the years with their clear-sighted vision. Their recent marketing campaign for the denomination, featuring the inclusive slogan "Open Hearts, Open Minds, Open Doors," had produced some sober but moving television commercials and advertisements. UMC is as effective as any agency I can think of at communicating the mainline Protestant emphasis on social ministry as Christian witness. In fact, they're probably better at it than many United Methodist ministers who do their communicating from pulpits on Sunday morning.

The top communicator and the executive producer of *God, Why?* is the Reverend Larry Hollon, whose official title is general secretary of UMC. Not surprisingly, he had little trouble explaining what needed to be done after the tsunami:

> We responded because we were receiving questions about how to help people as they sought to understand these disasters. People were trying to put it all into perspective from the standpoint of faith and belief in God. How does God fit in all of this? What is the appropriate response from someone of the Christian faith to the death and destruction, the pain and the suffering? Our church tradition, as most traditions, says that God stands with us in human suffering and is not a cause of human suffering through natural calamities. And the appropriate response is to see the presence of God as a healing presence in the midst of these calamities, rather than as the cause of them. We wanted to say that in fairly clear and straightforward and simple language that would be helpful to people.

When watching the DVD, I had several impressions. First off, I was impressed by how it dealt directly and unflinchingly with the mystery that is at the heart of any natural disaster. It acknowledged up front that "Our trust in God's compassion can be shaken," a somewhat risky admission for a teaching resource that was designed for not only adults but high school students. As the DVD showed footage of the devastation in Banda Aceh— entire communities reduced to piles of driftwood—the narrator had the courage to even raise the question "Was God a part of this?"

My second impression was that UMC was quick to fall back on a traditional mainline Protestant line of reasoning: "Perhaps God was in the rubble." In other words, we believe that God was with those who were suffering, even if we can't explain why he didn't prevent their suffering in the first place. The DVD quoted several lines from Scripture to back up this conclusion, such as "God has said I will never fail you nor forsake you (Hebrews 13:5)." Instead of digging deeper for God's possible motivations, the program focused largely on the appropriate Christian response, which of course is to help the suffering through relief efforts. "To reach out to others as we cry out to God is to heal the wounds of those we help—and our own," the narrator intoned.

I asked Hollon about my impressions. What message *was* he trying to get across? On my first point, he said it was vital to acknowledge that people were asking painfully difficult questions about God.

Our thinking is that people really want an authentic response. They are not looking for bromides or easy answers to complex questions. By being honest about the challenge that a tragedy like this presents, we can actually grow and develop a deeper understanding of God and of our place in the universe. It was an attempt to be very straight with people. This was an unprecedented time of media attention around human suffering. Some of the basic support systems we have are undermined.

On the question of how to move forward in the face of suffering, in the absence of any reliable answers about God's role or presence, Hollon was equally direct. Christians pray and Christians act. That's all we can do, so that's what we must do. "We believe that the rescue efforts and relief efforts and the rebuilding are in fact are form of prayer," he told me. "Prayer is not disengagement and reflection only. It is that. But prayer can also be what you do with your hands and with your feet to express healing and to heal brokenness."

Hollon has documented a lot of brokenness. After pastoring a church in Omaha, Nebraska, for a decade, he began a career of producing films that tell the stories of the poor, the suffering, and the marginalized. He's been to more than thirty countries, documenting civil wars and natural disasters. He received much notice for documentaries about the rebuilding of Cambodia after Pol Pot and about the lives of street children in Brazil. Hollon has seen a lot of things that might shake the faith of the faithful, and yet he ministers by telling the stories of what he's seen. There is something particularly honest about this approach.

He told me about visiting downtown Banda Aceh a few weeks after the tsunami and seeing a young woman wearing a Red Cross vest who was wrapping something in the street.

It dawned on me that it was a body bag at the side of the road. I went over to see. There was a picture of a young woman on top of this body bag, a wedding picture. Apparently this was the means of identifying her. Someone had reclaimed her body, found her in a house that had been flattened. This young lady wearing the Red Cross vest had pulled the body from the debris and was crying, very somber. It just struck me how tragic this is, that folks are doing this work of recovering bodies, doing it in a very anonymous sort of way. We don't know the people who did this very important and very sacred work. The young lady who was recovering bodies was engaged, in my opinion, in an act of prayer. She may not have been Christian. She may have been Buddhist or not religious at all. Nevertheless, in that act of hope and of rebuilding, hands are already at work, as if in prayer.

Hollon told me that United Methodists felt compelled to produce the DVD and other materials because of two experiences in Banda Aceh. First, bodies had literally washed up against a United Methodist Church there. A decision had been made to clean and repair the building, inside and out, as a sign of hope. "What do you say to people when, as a worshiping community, bodies are delivered to your very doorstep?" Hollon asked. Second, everyone in the community had heard that a nearby pastor from another denomination had preached that the tsunami was God's way of "cleansing the beaches" of people who were not favorable. "We got a few calls from folks and emails from people saying 'I heard this. What do you have to say about it?'" Hollon told me. Something had to be said. The DVD, a teaching tool, was one result.

It's important to note, I think, that Hollon's DVD showed mostly Muslim survivors, women and girls with their heads wrapped in modesty even during the most filthy stages of cleanup. But it made no mention of religious differences. The overriding message, as far as I could tell, was that Christians witness through action, regardless of who needs help. There was no mention of the need to evangelize. The DVD sought to provide education and inspiration through scenes of relief work, accompanied by gentle music.

Months after I watched the DVD, I saw UMC at work again. After Katrina, Hollon's agency placed commentaries in newspapers across the South. The ads, headlined "In Rebuilding, Set a Place at Table for All," urged politicians and planners to give a voice to the voiceless—the victims—as communities were rebuilt. "By supporting equal access to housing, education, employment and medical care, rebuilt communities will be even stronger than before," it read.

Here was the United Methodist Church streamlining its socially conscious, politically charged, mainline Protestant message: equality, inclusion, tolerance, pluralism. Hollon told me that since the United Methodist Church has many churches along the Gulf Coast, and ministries in numerous communities, it had an obligation to stand up for the people it serves. "We just felt it was important to say to them that we as a church are with you, and we as a church stand with you to call upon political leaders to include you in the rehabilitation and reconstruction," he said.

It is the church's responsibility, Hollon told me, to communicate with the people in times of suffering—to help them deal with questions of faith, to get them food and shelter, to represent them before the powers that be, and to simply be with them. It's about *presence*. And it's all circular. To do relief work and hold the hands of the suffering is to offer Christian witness and attest to the power of faith, which can be part of the theological answer that people are searching for. For United Methodists, and most mainline Protestants, prayer and Scripture are not separate from relief work. One blends into the other, becomes the other.

> The obligation is to say to people who feel that their lives have been torn apart that they can recover by drawing upon the strength that God gives them and that the larger community can offer. I was in a tornado, when our little town was blown away in Oklahoma. You feel awfully isolated. You feel like things have been turned upside down. "What am I going to do?" "Where am I going to go?" You need to know that there is someone who is standing with you, to help you refocus and look to the future. Things were pretty darn bad in the Gulf Coast and after the tsunami. We have to offer that hope. We have to offer that presence. The people of all the churches have done that by physically going down, being with people, cleaning up, rebuilding. I think that's a powerful expression of human community that we need at a time like that.

THOUGHTS

It's given that mainline Protestants react to tragedy by rolling up their sleeves and getting to work. They believe that they must act as Jesus would want, rather than telling other people how to behave. So it made perfect sense when Hollon told me that action can *be* prayer and that a church community can sooth victims of tragedy simply by being present. I understood why Premawardhana was content to face the tragedy of the tsunami in silence, while doing all he could to organize relief efforts. He felt God's presence with the survivors of the tsunami and with relief workers and could be comforted by this knowledge alone. Hollon and Premawardhana were willing to chat about the question of God's involvement in disaster, but I began to see that it wasn't important to them. If God suffered along with the victims and inspired compassion on the part of others, that was enough. The mainline approach is all heart.

But does it go far enough in trying to grasp God's role in a calamity that inflicts savagery on teenagers who are full of hope and seniors who deserve some rest after living quiet, heroic lives? I think mainline Protestant leaders could probably do a better job of talking about the challenges to faith—without losing their commitment to compassion and presence. Henderson took this step when we spoke, saying that there is a huge element of chance in our lives and ridiculing the idea that God directs our fates, good and bad, like a superhero above the clouds. He didn't claim to know what God was doing during the tsunami. But Henderson made the moving observation, at least to my ears, that the crucifixion of Jesus was not special, but *typical*, because innocent people suffer unjustly each and every day. This point struck me as classically mainline, focusing on humankind's hurts, but it was somehow more stark, realistic, and challenging.

Adams and Lim probably represent the two ends of the mainline Protestant spectrum. Adams is off the spectrum, actually, but talks like a mainliner (although Episcopalians are not exactly Protestants). I think his upstart point of view—that God is beyond our understanding and does not intervene in our lives in any way that we can grasp—was important to represent here. Why? I can't help thinking that many mainline Protestants and others may, at weak moments, draw similar conclusions. Lim shares the mainline emphasis on empathy and action but has a grounded Christian faith that rings of evangelicalism. He may be turned off by the certainty that evangelicals often possess, but he shares with them an ultimate belief in Christian salvation as the final answer to suffering.

6 THE EVANGELICAL CHRISTIAN PERSPECTIVE

While mainline Protestants transform their faith into action, seeking to fight injustice and suffering, evangelical Protestants are more likely to keep the focus on faith. That's not to say that they won't reach out to the victims of a hurricane—they did after Katrina. But it is clear that certain principles guide their views about the physical world, the suffering of man and the path to salvation. Evangelicals will look to the Bible for their ultimate understanding of all natural events, even if they also embrace science. They see all forms of disorder and pain as the inevitable result of a fallen world and a fallen human race. And they will always emphasize that men and women can only be saved through Christ. So people who face unfair suffering—and those who manage to avoid it—will wind up in the same place, needing to be saved in order to find everlasting life.

KENNETH R. SAMPLES/THE ANSWER MAN

He'll try his darnedest to give you an answer to any question. The harder the question, the harder he'll try. Of course, the answers all come from the Bible. Kenneth R. Samples' job is to find them in the pages of Scripture and to explain them in such a way that people's faith in Jesus Christ will be strengthened, repaired, patched, and even found. He is a professional apologist, an evangelical Christian answer man. But he's no fire and brimstone prophet hurling the threat of damnation at every questioner. He has an even-keeled, *aw shucks* manner that says he has the utmost confidence in the answers of the Bible. You just have to read God's word and sort it out for the modern world.

"I've been asked these questions at church, by skeptics, by friends, on radio and TV. I think the greatest challenge to Christianity is the problem of pain and suffering," he told me.

> Instead of wondering why God allowed Hitler and Stalin to do what they did, the question now is why nature seems so inhospitable to us. I would suggest that the greatest amount of evil in the world still comes from the will of the creature—human beings. But when you're dealing with natural disasters, it takes the question of theodicy to a different realm. A difficult realm.

Samples is vice president of theological and philosophical apologetics at Reasons to Believe, an evangelical group that doesn't simply insist that Jesus is the way, the truth, and the light, but that tries to show the harmony between what it says in the Bible and the facts of nature in the world around us. Instead of aiding the age-old religious cause of questioning or downplaying science, the group seeks to explain that science in most cases reflects the revealed word of God. Samples is also cohost of a syndicated radio show, *Bible Answer Man,* and the author of a straightforward book of apologetics, *Without a Doubt: Answering the 20 Toughest Faith Questions.* Among the questions he answers: Are the Gospels trustworthy accounts of Jesus' life? (Yes.) Don't all religions lead to God? (No.) How can a good and all-powerful God allow evil?

In answering the latter question, he surveys various positions on the problem of evil and considers the pure logic of several lines of reasoning. He posits that God has not fully revealed his reasons for allowing evil, that God will ultimately prevail over evil, and that God allows suffering because a greater good can come from it. His ultimate answer: "The suffering of God in Christ is the solution to the problem of evil for human beings."

Samples has a sincere eagerness to work out the tough questions and has been kept quite busy the past few years facing the challenges posed by natural disasters. He told me that he listens with great interest as others sort out the meaning of earthshaking events, especially how God's goodness can jive with the suffering of good people. "I think there is a burden on those of us who believe that God is loving and caring to deal with this up front," he said. "I don't fault people for asking those questions. Maybe it's during the most difficult times in our lives that we're most perceptive to the most meaningful things in life."

Right off the bat, Samples made it clear that he could not entertain the possibility that God was somehow unable to stop the tsunami. But there is much we can never understand about how God relates to this world.

I believe that God has purposes, even in calamity and disaster. I don't think we always know the specifics, but there are general principles we can draw. As to why it happened to a particular community at a particular time, I would be cautious in drawing conclusions. In terms of the broader purposes, I really like C.S. Lewis' statement that "God whispers to us in our pleasures. He speaks in our conscience. He shouts in our pain. It's his megaphone to rouse a deaf world." What I draw from that statement is that God does have purposes in pain, suffering, trial, difficulty. It may be transforming our character, getting people's attention, getting them to focus on moral issues. I'm only comfortable speaking to it generally. I'm much more deliberate when speaking to specifics.

In other words, Samples has faith that God has a purpose even when there is no clear purpose to be seen. But he's unwilling to make the leap and try to ascertain God's purpose from, say, circumstantial moral evidence. So I nudged him to consider examples from Scripture where God voiced his displeasure through acts of nature like the great flood. How can a Bible-believing apologist discount the notion that God could have been doing it again by cracking open the Indian Ocean floor? I was concerned at first that he thought I was pushing him to condemn this group or that. During the period when we spoke, several people, including New Orleans Mayor Ray Nagin, made headlines for suggesting that Katrina was punishment for sinful behavior. But Samples understood the inevitable nature of the question. So he took a breath and answered in his typically mannered way.

I think one could make a case, in broad strokes, that God has used calamity, natural disaster, as a means to reflect his anger or his wrath upon people, as an instrument of judgment. The problem I have as a Christian theologian in saying that it happened to these people because they're Muslim and not Christian or those people because they are given to occultism, is that I don't feel I know enough to draw that conclusion. God could have hit New Orleans or he could have hit downtown L.A. or Las Vegas. I don't feel I'm in a position to draw the kind of conclusions that would set up why God did what he did. Is it possible he had a component of judgment in it? Yeah. I don't think I could argue with that in light of the Old and New Testaments. But I don't have the capacity to be a Noah or a prophet who says *Thus sayeth the Lord.*

Like others, Samples emphasized that human failure almost always contributes to the suffering that follows a natural disaster. We're not making the most of the world God gave us using our gifts to the fullest, so we are unnecessarily vulnerable to being flattened by God's laws of nature. The Indian Ocean could have had a warning system. The people of New Orleans could have been more protected. When I spoke to Samples, he sounded reluctant to make this point, as if he did not want to sidestep the question of God's involvement. He sounded as if it was his duty not to let human culpability slip between the cracks. "I believe God has created a universe that is incredibly majestic and eloquently designed and provides an incredible habitat for us to thrive as humanity," he said.

> Yet I also believe it is a potentially very dangerous place because God has created a world that is governed by the laws of physics. Just as we have to be cautious in our dealings with each other, we have to be cautious and prudent and reflective about the way we live in the world. If you build a city right next to the ocean, we have to bare some of that burden in terms of prudence.

Through our talk, Samples kept coming back to a point that was clearly important to him: that good comes out of evil. He is certain that it does and that good must have come out of the tsunami. He offered several possibilities, none particularly new or likely to interest a skeptic: we're reminded of the fragile nature of life; we're shaken out of any sense that our security is guaranteed by money and influence; we remember how important it is to comfort and clothe those in need; we see that government can't protect us. "You can seek shelter from the storm in only one place," he said. "God."

Thinking back on our long conversation, Samples' ultimate hope kind of crystallized before my eyes. Even if the tsunami raises questions about God's motives and actions and causes one's faith to flicker, the greatest suffering can still drive people to God. The only alternative is darkness. What better refuge is there than Jesus? This is the evangelical end game.

> Good things can come out of evil. Out of evil, the son of God is subjected to judgment and crucifixion, but out of that evil comes salvation. I think that is a very, very powerful message that God is not empathetic, he's sympathetic. He's in the midst with us. God knows what it is to suffer. We don't have a God who is far away. We have a God in space and time. I think that is the central answer to the problem of pain and suffering. Good things come out of evil. I can't think of another religion that proposes that answer.

DAVID LEFLORE/GETTING YOUR ATTENTION IN 1,000 WORDS OR LESS

Nothing boils down faith like a good, old-fashioned tract. And nothing boils down evangelical Christianity like a tract that urges and pleads with its reader to repent and accept Jesus as Savior. A tract is just a sheet of paper, usually folded twice so that you can slip it in a pocket. It is designed and written to grab the attention of anyone who is handed one in a crowd or picks one up from a bench. There's no room or time for blather. A tract must be direct and simple. It is most effective when it addresses the circumstances that the reader is facing *right now.*

A couple of weeks after the 9/11 terrorist attacks, I walked around downtown Manhattan to write an article about all the religious activity that was going on. Street preachers did their thing on every other corner, some predicting the end of the world. Church groups from across the country looked for ways to help, smiling hopefully at dazed New Yorkers. Anonymous men, some in expensive suits, some glassy eyed with religious fervor, handed out tracts. Most of the tracts bore images of the World Trade Center and warned city dwellers to repent before something else happened (presumably, the next attack).

If you think about it, there is no better time to hand out religious tracts, whatever their message, than when people are searching for answers. When are more people likely to be searching for answers than after a life-altering disaster? So the past few years have been a time of opportunity for the American Tract Society, which has been writing, printing, and distributing Christian tracts around the world for 180 years and packaged tracts for relief workers heading to the battlegrounds of the Civil War. This is not to say that the Society takes any comfort in humankind's suffering. It's just that the Society has an urgent message to spread about the saving power of the Christian faith. If people are more open to that message when the world around them has fallen to pieces, the Society will make sure that Christian relief workers set off on their journeys with as many tracts as they can hand out. "Typically, I think a disaster makes things easier," David LeFlore told me. He is vice president for evangelism and outreach for the American Tract Society. "People are asking 'Why? Why did this happen?' A believer in Christ can say that we don't always have the answers, but here is the solution to the ultimate problem."

The American Tract Society, which is based in Garland, Texas, "experienced a wonderfully busy and productive year in 2005," according to its literature. Its international division distributed 2.4 million tracts to tsunami victims in Sri Lanka, Thailand, and India (translated into the local languages). Another 1.5 million were passed out in India that deal with various other disasters. Some 200,000 AIDS-related tracts were distributed in Africa, and 100,000 tracts dealing with Pakistani disasters were handed out there in the Urdu language.

When I spoke with LeFlore, he told me up front that he was not a scholar. He might not have answers for high-minded questions. But I learned that he is very much an evangelist—with an extremely large and overlooked audience. LeFlore spoke with the directness and sense of purpose that you would expect from someone who produces tracts. He told me that his tracts should be between 250 and 1,000 words in length and should be written at a third- or fourth-grade reading level. "You want it to be something that people will actually read," he said.

I asked him: What is the immediate message that a tract should deliver to someone whose world has fallen apart—or to someone whose faith has been shaken by a faraway disaster. He answered:

> What we try to do at the American Tract Society is to say that through the hurt and pain—whether it's something as unfortunate and minute as a divorce, or whether it's a tsunami or hurricane—God is still in the picture, if you allow him to be in the picture. Many times, even in the Bible, we see that God allowed bad things to happen so he would be made more prominent. First and foremost, we want to present the gospel to those hurting people. We let them know that God is not punishing you, this is not God's way of getting back at your country and your family. It's more of: Through this circumstance, let God show you his love.

The Society has a tract called *When Disaster Strikes: Will You Be Ready?* which was widely distributed after recent natural disasters. The tract offers a quick rundown of prominent hurricanes, tsunamis, floods, landslides, earthquakes, and volcanic eruptions. Then it offers: "Natural hazards are part of the way the Earth operates...but there is hope." So the tract quickly dismisses the cause of natural disasters before getting to the heart of the matter: the hope offered through Christian salvation. It explains that death is the natural event we *can* prepare for and that "God offers us all the way to safety."

LeFlore told me, in so many words, that he is not particularly interested in studying God's role in unleashing natural disasters—at least not in his tracts—although he has no doubt that God is out there.

> There are so many different philosophies on who God is. Is he this great watchmaker in the sky who put this watch together, winded it up and said "Okay, let's watch it tick." I don't believe that is the God that I follow. I think that God is active and present in everyday life. Natural disasters and hazards are just part of the earth, part of the way he created the earth to work.

Neither is the Society interested in placing blame. Its tracts never evangelize—as far as I can tell—by warning readers that they may be suffering because of their behavior or belief. Their messages only look forward by offering God's love and consolation. "God is not unaware of your troubles," reads a tract called *When You Lose It All.* "His love reaches out to you at this moment." In a tract called *Why? Trusting God When You Don't Understand,* Anne Graham Lotz, Billy Graham's daughter, explains that faith can only grow in the face of suffering. This is the state of the world because of original sin. "Death was not part of God's original plan," she writes. "He created you and me to live with Him and enjoy Him forever in an uninterrupted, permanent, personal, love relationship. But sin came into our lives and broke that relationship."

The Society's tracts hardly contend with personal sin. But they give original sin a prominent place, as part of a final plea with the reader to become a Christian. Most tracts end with a three-pronged plan for the reader: admit you're a sinner; acknowledge that only Jesus can pay for your sins, personal and original; and confess faith in Jesus.

As I talked with LeFlore, he was very modest in regard to his abilities and understanding of the world around him. He's only doing the work that all Christians should do, but in a particular form, he told me. Eventually, though, he drew a link between the simple messages within his tracts and my real interest—explaining natural disasters:

> Let's face it, if Adam and Eve hadn't eaten that fruit in the Garden of Eden, we wouldn't have sin. We were created in a perfect likeness of God. Because man had the choice to sin, sin is what caused death and what causes these natural disasters and man-made disasters. If you go back and read the Book of Genesis, I think there was a perfect world at that time. When God created the earth, he created a very mature earth. From what we know about the earth, it was perfect. I mean, the Bible says that Adam named all the animals. He must have been able to walk up to a lion and say "You're a lion" without the lion wanting to eat him. At that point, when God banished Adam and Eve from the Garden of Eden, they got a taste of what the world really is. It's harsh and cold and hard and there's a lot of evil.

For LeFlore, musing about the animals in the Garden of Eden was nothing more than a diversion, a detour from the real work at hand. I had no doubt that he believed in a real connection between Eve biting the apple and modern-day earthquakes. But the theme of a tract, whether it is natural disasters or divorce, is only an attention-getter on the way to the final push for salvation. Going into 2006, the American Tract Society had plans for new AIDS prevention tracts for Africa, Russia, and China, as well as soccer-themed tracts for the World Cup in Germany. When I spoke with LeFlore, the Society's hottest tract was electronic, a Web site called www.biggest-bet.com, which draws people in by appearing to be just another poker site.

"When they sit down at the (virtual) table, instead of being asked to make a deposit, they push a button and here comes the gospel message," LeFlore told me. "It's really a pretty neat site. By whatever means we can, if it is morally, ethically, biblically right to do, we want to share the gospel."

THE REVEREND TONY CAMPOLO/NOT YOUR FATHER'S EVANGELICAL

I didn't expect to interview anyone for this book who would also appear on Comedy Central. But there he was, just two weeks before I spoke with him. Tony Campolo on *The Colbert Report*. Faux journalist Stephen Colbert, who plays a Fox News style, conservative TV "personality," introduced Campolo as a spiritual advisor to Bill Clinton. Then he hit Campolo with an opening question that he might very well be asked by a real television commentator: "You claim to be a member of the evangelical left. Doesn't that seem a contradiction in terms to most Americans?" Campolo, always good natured and clearly aware of what he was getting into, answered that Jesus could not be a strict Republican because he cared about the poor and about love and justice. Colbert didn't miss a beat, responding "You're saying that Jesus hated America?" The audience laughed heartily, as did Campolo. As the segment progressed, he tried to get into the spirit of things. "Putting religion and politics together is like mixing ice cream and horse manure," Campolo insisted, offering Colbert some fodder for a number of jokes. Overall, Campolo came off looking pretty good, a lefty evangelical with a very necessary sense of humor.

There are many evangelicals who would contend that Campolo is not one of them. Before I spoke with him, I thought that was solely because of his political inclinations. Instead of focusing on questions of morality like so many evangelical leaders do, Campolo concentrates on Bible-based responsibilities to serve the poor and the helpless. He founded the Evangelical Association for the Promotion of Education almost three decades ago and has since helped develop schools, literacy centers, orphanages, AIDS hospices, and youth ministries in America's big cities as well as in Africa, Haiti, the Dominican Republic, and elsewhere. His approach to living out the Christian faith has much in common with what mainline Protestants preach, but Campolo carries out his ministry with what might be called an evangelical fervor. He wants to help usher in the Kingdom of God—but says that promoting social justice is the way to do it. As a result, he has become a unique and controversial figure in the evangelical world, even if he can be seen as a model for Rick Warren and other mega-pastors who are heralding global poverty as their next big target.

I understood that Campolo was really different, though, when I spoke to him about natural disasters. I wanted to pick his brain not only because he is so hard to categorize but also because he travels almost year round and has a real ear-to-the-ground sense of what Protestants have been saying and wondering in the wake of the tsunami, Katrina, the Pakistani quake, and the rest. It was a subject he seemed eager to dig into, and he surprised me right off the bat with his take on much of what he had heard:

> We have some people who think that God is in control over everything that goes on in the world. If you believe that every single thing that happens is planned by God, you have to hold God responsible for a disaster. As a result, you have all kinds of crazy attempts to justify God. People say that it's part of some great plan of his to do something wonderful in the world. Another option I've heard is that God is somehow punishing America or the people of New Orleans for their sin. All of these attempts to explain why an all-powerful God would allow such things to happen seem to discredit God. My own sense is that God is not in control of everything.

I know that Harold Kushner has taken a lot of heat over the years from Orthodox Jews for his conclusion that God cannot be all-powerful and allow such suffering in the world. Evangelical leaders are not shy about criticizing each other in public, so one has to figure that Campolo's stance may not go over all that well. Then again, many are already perplexed by his focus on social justice rather than moral behavior. Before I could even ask Campolo about Kushner—who, it turns out, is a good friend—Campolo volunteered that his position is a bit different from the rabbi's.

> The only place where I would differ with Harold Kushner is that I believe that God has *chosen* to not be all powerful. The reason God has chosen to not be all-powerful is simple: if God were in control of everything, there would be no such thing as human freedom. Without human freedom, we wouldn't be human in the first place. We would have no capacity to love, either God or other people. Love requires freedom. In the economy of God, love is more important than power. The loving God, in order to give us the capacity to love, has limited power. It was a choice. God made it.

Like George Coyne, Campolo told me that he views God as a loving parent who ceased exercising total control over his children in order to allow them, and their world, to mature. Among the consequences of God's decision to put down his universal cell phone and go easy on humankind's curfew is that people are subject to all kinds of dangers. The laws of nature have been set free to shake up the land and the sea, so humankind has to make wise decisions that minimize the impact of natural disasters. "I believe God has said 'I'm no longer going to protect my children from every disaster that comes their way because I want them to come of age,'" Campolo told me. "I would contend that when the earthquake in Pakistan took place and this incredible suffering followed, God was the first one who cried."

The idea that God is less than all-powerful—whether or not it is God's choice—is certainly not mainstream thinking in the evangelical world or even in the larger Christian world. I made this point to Campolo, who initially resisted. I got the sense that he did not want to be portrayed as a radical in his conception of God. He finally explained that his position would be mainstream if people would only stop and think about it. "I don't think that people really think through a lot of the things they say they believe," he said.

> I don't think anybody wants to make God the author of evil, and when you say everything is controlled by God, you do make God the author of evil. If God is all-powerful, God ought to be able to accomplish good without creating suffering. I think that Christian people, if they stopped and reflected, would agree.

It's hard to imagine. But Campolo does meet a lot of Christian people. He just about lives on the road, speaking more than 400 times a year—yes, often twice in one day—at evangelical and mainline churches, universities, crusades, professional events, and wherever else they'll have him. He's booked almost two years ahead and negotiates his fees for each event, depending in part on a sponsor's ability to pay. He talks about his work and the importance of service to the poor in living out the gospel. During the month I spoke with him, March 2006, he had engagements on 30 of 31 days. He called me from Winston Salem, North Carolina, where he was to address insurance and financial advisers.

Campolo talked to me for quite a while about the idea that God is not all-powerful. Whether people like it or not, it is a formula that could explain why a world created by God cracks and shakes without regard for the suffering that will result. Like a good evangelical, Campolo went to the Bible to support his case. Neither the Old Testament nor the New Testament claims, he said, that God is all-powerful:

> What the Hebrew Bible says is that God is more powerful than any other force in the universe and that ultimately—and here is a big word, ultimately—God will bring all things under control. But between now and then, there is a struggle going on between good and evil. It's a struggle that God will win. But the word omnipotent does not appear in the Hebrew bible. In the New Testament, the word omnipotent appears once, and that is in the Book of Revelation.

And it only says that God is omnipotent at the end of history. It doesn't say that God is operating with omnipotence right now. If you want to get theological about it, the Bible doesn't really make the case for God that many Christians make. What the bible does make clear, particularly in the New Testament, is that God's love is infinite and God wants us to love infinitely. So he chooses to limit himself, as I've said.

Something was still nagging at me. If God has chosen to be something less than all-powerful, in order to give humankind real freedom, why did he have to pull back from overseeing the physical universe? Couldn't God give people free will and limit his power to intervene in our world without allowing the forces of nature to cause havoc? God could presumably allow the physical world to regulate itself in a safe way, without slipping disks, even as humankind has to make its own decisions. Campolo saw where I was going with this and conceded that God did not necessarily have to give up power over the physical world in order for people to have the capacity to love. But he told me that there are other forces in the world that may take advantage of a less than omnipotent God by manipulating the physical world. "I'm one of those persons who believes there are evil forces at work in the universe," he said. "Anybody who doesn't believe in the reality of evil has to be naive. As George Bernard Shaw said, 'I question the existence of God, but never the existence of Satan.' Some evil forces work through human means and some through natural means. But there are evil forces out there."

Campolo had to go. He seemed pretty satisfied with his answers to my inquiries, and I wondered if he might refer to our talk in the days ahead. After all, if God has chosen to be semi-powerful so that we can be free to love, that is an awfully good reason to get involved with his campaign to serve the poor and sick and illiterate. "I think I'm ready to live with the fact that God has chosen to be limited in order to give us the freedom to express love," he said. "If that seems a bit unorthodox, let it be."

VINSON SYNAN/THE HOLY GHOST IS AT WORK

April 2006 was the 100th anniversary of the opening of the Azusa Street Revival, one of the seminal events in American religious history, even if many Americans know nothing about it. As the story goes, an African American preacher in Los Angeles by the name of William Seymour began to speak in tongues—the Holy Spirit working through him. He and some followers founded a small church in a derelict downtown building. Word spread of what was happening there—a fiery, ecstatic form of worship that had baptized believers speaking in an unknown language—and people began to come from all around. The revival, on Azusa Street, lasted for three years. It became known as the turning point for Pentecostal Christianity, transforming a small, mysterious cult into a worldwide religious force.

I spoke with Vinson Synan, one of America's leading historians of Pentecostalism, a few weeks before the anniversary. He had just returned from Lagos, Nigeria, where he had worshiped in what might be the largest church sanctuary in the world. The church, a stadium that holds 55,000 people in pews, is home to a Pentecostal congregation that grows by the day, if not the hour. A nearby Pentecostal church draws 1 million people to monthly prayer meetings on a campground outside Lagos. Nigeria is only part of a Pentecostal reformation that is changing the face of Christianity in Africa, in Latin America, in Asia and—a bit more slowly—in America. After only one century, more than 600 million people practice "tongues" as evidence of Spirit baptism and take part in divine healing of the sick.

Synan is a professor of divinity at Regent University, a Christian graduate school founded by Pat Robertson in Virginia Beach, Virginia. A believer himself, he has studied every major period of Pentecostal growth. When we spoke, he told me about doing research on the Azusa Street Revival. He had been going through the *Los Angeles Times* on microfilm, an always laborious process that quickly tires the eyes and seems particularly primitive in the Internet age. Although the opening of the revival is officially considered to be April 9, 1906, the day that Seymour began to speak in tongues, what was happening on Azusa Street did not make the *Times* until April 18. "I was reading a prophesy at the end of that very first article," Synan told me. "Someone prophesied great destruction unless people turned to God and this new outpouring of the Spirit. I read this prophesy and then turned the crank on the microfilm. The next day the headlines were four inches high. SAN FRANCISCO DESTROYED. Well, that's kind of chilling."

On the day that the prophesy was quoted (probably as an afterthought) in the newspaper, more than a third of the 700-mile San Andreas Fault ruptured. An earthquake shook San Francisco for one solid minute, ripping open gas lines that started fires across the city. Water mains also snapped, leaving firefighters unable to put out the flames. Around 3,000 people died. Earthquakes were studied with a new intensity after the San Francisco quake, and scientists began piecing together how the shifting of tectonic plates causes quakes. Previously, the faults beneath the earth's surface had been thought to be the *result* of quakes.

Not surprisingly, those who had been praying on Azusa Street thought they had the goods on the earthquake. "They put two and two together and said that a spiritual earthquake hit Azusa Street, while God brought judgment to wake up the world with the San Francisco earthquake," Synan told me. "God brought two earthquakes to California. The early Pentecostals made a big deal of that."

Pentecostals generally are among the most strict adherents to fundamental Christian doctrines. They break away from other evangelicals by emphasizing the profound physical effects of the Holy Spirit in this world. The word of the Bible is central and beyond question to Pentecostal Christians. So I was prepared when Synan, who is as immersed as anyone in Pentecostal history, culture, and belief, gave me a classic Bible-based, evangelical explanation for the continuing eruption of natural disasters in God's world:

> The earth was created perfect. In the Garden of Eden, no one would ever die, there was no sickness, birth was without pain. There were no weeds, you know the story. Then the fall. The curse. The curse of sin fell not only on mankind, but on all of creation. It fell on the earth. After the fall, weeds would grow, childbirth would be with pain and travail, the Bible says. So the whole natural order was affected by the fall and sin. All of creation has been under a curse. Christ came not just to redeem mankind, but to redeem the whole world and the universal order. I was taught in school that in the garden, fire would not burn and water would not drown. There was nothing dangerous in nature. After the fall, fire would burn and kill, water would drown, and all of nature could be destructive. I think God allowed that to happen. Natural disasters come as a general result of the fall.

Synan told me that he sometimes preaches a sermon that he calls "Kingdoms of this World." He focuses on Revelation 11:15, which says "And the seventh angel sounded; and there were great voices in heaven, saying, the kingdoms of this world (have) become the kingdoms of our Lord, and of his Christ, and he shall reign for ever and ever." People might read this passage to mean that God is taking over the kingdoms of the world in a political sense, Synan told me. But you have to read it in a broader sense, to cover the entire created world. "When the whole created order is redeemed, there will be no more natural disasters," he said. "Until then, there will be random disasters that God has permitted. I don't know that God likes it to happen, but it says in Scripture that God was in the whirlwind." He also quotes Isaiah 11:9, which says "In all my holy mountain, nothing shall hurt nor shall destroy." This is a promise that after the final redemption of all things, Synan told me, the curse on the land will be lifted and the physical world will no longer cause pain. "In the meantime, from the fall of Adam until the final redemption of all things, there will be natural disasters," Synan explained casually. "Man is subject to this. God allows it. Maybe the Lord allows Satan, who is the destroyer, to do this. In the end, when the natural disaster hits, people are mute. It is an act of God and shows us there are powers far beyond anything man can do."

Synan told me that many theologians are not satisfied with his most basic biblical explanation, that original sin makes natural disasters possible. He mentioned Calvinists, in particular. Some don't want to see that God allows random things, so they form what Synan calls a "naturalistic" explanation. This involves God creating a world in which conditions must be perfect for humankind to survive and thrive. In order for this world to carry on, though, earthquakes, hurricanes, and the rest must regulate the conditions of the planet. "They are the price of making a paradise in which man could live," Synan said. "It's just like how out of so many babies who are born, so many will die, but so many will survive." He had no specific problem with this concept—other than that it goes beyond what is biblically necessary. "The theological answer remains what I said—the curse of sin on all creation," he told me.

> In the end, God will redeem and sanctify and bring into order all things. I like that verse, "In all this holy mountain, nothing shall hurt nor shall destroy." That means drugs. That means earthquakes. All the disasters that could happen. There will come a time when none of these things will happen, if you believe the Bible.

Synan has little interest in trying to read God's anger. While Scripture tells of God's willingness to punish the wicked, he feels that it is impossible to decipher whether a natural disaster has been directed at a given people or nation.

> There were those who said that the sin in New Orleans—and there is a whole industry based on sin and sex—received God's judgment. Many people said that. But what about the innocent people who were not involved? And a lot of what happened was man's fault, building in what was once marsh, which God created to be wetlands. Then they drained it to build houses where they shouldn't build them. And it was man's fault for not building high enough levees, not strong enough. People have a need to explain things. There are those who think that someone must have sinned greatly in order for these things to happen. But I don't think that these things happen because of the specific sins of certain people. It's the general result of sin. It's the state of the world.

All disasters, all day-to-day problems, all pain, come back to the Garden of Eden. Adam and Eve. The apple. That's not just the bottom line for Synan, but the only line. Until the redemption of the world, though, Christians who have been baptized in the Spirit can feel God's presence in this broken, sinful world. For Synan, the need to feel that presence is why Pentecostalism is growing at the expense of Protestant traditions that prefer to focus on thinking instead of feeling. "It makes you think," he said, "that the Azusa Street Revival and the outbreak of the Pentecostal movement is a kind of a spiritual tsunami."

The Reverend Erwin Lutzer/God Made it Happen

I was telling someone about this project of mine, and how most religious thinkers jump through theological hoops in order to separate God from any real responsibility for natural disasters. Even evangelicals, in blaming original sin, set up a scenario in which God is a loving but disappointed parent who sits back and lets the fall of the world play out. He's running the show, of course, but there is a script in place that will allow for all kinds of suffering until the Second Coming of Jesus.

But this associate of mine told me about a pastor of a big evangelical church in Chicago who had been preaching about natural disasters in such a way that word of his sermons was getting out. I had heard of Erwin Lutzer and his church, The Moody Church, but didn't know much about him. So I looked him up and found a book he had written called *Ten Lies About God*. The lies at which Lutzer took aim were of the no-nonsense, Bible-centric variety: God is whatever we want him to be; many paths lead into God's presence; God is more tolerant than he used to be; and God is obligated to save followers of other religions. But the lie that caught my eye was that *God takes no responsibility for natural disasters.*

Then I came across a newsletter that his media-savvy church had produced shortly after the tsunami, which opened with this question: "God didn't have anything to do with the tsunami...did he?" Inside, Lutzer brought the hammer down on those who deny what cannot be denied. "Yes, let us boldly say, that God willed that the tsunami happened...Let me say simply that what happened in Southeast Asia is consistent with the God of the Bible, who is both powerful and loving."

When I spoke with Lutzer, I told him that his position was out of step with that of many others with whom I had spoken. He understood and was eager to push ahead. "The bottom line is that you either believe the Bible or you don't. In the Bible, God stands back of these things very clearly."

Lutzer started to tell me that he had heard something about Campolo explaining natural disasters by deciding that God is not all-powerful. I told him that I had spoken with Campolo only weeks before. Lutzer was intrigued. "Did he really say that God is not omnipotent?" he asked. I explained that

Campolo did say this, although his position was that God has chosen to be less than omnipotent. Lutzer was not impressed. "His view is just a human construct to distance God from natural disasters," Lutzer insisted.

> His view, like Kushner, is that it makes God look bad. But where is Tony getting this from? Not from the Bible. Nature reflects God's attributes, both in terms of his care for the world, with the sunshine and rain and so forth, and also the other side of God's nature, his judgments.

I was eager to get into it. I asked Lutzer what exactly he means when he says that God is responsible. He answered:

> If you believe the Bible, you can't help but realize that God stands back of natural disasters and that he takes responsibility for them. Here's a point I like to emphasize: People say "Can we blame God?" Well, blame implies wrongdoing, so the answer is no. Even the world responsibility often implies accountability, and that's not right. I prefer to simply say that God is in charge of this world, so *nothing* happens without his express permission and, I would even add, his decree. When you think of it, if God is totally sovereign, even if he permits something—because he could choose to not permit it—he isn't removed from it. So that's the way in which I understand natural disasters. God is in charge.

You can call Lutzer's position complete submission to God's omnipotence. God is truly all-powerful, so nothing happens by chance. Nothing happens without God's awareness and approval and decree. When I was listening to Lutzer, I knew that his stark position would make many God-fearing people mighty uncomfortable. But I couldn't help feeling that there was something refreshingly direct about his logic. I had spent a lot of time listening to good, sincere, and insightful people trying to defend their all-powerful God from charges of brutality, sometimes by simply refusing to put God at the crime scene. And here was Lutzer saying that God made the tsunami happen. He must have!

To further illustrate his conviction, Lutzer began reciting a verse from an old hymn called "I Sing the Mighty Power of God." The hymn was written by Isaac Watts, an English pastor who wrote hundreds of hymns during the early eighteenth century and whose work was brought to the United States by Benjamin Franklin. Lutzer went on:

> There's not a plant or flower below,
> but makes Thy glories known,
> And clouds arise, and tempests blow,
> by order from Thy throne;

While all that borrows life from Thee is ever in Thy care;
And everywhere that we can be,
Thou, God art present there.

"What that shows," Lutzer told me, "is that the particular supervision and hand of God is in the smallest details of nature, including disasters."

He told me that he gave a series of sermons in early 2006 about natural disasters and that he was planning to publish them. He said that he deals with the questions that people really ask: Should God be absolved of responsibility? How do we harmonize faith with such devastation? Can we still trust God? Are natural disasters judgments of God?

Okay, I said, let's delve into the question of God's judgment. If you believe that God causes natural disasters, the obvious follow-up question is why? He agreed that this is a key point:

> People ask whether these are judgments. The answer is yes. But not in the manner that some people imply. We cannot look at Southeast Asia and say that they are more wicked sinners than others. Sure the sex industry is there, but Bangkok was spared and it's the hub of the sex industry. Are we to say that New Orleans is a more sinful city than Las Vegas? We as human beings cannot look at these disasters and say "They got it because they are more sinful." Remember, the righteous die with the wicked. Whether in New Orleans or in the tsunami, there were many believers, many Christians, and they died with the non-Christians. We cannot read the fine print of God's purposes. We cannot look at a natural disaster and say we now know which religion is right or who is wicked and who is righteous. You see, we as Christians believe that Jesus died for our sins, and yet we're going to die because of sin. In other words, we are part of the judgment, too. People need to understand that—that the curse and the judgment fall on all of mankind as we live on this planet.

So God causes natural disasters, but we really don't know why—other than to conclude that all the rumbling and tumbling is part of God's overall judgment against humankind. I asked Lutzer why so many people, including fellow evangelicals, do try to read the fine print and figure out who has angered God. He was very practical on this point: "We're all looking for verification of what we believe, so we read into it. Somebody said that many people try to convince God to be mad at the same people they are mad at."

I asked Lutzer if the wave of natural disasters in recent years would affect the godliness of the culture, one way or the other. He was silent for a few moments. Then he seemed to conclude that the evidence of God's might would only harden people's positions. "I'm sure there are many people who are angry with God," he told me.

There are also people who have no doubt pursued God as a result of natural disasters. The Lisbon earthquake did split Europe in two. Many began to flock to the churches to try to find help and answers and to prepare for eternity. But you also had the Enlightenment.

These days, more and more people focus on the scientific explanations for natural disasters, he said. "I think that people recognize that there is a scientific explanation, an immediate cause, but the *thoughtful* mind recognizes that if God exists, God must be the ultimate cause."

THOUGHTS

If you're looking for a full-blown theology to shed light on God's presence during the tsunami, evangelical Christianity is likely to disappoint. This is not to say that evangelicals don't have a unique perspective on the suffering of innocents. They do. But it's not that different from evangelical thinking on any question when it comes to the miserable state of humankind. People are stained by original sin. We are sinful, hopeless, and irredeemable, unless—*unless*—we are saved by Jesus Christ. Then all sins are forgiven and eternal life is assured. Natural disasters are simply one part of a fallen world inhabited by fallen creatures. We encounter all kinds of wretchedness—sickness, deceit, violence, you name it—because nothing in this world is as it should be. Nothing. The victims of the tsunami only suffered in a different, temporarily more agonizing way than most people. But if they were saved, they were quickly rewarded. If not, well, they ran out of time.

So it's hard to separate or tease out an evangelical philosophy on suffering—let alone God's role in natural disasters—from the overall evangelical understanding of the world. Everything goes back to Eve eating the fruit of the tree of knowledge of good and evil. Synan told me as much: natural disasters are a result of the fall of the world. LeFlore said that everything was perfect in the Garden of Eden (Adam could walk up to a lion) and that the world will return to this state after Christ's return. Lutzer told me that, in a fallen world, every person must face up to God's disappointment and that one symptom of divine judgment was the tsunami. Lutzer believes that Acts of God really *are* Acts of God.

I should note that people always hear about evangelical personalities like Pat Robertson and Jerry Falwell blaming particular groups of the sinful for incurring God's wrath. The evangelical scholars I interviewed had little interest in trying to read God's mind. They go by what the Bible says, which is that everyone is sinful.

The answer offered by evangelical Christianity is, more or less, a take it or leave it choice. Either you believe that salvation is a necessity and comes from Jesus alone or you're probably not an evangelical. Samples, the professional apologist, tried to answer some of my questions about natural disasters, but his answers—that God hasn't revealed the reasons for evil, that good comes from suffering, that good will ultimately prevail—did not give me much to think about.

Campolo was the odd man out, of course. Looking back on our conversation, I'm not sure that he fits within the evangelical camp. It's not that he talks about social justice more than he does salvation. When he insists that God has chosen to be less than all-powerful and that the Bible doesn't claim God to be all-powerful, it's hard to think of him as an evangelical, according to the modern understanding of the term. A 2004 poll by ABC found that 87 percent of evangelicals believe the story of creation to be literally true. For most of those folks, the tsunami, while shocking and terribly sad, was only another result of the bite in the apple.

7 THE AFRICAN AMERICAN CHRISTIAN PERSPECTIVE

The black church tradition occupies a unique place in American Christianity. It is well known for leading the fight for social justice, with a similar agenda to that of the mainline Protestant churches. But the black churches—mostly Baptist and Methodist—also share a conservative reverence for Scripture that overlaps in many ways with the evangelical approach to the Bible. African American Christianity is a distinct tradition. You can make a strong case that African American Christians have relied on faith to get through hard times more than any other group. The church has been the very foundation of black culture and community. From slavery on, African Americans have seen the struggle for freedom and equality as part of their Christian expression. To this day, the most respected leaders in black communities are often preachers. The black church tradition has put its energy and prayers into facing down moral, human-made evil. Natural evil, on the other hand, is hardly an afterthought.

PROFESSOR ANTHONY B. PINN/WHEN TRADITIONAL ANSWERS FALL SHORT

When I started doing my initial research on how African American Christians have explained natural disasters, two things quickly became clear. The first was that I was not going to find much. There is a tremendous amount of literature related to suffering caused by *man* but hardly any on suffering caused by nature. Fair enough.

The second thing was the work that had gained the most attention in recent years among black theologians—and had caused the largest stir—was a 1995 book called *Why, Lord? Suffering and Evil in Black Theology.* In this work, Anthony B. Pinn presented the traditional African American Christian belief that suffering can be redemptive. That is, that pain can bring greater understanding and meaning. Then Pinn rejected the whole idea. He argued that nothing good comes from the suffering of innocents and that the notion of an all-powerful, all-loving God is ultimately challenged by the reality of suffering in this world.

When Pinn focuses on evil, he's almost always thinking about moral evil. Immoral behavior directed at black people. In other words, racism (accompanied by other "isms," which we'll get to). He's willing to question God's presence and power based solely on God's inability or unwillingness to intercede on behalf of African Americans through their long and troubled history. He does not even need to address God's possible role in *delivering* pain and suffering in order to reach this conclusion. The suffering of thousands of African Americans in New Orleans after Hurricane Katrina—homeless and humiliated, without clothes or food, begging for help from homemade rafts and rooftops—is a strike against God. The cause of natural disasters is beside the point.

"There isn't a great deal of energy put into the question of natural evil," Pinn told me early into our conversation. "It seems to me, that in terms of African-American Christianity, little energy has been put into how to respond to natural disasters. What raises the theodicy issue are the larger questions of racism, classism, sexism. That's where the problem of evil surfaces."

It started to make sense. Even though there was so much written about God's role in the tsunami during the first weeks of 2005, I could find very little authored by African Americans. I don't think I came across a single column or sermon that considered the meaning of the tsunami—not the response to the victims, but the meaning of the great wave itself—from a black Christian perspective. Hurricane Katrina, of course, became the seminal African American event of 2005, laying bare old questions of generational poverty and institutional racism that many Americans thought and hoped had been put to rest. But even in this case, when black scholars responded in great numbers and with great emotion, the focus was almost entirely political. The black Christian response was to call on the powers that be to deliver justice, not to demand an accounting of God for creating a hurricane that the poor were ill-prepared to face.

Pinn, who is a professor of religious studies and humanities at Rice University in Houston, has probably focused on the question of evil in African

American religious thought as much as an anyone in the modern era. It was the subject of his doctoral dissertation at Harvard. In addition to writing *Why, Lord?* he edited a collection of essays and articles about the problem of evil by leading black thinkers, past and present. He is also executive director of the Society for the Study of Black Religion. Still, when we spoke, I couldn't entice Pinn to spend much time weighing the religious significance of natural disasters. He told me that, with the exception of a small percentage of conservative preachers who might say that God punishes the sinful with rain, wind, and earthquakes, most black Christians simply are not drawn to this question.

> Some African-American Christians on the fringe will argue that what took place in New Orleans was God saying no to a particular kind of lifestyle or a liberal attitude toward sexuality. But I don't think their perspective is representative of what most African-American Christians think. The vast majority of black ministers will preach the need for charity. How do we respond to this in light of the teachings of the gospel? How do we provide assistance? How do we put our Christianity into work? African-American Christians would tend to say that God sends the rain on the just and the unjust. The question becomes how do we respond to that rain? How do we help those who have been flooded? I think very few will see an opportunity to raise questions about God's justice—at least until questions of race and class come up.

Pinn reminded me that it is often difficult, if not impossible, to separate the political and the spiritual in the eyes of black Christians. To demand justice is a political act and a spiritual act. The black church helped foment and lead the civil rights movement at least in part to put flesh on the words that black ministers preached on Sunday mornings. "The Reverend" was not just a title that Martin Luther King Jr. put in front of his name. He was working from the gospel when he marched, and—if you think about his words—he worked with a confidence and an authority that he believed came from God. "Black Christians are still deeply committed to notions of the social gospel," Pinn told me. "The question becomes what kind of impact does the gospel have on socioeconomic and political issues. For many black Christians, there isn't a significant distinction to be made between explicit theological conversation and political conversation, because both are motivated by a deep commitment to Christ."

The reaction to Katrina, then, from black preachers was predictable. There was no time or energy for musing about God's presence when the skies opened up or when the levees started to fail. It was humankind's job—humankind's God-given duty, that is—to have an adequate levee system in place, to prepare a realistic evacuation plan, and to have all necessary services and personnel ready to go when Katrina hit. African Americans can live with the suffering caused by a natural disaster, Pinn told me, because the pain inflicted is random, affecting white and black, rich and poor. Besides, there are scientific explanations for natural disasters that show us how earthquakes and hurricanes are part of a much larger system that makes the earth a habitable place. Problems arise and fingers may be pointed at God when the suffering caused by a natural disaster is *disproportionate,* leveling the poor and marginalized because the world they live in is already unfair.

"When a hurricane or tornado goes through an area, it doesn't simply pick out the black folks," Pinn told me. "The issue of theodicy comes up for African Americans when they suffer in ways that others do not. This raises questions of what God is interested in and what God's motives are. After Katrina, the political issues were so glaring. How can God allow *this?*"

The answer for most black Christians is the traditional explanation for suffering that black Christians have relied on since the days of slavery: Jesus suffered on the cross, so there must be redemptive power in following his example. "In terms of the problem of evil, the dominant attempt to resolve this problem comes through the Christ event," Pinn said. "It is the dominant paradigm to understand God's relationship to human misery."

Pinn grew up in a culture that draws strength from the redemptive powers of suffering and the promise of salvation. His mother, the Reverend Anne Pinn, was a minister in the African Methodist Episcopal Church, a national black denomination that was formed long ago by black Methodists who fled the open racism within the conventional Methodist church. In 2002, Pinn coauthored a book with his mother, the *Fortress Introduction to Black Church History.* She died in 2005. "Her perspective was that there are some things we just cannot understand with respect to the ways God works in the world," Pinn said. "Suffering doesn't make sense to us, but God is all-knowing and God is compassionate, so ultimately things will be worked out. God is all about justice, and we may not understand how justice will come about, but we should remain confident that it will."

For Pinn himself, this most traditional African American belief proved wanting. He openly rejected it in *Why, Lord?*—unable to reconcile the suffering endured by African Americans with the traditional belief in an all-loving, all-powerful God. His conclusion did not go over well with many black scholars: "Some folks said I had lost sight of the tradition. Others thought this made no sense because black folks are Christians. Some said this was an Enlightenment idea that doesn't fit with the attitude of African-Americans. Some had a response that was even worse: silence." Pinn recalled that at a meeting of scholars, one black theologian stood up and said that Pinn's book had nothing to do with how black people live and understand themselves or with the struggle for justice.

Pinn told me that there has always been a strong current of nontraditional religious thinking among African Americans who have been unable to accept a redemptive understanding of suffering. But this reality is hardly acknowledged.

> It can be difficult in black communities to talk about this openly. But I would suggest that there are a healthy number of African Americans who are skeptics, free-thinkers, humanists, atheists, people who move in that direction because they can't find a satisfying response to the problem of evil within the context of black churches. It's not a very popular perspective. There seems to be a tendency in the United States to blame atheists for things that go wrong. For African-Americans to bear the burden of race and on top of that, to bear the burden associated with atheism in this country, well, that's a bit much. That said, there are African Americans who belong to Unitarian Universalist congregations, who are not involved in any kind of institutional religion and say "What I do is try to help people," who move toward an appreciation of nature as their form of spiritual engagement. As far as I can tell from the historical record, there is a long history of African Americans who have been free-thinkers or skeptics or have been involved in religious nationalism or have labeled themselves humanist. You get this perspective very early on from the blues. We don't know when the blues began, but we do know the blues often raised questions concerning the existence, the goodness, the righteousness of God. This sort of perspective became explicit during the early 20th century, when African Americans became involved in the communist party. A significant percentage sought political involvement in place of participation in the church. They didn't see God doing much to make things better.

Pinn does not need to dwell on God's presence or motivation during a natural disaster in order to declare himself a humanist. Day-to-day injustice, on a much smaller scale, is enough for him to ask "Where was God?"

CHERYL KIRK-DUGGAN/DELIVERANCE FROM INJUSTICE

There is an old "spiritual," sung by slaves and their ancestors, that went like this:

> Oh, freedom, oh, freedom,
> Oh, freedom, oh, freedom over me;
> And before I'll be a slave,

I'll be buried in my grave;
And go home to my Lord and be free.

The singers, whether they were slaves or felt enslaved by Jim Crow laws or other historical adversaries, denied being slaves when they sang. Instead, they anticipated being freed and saved by the Lord. No earthbound powers could stop it. Their ultimate victory was assured by God. The singers of this spiritual could not be further removed from blaming God for their troubles.

Cheryl Kirk-Duggan, an ordained elder in the Christian Methodist Episcopal Church, one of the three historically black Methodist denominations, grew up singing this and other spirituals in church. She knows their power and can imagine how singing them gave solace and strength to men and women facing torment without end. "The slaves did not blame God for slavery," she told me at the start of a long conversation that covered history, sociology, literature, politics and the connections among them.

> They understood that white slave owners made these choices. While they knew they were physically slaves, they did not concede to being slaves holistically. It's like they were saying "You may have me bound up physically, but you're not really in control of me. First chance I get, I'm leaving."

Into the arms of God. The ultimate destination and the only salvation. The spirituals, the prayers, the preaching, the whole African American Christian tradition, are all about deliverance from a world of inequality to an eternity of justice with God. There's not much room in this tradition, Kirk-Duggan told me, for blaming God.

> I know there are folks who say God is punishing people when a hurricane strikes. But I don't see any tornadoes or hurricanes blowing through Las Vegas or Atlantic City. It's ludicrous to put things into the mind of God. First and foremost, we are human and use anthropomorphic language to talk about a God we think we kind of know about, but can never fully understand. People try to find easy answers, words of consolation. It's like when something tragic happens, a drunk driver hits a 4-year-old, and someone has the audacity to say it was God's will. What kind of god would want someone to get drunk, to get inside a vehicle, making it a deadly weapon, and would want that driver to hit a child and cut her life short? Is that your idea of a god? I think that's ludicrous. I believe that God is there with that child and her family. I don't believe that God forsakes us. But sometimes people try to come up with answers when we're better off saying *I don't know.*

Kirk-Duggan prefers to focus on what we do know in her job as a professor of theology and director of women's studies at Shaw University in Raleigh,

North Carolina, the oldest historically black university in the South. She has written, for instance, about the history of religious traditions fomenting violence even as they have preached against it. She has written about domestic violence. And she has written a history and analysis of African American spirituals called "Exorcizing Evil," looking at the powerful role this music played during slavery and again through the civil rights era. In other words, Kirk-Duggan focuses on violence carried out by knowable, flesh and blood culprits. She is mostly forgiving of God, preferring to bypass theological questions without answers in favor of the many questions that do have answers, however difficult and challenging. This seems to be true of the African American Christian tradition, by and large.

"In terms of things like the tsunami and Katrina, most African-American pastors would say that we understand that we live in a world that is shaped by nature," Kirk-Duggan told me.

> If you live on a fault, by definition, expect an earthquake. The earth has to have earthquakes to regulate heat or the planet would be too cold for us to exist on. If you live in California, where I lived for seven years, that was the risk: I knew that if I was driving on a bridge, the bridge could collapse during an earthquake and I could die.

I kept prodding about God's presence in natural disasters, as I was prone to do, and she answered me directly:

> I would love for God to stop the universe and be there, fixing things, like in that TV show they took off, *Joan of Arcadia*. But we know that life is not fair. There is no place in the Scriptures that says that life is fair or that we understand everything. If we take the Hebrew and New Testament Scriptures seriously, then we are made in the image of God. It's my job to be God's presence whenever I can.

Unfortunately, Kirk-Duggan told me, people of means and power often fail to be God's presence when it comes to taking care of those in need. It happened before the tsunami hit, when a host of governments failed to set up an early warning system. It happened again when Hurricane Katrina was coming and no serious efforts were made to determine who was likely to evacuate and who was likely to stay behind. Kirk-Duggan still sounded exasperated five months after the hurricane.

> You had all these poor people, many of them living in New Orleans all their lives, generations in the same homes. They had been able to do okay because the family owned the house and you can get by with bus transportation. There are also lots of extended families to help. But they didn't have money.

What I cannot wrap my mind around is that if you've been talking about the storm from the Wednesday before it hit on Friday and Saturday, why didn't someone say "I want every Greyhound bus, every Trailway bus, every school bus. We'll meet at fire stations or churches. And tell the hospitals to let us know what you need." There was enough warning and time. I don't see how people can blame God for human incompetence.

Americans may have been horrified by the tsunami, but no one was surprised that the governments of Indonesia, Sri Lanka, and India failed to protect or care for their people. That's the Third World, where we are told the governments are corrupt and the people don't have the same civil spirit that requires looking out for your fellow citizens. But something like this was not supposed to happen in America, Kirk-Duggan said. The moral failings of our leaders easily overshadowed any questions that might be asked of God. "The thing is that in the West, certainly the U.S., we have developed a real sense of arrogance," she told me.

We have all this technology, all the scholars, we are the wealthiest country, therefore we are immune to disaster. We think it should not happen to us. No, we're not immune. We have thousands of miles of borders that cannot be protected. We can't patrol all of that. We should be thanking God we haven't had more terrorist attacks, given how we've treated people around the world.

Kirk-Duggan went on to give me a lengthy lecture on the major social failings of American culture and government. We unnecessarily angered the Arab world by having too large a military presence there. We support dictatorships and spend too much on the military. We disregard the poor and, by putting our poorest kids in the worst schools, perpetuate poverty. We focus too much on test scores in schools and not enough on developing critical thinking skills, making it harder for undereducated poor children to catch up. None of this had to do with explaining why a just God allows suffering, let alone natural disasters, but what Kirk-Duggan gave me was a primer on the African American Christian pursuit of justice. There is just too much work to be done right here, right now, to spend much time worrying about why God chose earthquakes as a way to spread energy.

From an African-American perspective, there was tremendous awareness of the poverty involved after Katrina and of poor people being blamed for being poor. A lot of African Americans are sensitive to the fact that poor people get scapegoated in this country. *I got mine, how come they can't get theirs.* Most people, on a daily level, are not concerned about poor people, in Appalachia, anywhere.

We are very much in denial about class issues in this country. We're in denial about a lot of things.

When I talked with Kirk-Duggan, she was in the final stages of editing a collection of essays and sermons about, of all things, class, race, and natural disasters. She told me that the book would deal with a wide range of issues, from the government's failure to help the poor to the long-term effects on evacuees to how family relationships were affected by Katrina. There would be no sustained focus on God's role in any of this. In fact, she chose a title for the book that not only took the heat off God but assumed that God is distraught over humankind's latest failings. The name of the book would be *The Sky Is Crying.*

THE REVEREND HENRY H. MITCHELL/OUR ARMS ARE STILL TOO SHORT

An important part of my job as a religion writer is reading as many religion magazines and journals as I can get to, over breakfast, in front of the TV, while my sons are scaling a jungle gym. The good ones, and there are many, give me a sense of what people are thinking and talking about. They lead me to potential sources on the subjects of the day. And they give me the chance to read the writing of clergy, theologians, and others who are sharp, argumentative, possibly prophetic, important, self-important, reflective, moving, and now and then, full of hot air. Thanks to the Internet, I can read as much as time will allow. One periodical I've enjoyed in recent years, thanks to the Web, is *The Living Pulpit* (http://www.pulpit.org/), whose motto is "Dedicated to the Art of the Sermon."

Some time ago, I clicked on the January–March 2006 issue, the theme of which was "the Reign of God." The first article I came to was called "Lord, How Long?" by the Reverend Dr. Henry H. Mitchell. It only took me until the second paragraph before I was hooked. Mitchell, it seemed, had been thinking about the very issue that I had been struggling with: How come African Americans hardly ever question God, at least in a public or church-sanctioned way? "As I reviewed this doctrine (of the reign of God), I discovered that through the years African American religion has included a factor that has apparently not been held in common with the majority culture: a gut-level gladness that God is in charge of history," he wrote. "Joy was and is so pervasive that I wondered why I hadn't seen it before."

I would soon learn that Mitchell was, at the time, 87 years old. His wife, the Reverend Dr. Ella Pearson Mitchell, was 89 years old. They had each held prestigious positions at colleges and seminaries and served together for a time as deans at Spelman College. Henry Mitchell, a Baptist minister, had been immersed in black church studies for a half-century. And yet, even he had not stopped to fully consider the meaning of the unconditional black surrender to God's providence. He wrote about it in 2006 as if he had stumbled upon the most obvious truth in the world—that African Americans have always put their complete faith and trust and confidence in God. Questioning God is not part of the equation. "It is not possible to survive without hope, and that hope for the enslaved was the reign of a just and powerful God," he wrote. "It was a hope that gave strength and courage, a light at the end of the tunnel, a reason for keeping on keeping on. It was the hope stemming from the reign of God that provided the slaves' phenomenal capacity to endure unspeakable cruelty."

A little later on, Mitchell confided that there is no demand for theodicy—for calling God to account—among African Americans. "One knows one's arms to be too short to box with God," he wrote.

When I called Mitchell cold at his home in Atlanta and told him that I wanted to talk about God's role in natural disasters, he laughed. At first, he didn't seem to know if I was serious. Maybe *he* didn't think I was serious. He was well aware that the disasters of recent years had provoked lots of big thinkers with big titles to think they could question God. Such a thing seemed as odd and bewildering to him as trying to hold God accountable for UFO sightings. He told me that black theology had been mixed up in many ways by its inevitable contact with white European theology but that blacks had retained the common sense not to wag their fingers at the Lord. "This goes all the way back to our roots in traditional African religion," he said.

> You don't ask. You don't question. Going all the way back, you don't assume that you have any particular standing in a discussion like that. There is a hymn—people call it a gospel because it was written by a black man, so it isn't a proper hymn—that says "We'll understand it better by and by," and you just wait.

Then he started to softly sing:

> *Trials dark on every hand,*
> *and we cannot understand all the ways of God*
> *would lead us to that blessed promised land;*
> *but he guides us with his eye,*
> *and we'll follow till we die,*
> *for we'll understand it better by and by.*

I later learned that this hymn was written by Charles Tindley, a son of slaves who taught himself to read and write, attended night school, and took correspondence courses from the Boston School of Theology. He became an AME minister and wrote some fifty hymns. He must have known something about having patience with God.

Mitchell told me that he sang Tindley's hymn at his 26-year-old son's funeral.

> That hymn sums it up for me. Anytime you think you're in a position to judge God, you're out of position. Whoever does that is on shaky ground. A common saying in folk religion, which I hold in high esteem, is that your arms are too short to box with God. There is no point in judging God, or trying to determine if God made a decision for something to happen. We might not understand it, but we won't question God, not even at our son's death. If something terrible happens and two people out of ten die, why ask God why he let those people die? Why not be thankful he let the others stay? How many people survived the tsunami? But we don't go into it. Why not? There were those primitive peoples on the islands who read the signs and knew the past. They got away. God gave them the chance.

Mitchell started digging into Scripture, not to prove his case—as so many others did when speaking with me—but to give me examples of passages that had given him strength throughout his long life. He went first to Romans 8:28, one of the most paraphrased passages in the Bible (as in, everything will work out in the end): "We know that God causes all things to work together for good to those that love God, to those who are called according to His purpose." He turned to some more time-tested words of encouragement in 1 Corinthians 10:13: "And God is faithful; he will not let you be tempted beyond what you can bear."

Mitchell read out these passages as if they tell him everything he needs to know. He's a man who has held some pretty lofty titles—professor of black church studies at Colgate Rochester Divinity School, director of the Ecumenical Center for Black Church Studies in Los Angeles, dean of the School of Theology at Virginia Union University. But he made clear during our talk that he holds a distrust of scholarly types. They miss the obvious truth because they're too busy tying themselves up in academic knots. "Nitty gritty people are not into the same kinds of thinking that academics are," he said. "I am supposedly an academic, but at heart have never been more than a pastor."

He continued:

> Theodicy is expensive. It demands a lot of us, trying to figure things out. We have no standing to be questioning God. That's why I go back to my favorite verses, like Romans 8:28. Black people have survived because we believe things like that. Otherwise, we would have gone stone crazy.

"Well, that's right," said his wife, listening in on the other line.

They started telling me about a joint sermon they sometimes give. The theme is that Lincoln did not free the slaves. "We were brought out of slavery by the will of God, not Lincoln," Henry Mitchell told me. "We preach it—that God is in charge of history," Ella Mitchell said.

At this point, I felt silly even asking about the possibility that God delivers natural disasters as punishment for humankind's sins. But it's one of the questions that I asked of everyone because the "blame game" is often played. Mitchell, still patient and even playful (he seemed to get a kick out of our spontaneous talk), said that it's always possible that God acts in this way. There are examples in Scripture of him doing so. But it's nothing more than foolishness, he told me, to think that we can discern God's intentions. "You can't blame any group specifically," he said. "How can you? Anyone who does it is playing God and judging God. How can our finite minds ever extend to that place? We face trials that we cannot understand. Don't even try."

I asked Mitchell about one, brief admission in his essay—that African Americans do sometimes lose their heads and look to God in an immature, if understandable, way. He answered this way:

The common cry when one feels oppressed and depressed is, "Lord, how long?" The complaints of modern African Americans, including me, are expressed to God and gotten off the chest, after which praise and commitment are resumed, as in the 22nd Psalm, repeated by our Lord himself on the cross. This sequence of cathartic cry, followed by positive praise and promise of obedience, is fairly common in the Psalms and in the spirituals. It even surfaces in the blues.

Mitchell told me that such catharsis is unavoidably human and allows people to recharge their faith. You can come back stronger and more faithful after letting down your guard just a bit. For African Americans, Hurricane Katrina undoubtedly inspired many such moments. They were stunned and saddened that the levees were allowed to fail, Mitchell said. They were deeply depressed that the evacuation of poor blacks was hardly considered. But the need to cry "Lord, how long?" was in response to the ongoing trial of racism—not God's role in bringing down a hurricane. When the waters receded, most African Americans returned to praising God and waiting on deliverance. Mitchell was certain.

"If we had to live by our guarantees in this world, in the hands of an oppressive majority, we would have been lost," he told me. "If you feel utterly exposed and endangered, you can live a miserable life. One of the most healing things I know is the basic assumption that God works in everything for good."

He turned to folk religion again to sum it all up: "We can squeeze the blessings out of every catastrophe."

His wife was still listening. "I've run out of numbers to count the blessings," she said.

PROFESSOR ANTHEA BUTLER/BLAMING POLITICIANS AND THE DEVIL

As I said, I was introduced to Henry Mitchell by *The Living Pulpit,* a Web site that deals with the concerns of preachers and the substance of what they preach. Another Web site that I read often—for very different reasons—is called *The Revealer* (http://www.therevealer.org/). It's long been said that "Everyone is a critic," and the Web has truly made it so (for better or worse). Not only can any citizen with a computer start up a blog to comment on Mel Gibson's ideas about Vatican II or what the Bible says about eating meat, but scholars and other professional critics can post their observations for niche audiences in a way that was never practical on paper. *The Revealer* is a Web site run by several people with connections to New York University that critiques media coverage of religion. It sticks mostly to the *New York Times,* national magazines, and other big guns. I skim it fairly often and critique their critiques.

It was on September 2, 2005, just days after Hurricane Katrina, that I banged out www.therevealer.org and read these words: "That port that took in the bodies and souls of Africans to enslave them in America is the same place in which their descendants are dying because of the neglect—and virtual genocide—foisted upon them by a lame duck and lame president and an ineffectual government."

A brief introduction to the column warned that "It won't be appearing in any mainstream press near you soon, but it should: This is the language appropriate to atrocity."

The column was written by Anthea Butler, an historian of African American religious history at the University of Rochester. I would later learn when I spoke with her that she had nine relatives in New Orleans when Katrina hit. She had spent the first couple of days watching television, amazed by the scenes of black people pleading for help like in a Third World country. In something like a fit of rage, she wrote the short essay that would wind up on *The Revealer.* She wrote: "Bush's Christianity makes me want to puke. If Bush can claim to be a Christian, after smirking in his Rose Garden address about people wanting the help quickly, then he should start to put anti-Christ before his name."

Butler also attacked the media for harping on supposed looting committed by blacks with no food or shelter, which I'm guessing is part of the reason that her essay was considered appropriate for *The Revealer*.

Regardless, it was harsh. When I first read it, I was taken back by the naked emotion and by Butler's mocking of not only the president's competence but his faith. I remember thinking that Butler's words probably captured bits and pieces of what many African Americans were feeling at that time.

When I spoke with Butler several months later, she wasn't angry at all. In fact, she laughed easily and seemed to have a hard time believing that she wrote what she did about President Bush. Not that her feelings had changed. But she wasn't used to losing control in such a public way. She and *The Revealer* had received hundreds of emails about her piece. "Boy, I never intended for that," she laughed.

> I was just mad. I was like those guys in Idaho with the rifles, the ones who fear the government and say "Let's take care of our own people." That's radical to say, but it was the basic Christian response after Katrina. That little, pitiful golden rule should have applied.

As an historian, Butler told me, watching Katrina unfold was like watching African American history flash before her eyes. It was impossible not to recall that slaves had been brought into the same ports on the Gulf. "The only thing different is that with Katrina, we had actual footage," she said.

> To see all this pain and suffering and to see no one coming, it was like "Oh, crap. Here we *go*." All this la-de-da about faith based initiatives and all this Christian shouting, it all just fell on deaf ears. If you're a white Christian, you can get help. If you are a black Christian, you don't get help.

I've included Butler in this section about black Christians even though she is neither a Baptist nor a Methodist. She has a very different perspective on things. She is a Roman Catholic who attended an evangelical seminary. She has focused her research on Pentecostals, even serving as a former president of the Society for Pentecostal Studies. When I spoke with her, she had just sent off a manuscript about the historical role of women in the Church of God in Christ, a Pentecostal denomination. But as an historian of African American religion, she has also studied the mainstream black experience in Baptist and Methodist churches.

I kept her broad Christian background in mind when I reread her essay, which asserted: "That's right, America. Slavery has never ended for generations of African Americans in Louisiana, Mississippi and Alabama."

Then I asked her whether her column was a purely political statement, a religious statement, or both. She answered:

It was *absolutely* a religious response. It was both political and religious. I don't mean it in a black church sense, because I know everybody will say that's just the response of the black church. But I'm Catholic. For me, it was the same response as—to use the evangelical line—*What would Jesus have done* in this instance? It was righteous indignation, because we're supposed to be this nation of plenty, we're in Iraq, but we ain't helping our own people? What? We have this president who has said unabashedly that Jesus is his favorite philosopher. If you are a follower of Jesus, then send some stuff down there and go get these folks! They are God's children. Period. End of story. It was not what happened. Even in the 19th century, when people thought blacks and people of color did not have civilizations, we got treated better than this. At least they would go missionize the natives. This time around, they weren't even passing out tracts at the Superdome. It was like New Orleans was the pit of Sodom and Gomorrah and everyone else was thinking "We should just leave 'em and let it turn into a pillar of salt."

We talked for a long while about the government's failures before and after Katrina and then about New Orleans itself. "It sounds funny to say, but you can't separate the sacred, the secular and the profane in that city," Butler said. I slowly started pushing her (as I had become used to doing with others) to put aside the government's political and moral failings, as difficult as that might be, and to consider God's role in all this. She knew where I was going and she laughed, as Butler did about most things. "Oh, here we go, here we *go*," she said. She dismissed the idea that God is responsible for natural disasters, as if the very notion is kind of nutty. The idea that God shakes the ground to punish specific groups of people was hardly worth commenting on. "It's nature and it happens," she told me. "Maybe it's a little deist to say this, but you can't stop the world from turning. It doesn't matter how perfect you live, (bad stuff) is going to happen."

Butler said she likes to lean on the words of her professor at Fuller Theological Seminary in Pasadena, California, Ray Anderson, who says that "When the worst things happen, God has not abandoned you. God is there in the midst with you." It is another version of the idea that God suffers with the suffering. "It's not like God waves his big hand and says 'I'm going to stop this disaster and not let anything happen to you,'" Butler said.

That's not what the human experience is supposed to be about. It's about a relationship with God. If you have a relationship with someone, that means that when bad stuff happens, the person doesn't leave you. It's awful when you lose a loved one—I wouldn't want to be any number of people going through things—but you can't have this terrible sense that God checks out and goes on a picnic or something. God is in the midst.

Butler, laughing, told me that too many Americans misunderstand the idea of "life, liberty and the pursuit of happiness." "How many Americans have been suckered into thinking that happiness means that nothing bad happens to you," she said. "That isn't the case."

Then Butler veered off in a direction I hadn't expected her to go. She said that, yes, black Christians are less prone to blame God for their suffering than are other Christians. "If you go to a typical black church, they'll say God is good all the time," she said. But they don't blame God, she told me, because they have another culprit: the devil,

> Black people are more apt to blame the devil than the average white person. They are more apt to see the good vs. evil thing than most white Americans, who don't really deal with it unless they come from a Pentecostal background. Black people are not afraid to talk about evil, but it's in the framework of "The *devil* is trying to mess me up. The devil brought this on us to break us as a people." That's opposed to blaming God, which is a very different place to come from. I try to keep my ear to the ground by talking to normal people, and many black people just blame the devil. God will get the *victory* over this and then we'll get the victory. That's the framework, as opposed to it being God's fault.

Some people might ask why God doesn't just shut the devil down, or at least minimize his evil doings. Butler laughed, agreeing that the question is a good one. But sometimes you've just got to throw your hands up and say that it will all get worked out in the next life. "You have a big job on your hands, asking these questions," Butler told me.

DR. JAMES CONE/A PIONEER IN GRAPPLING WITH EVIL

Not long into my conversation with James Cone, a legendary figure among African American theologians, I told him how difficult it was to find black clergy or scholars who had given much thought to natural evil. Cone, who virtually created the concept of a separate black theology four decades before, knew exactly what I meant and got right to the point:

> You don't have many African Americans who sit around in seminar rooms talking about natural evil. That is a luxury for people who don't suffer much from moral evil. You read the books in theology and in philosophy about evil, it's

not until you get to the Holocaust that you really begin to talk about evil created by man. Or Hiroshima and Nagasaki. That's when moral evil comes in for most privileged whites. For us, it comes long before that. For most of the people who write the books, they focus on evil created by natural causes. For example, in 1755, with the Lisbon earthquake, that's when the questions about evil begin to emerge. But you had colonialism and you had slavery before that. Nobody asked questions about moral evil back then because the people doing the writing were doing the enslaving.

I've interviewed many people with impressive reputations. Some live up to them. Others do not. Cone surpassed his reputation. He seemed to know what I was going to ask before I asked it. And his answers to my questions were both concise and penetrating, as if he had just been talking to someone about white academia's luxury to muse about God's hand in earthquakes. I understood why Cone is credited with inspiring the work of dozens of black theologians. His 1970 book, *A Black Theology of Liberation,* indicted white Christian churches for failing to live up to Christ's message and urged the development of a black theology that would focus on the liberation of the oppressed. Any message that is not related to the liberation of the poor "is not Christ's message," he wrote.

All these years later, Cone is still a distinguished professor of systematic theology at Union Theological Seminary in New York. And he is still focused on deliverance from oppression. The main oppressor of African Americans, he told me, is not God, but human beings. "We've suffered from hurricanes and tornadoes before, but it's on a low-scale," he said. "We attribute that to the mystery of God. We don't know what's happening. But there is no mystery where most of our suffering has come from. It is very clear when you got lynching and slavery and all kinds of government policies where the suffering is coming from."

Cone was not as focused on Hurricane Katrina as others I had spoken to. I got the feeling that nothing about what happened surprised him. It was just a new chapter added to the back of an old story. "Everybody already predicted it was going to happen—and nobody did anything about it," he said. The encroachment on the New Orleans waterfront by developers and big business gradually made life less safe for blacks living in the city. "You can't beat nature with man-made dams," Cone said. "Nature will beat you every time."

Even in the case of the tsunami, Cone told me, it was mostly poor people living by the water, working menial jobs in the tourist industry, who got washed away. It's not only in America that the poor suffer disproportionately. His theology of liberation has no national boundaries. "Anytime poor people bear most of the suffering, there is more than the mystery of God at hand," he said. "Then it's a question of not just theodicy, but anthropodicy (the problem of human evil). How do we justify ourselves in the face of all of this?"

Our conversation turned to the earthquake in Pakistan and how it seemed to slip the American consciousness. Not surprisingly, Cone had a theory about this, too:

> It's happening to people of color who are not Europeans. If it had happened in Germany, everybody would be on that. The people who control public visibility about suffering—Who's suffering counts?—are the people who control the media. That's why you haven't heard much about it, about Pakistan, or the mudslides in the Philippines. With the tsunami, it was so overwhelming, so surprising, it was a curious event. How did that happen? Then people begin to say "Can it happen to us?" We are bounded by the Pacific, by the Atlantic. Can it happen to New York? To California? We don't worry as much about mudslides.

Cone wanted to make something clear to me. There is no doubt, he said, that African Americans are far more interested in human evil than natural evil. But that doesn't mean that black Christians are unwilling to question God. They do so all the time, he said. But they're willing to give God a pass on natural disasters, knowing that they are an unfortunate part of God's global system. From time to time, though, blacks are forced to question why God would allow racism and oppression to keep people of color down. People cannot develop deep faith, true faith, unless they face the moral contradictions before them.

> The question that African Americans have raised about God is how in the hell we got into the situation we're in. God must be addressed on that. But not in the sense in which faith feels itself crushed. Only in the sense that when you question God, you deepen faith. People who do not question God do not understand the Bible very well. Job questioned God. Isaiah, Jeremiah questioned God. Even Jesus questioned God—"My God, my God, why have thou forsaken me?" So in the depth of suffering, questioning God is to be expected. But it is for the purpose of keeping the faith, not as it were, rejecting faith.

Cone has been teaching a course on the problem of evil for the past few years. "God and Human Suffering," it's called. Students want to talk about the tsunami, Hurricane Katrina, all of it. Disasters can challenge faith, Cone told me, and he's more than willing to talk to students about it. But he won't let them lose sight of the more insidious source of evil. "The real issue is man-made evil, what human beings do to each other," he said.

Thoughts

Cone said it all: that African American Christians haven't had the luxury of questioning God. Going into this project, I didn't see how it could be a luxury to practice theodicy, the balancing of God's presumed love with the suffering in the world. After extensive conversations with Cone and the others I interviewed for this chapter, I learned otherwise. The act of questioning God is reserved for those who don't have to burn up their time and energy defending themselves from their fellow humankind. Cone, again, put it all into perspective when he noted that European philosophers treated the Lisbon earthquake of 1755 as a history-changing event in the course of understanding suffering. But what changed for blacks? The Atlantic slave trade had not yet peaked, and it would be decades before slavery was seriously questioned in much of Europe.

For these reasons and others, African American Christians have very little to offer when it comes to questioning God's presence in a natural disaster. Kirk-Duggan told me that there are too many social problems to deal with right now—housing, education, the military's demand for resources—to worry about an occasional disaster. Butler was furious with her Christian president's response to Katrina, not with God's challenge in delivering a hurricane. Pinn noted that at least natural disasters are *fair*. Their victims are not chosen by race, class, or culture. Cone said that black Christians and the worldwide poor do have a reason to question God now and then—about the way they are treated in this world, not the cause of natural disasters.

Even when leaving the question of racism and facing their relationship with God, black Christians are not all that interested in calling God to account. They rely too much on God for hope, strength, and the promise of a better day. As Kirk-Duggan said, their faith is in deliverance from injustice. Mitchell explained it best: that it's not possible to survive without hope and that African Americans have joyfully surrendered to their faith in God and ultimate salvation.

These weren't the answers I came for. But I came to accept them as somehow sufficient. Human beings have to deal with the problems before them before tackling the bigger questions. Maybe theodicy is a luxury.

8 THE MUSLIM PERSPECTIVE

All Christian traditions believe in the afterlife, the final reward after this life of pain and incompleteness, although they emphasize it very differently. Evangelical Christians insist first and foremost that we be saved, in order to guarantee salvation. African Americans see heaven as their deliverance from worldly injustice. Many mainline Protestants focus on their duty in this life, figuring God will take care of the rest. Roman Catholicism includes elements of all three. Muslims have a much more unified view of why we suffer in this life: The Quran says all that people need to know about God and how to live in this world. True knowledge will come only in the eternal life, so this earthly life is destined to be a struggle and a series of tests. Faith must be maintained in the face of all challenges and calamities, whether brought on by human behavior or by the laws of nature. The Quranic concept of Tawhid—the unity or oneness of God—requires that Muslims acknowledge God's presence in everything. They cannot understand or perceive God in this world, but they know he is there and involved in all things. This life is a step to the next.

DR. SAYYID SYEED/WHY A MOSQUE SURVIVED

As general secretary of the Islamic Society of North America, Sayyid Syeed is one of the American Muslim community's main ambassadors, both abroad and at home. He was telling me about his visit to a new, multimillion-dollar Islamic center in Bowling Green, Kentucky. While he was touring the grounds, he was touched by the hard work and dedication that a small community of mostly Bosnian immigrants had put into planning such a magnificent structure. Syeed soon found himself talking to those assembled about another mosque, one in western Turkey.

The mosque in question had become quite famous for surviving a massive earthquake in 1999. The quake occurred on a vast fault inside the earth's crust that had produced a series of quakes since at least the early twentieth century. This quake took more than 14,000 lives and left much of the region in ruins. But in the town of Golcuk, some 60 miles east of Istanbul, a mosque continued to stand, its dome surrounded by rubble. Pictures of the mosque were published around the world, and many Muslims declared that God had spared his home. Six years later, similar stories were told about a church in Sri Lanka that survived the tsunami.

Syeed told the Muslims gathered in Kentucky about the mosque in Turkey because he wanted to make a point: that mosques and other houses of worship do not stand for long periods—and survive natural disasters—because God protects them. They last because of how well the *faithful* build them out of devotion. "They are an expression of our love for God," he told them. "When we build a church or a mosque, we want to make it strong, everlasting, so we use the best materials, architecture, engineering. That's why they are stronger. It is your expression of love and religiosity that makes the center beautiful and strong, not God wanting to protect it."

He told me this story to show how interpretations of natural disasters have gotten so out of hand. Because of global communications, we hear about and see every major disaster. Everyone, it seems, has an immediate analysis, an armchair theory. A mosque that survives an earthquake becomes *proof* of God's will to people who know nothing about architecture or earthquakes. "It would be a travesty of the divine justice that God destroys the people around the mosque but saves his mosque, or his church," Syeed told me. "For the God of all mankind—Christians, Jews, Muslims, Hindus, atheists and everyone—to do that would be strange. How unethical. How unjust. It would be ridiculous."

Syeed has a patient way of explaining things, which is a good thing. He has been one of Islam's chief spokespeople in this country for several decades. It's never been an easy job. Since 2001, it has been about as difficult a cultural and religious role as one would want to assume. All of the Muslim scholars profiled in this chapter have become spokespeople for their religion, to varying degrees. Syeed first took on a leadership role as president of the Muslim Students Association of USA & Canada during the early 1980s. Then he transformed that group into the Islamic Society of North America, one of the first national organizations to actively speak for America's growing Muslim community. He is the founder of a respected academic journal on

Islamic social sciences. And he has been deeply involved in interfaith relations, in Indiana—where the Islamic Society is based—and at the national and international levels. Syeed has appeared on many American news shows, trying to explain Islam in 2 minutes or less, and has talked about the American Muslim community on the national television networks of Turkey, Malaysia, Sudan, Pakistan, and Saudi Arabia.

The Islamic Society of North America aggressively raised money for relief after the tsunami, the Pakistani quake, and Hurricane Katrina. Syeed was quite prepared to talk to me about natural disasters, having discussed the great events of the day within his own community and with his non-Muslim colleagues. The first thing he wanted to tell me was that the natural disasters that have shocked the world in recent years are evidence of a far greater power than ourselves. There may be much that we struggle to understand about these events, but they are stark reminders of our small position in the world and of the vastness of God's dominion. This would be the main point made by each Muslim scholar I would interview. None questioned God's involvement in each calamity (just as they would not question God's involvement in anything that happens in this world). Islam preaches complete submission to God's will and desires. So it makes sense that Muslims would see natural disasters as swift and painful messages that humankind must not lose sight of its minuscule role in this world.

"This kind of colossal disaster makes us feel that, in spite of all of our progress and all of our might, there is some superpower over and above us," he explained, slowly and patiently. "This kind of disaster reminds us of the overlordship, the control and power, of God in the universe. Is God involved? Definitely."

As I talked to Muslims about the devastation caused by natural disasters in this world, they would inevitably veer our conversations toward the next world, the eternal world. Syeed told me that even very religious people periodically lose sight of the fact that this life is only preparation for the next. It's easy to become transfixed, almost hypnotized, by stature and materialism, things that disappear like dust in the wind upon death. Even the worst disasters in this life, Syeed said, should serve to remind us of how briefly each of us is here and how suddenly our deaths may come.

It only emphasizes that we here on this earth, whatever we see, whatever we do, are part of a much bigger plan, that the life we spend on this earth is ultimately for a very limited span of time, that we are going back to God, that our life on this earth is an opportunity he has given us to serve him. So, therefore, when something like this happens, it emphasizes that we must have consciousness and awareness of the spiritual aspect of our life. We should not get overwhelmed by the material aspect of our life. We should plan our lives in a way that factors in the spiritual dimension.

God surely understands the impact of the media on all lives across the continents, Syeed told me. The sweep of modern global communications makes an earthquake or a tsunami a forceful message to the world, more so than at any point in history. But Syeed rejected any arguments that disasters are aimed at particular groups of people, saying that every group, in any corner of the world, is guilty of sinful behavior. "We can't identify the people affected as having more sins than those who are not affected," he told me.

> The message is to all of mankind. The major events of the last two years, if you look at them, are so big, so unprecedented, so global, maybe it is by design. But they are not against one particular nation, one state or city. They are lessons, in a global world of communication, to all of us.

Then Syeed made a very perceptive point about whether God can afford to reward and punish us in this life. If God punished particular groups each time they sinned, he told me, the world would get bogged down in a dreary cycle of sin and punishment. Our freedom to live our lives would be restricted by the threat of God's hammer always overhead, and there would be no need for God to judge us at the end of our lives. "The whole scheme of things, that man has been given a special role, the whole concept of heaven and hell, the day of judgment, would become irrelevant," he said.

As I said, the Muslims I interviewed for this project stressed that people must not view suffering in this world without considering the greater meaning of the next life. But I was still surprised by how willing they were to talk about the victims of natural disasters—far more so than any other religious group. They seemed eager, in fact, to talk about the dead. This, I would learn, is because of the Muslim belief that people who suffer needlessly in this world are forgiven of sins by God and rewarded in the hereafter. "There is a concept in Islam that a person who walks on the street and is hit by something that give him some pain is not being punished," Syeed told me. "The very experience is spiritually rewarding for him. Many sins are forgiven from his accumulated sins. You can multiply this experience for a bigger tragedy. A test of patience and endurance will be amply rewarded by God."

For those who are uninvolved in a catastrophe—the millions who watch devastated survivors on CNN—Islam's requirements are similar to those of the other great faiths: to pray for the victims and to raise money for the survivors. There are many requirements for charity in Islam. "It is an opportunity to come forward and show solidarity," Syeed said. "God put us on this earth with freedom of will. Some enthusiasts, religious zealots, want to see God's retribution in disasters. We should be expressing sympathy and charity."

Syeed continued on the central importance of free will. Because God gave us such power, he told me, God expects us to advance our knowledge of the universe and to do a better job of running the physical world that he created. Natural disasters, in addition to serving as reminders of God's dominance, may be tests of how well humankind is running the ship. How come there was no early warning system in the Indian Ocean? Why was New Orleans so vulnerable to a great hurricane when the city's vulnerability was predicated for decades? Why were millions still homeless in Pakistan one year after their earthquake? We may fail these tests, Syeed said, because of political reasons and a lack of will. But will God accept such excuses?:

> God has delegated to us certain powers as human beings. We are his servants, his trustees on this earth. He has given to us this intellect, this innate intelligence. We are challenged by him to understand him and to understand his hand behind the universe. Over the generations, we have developed science, technology. We can blunt some of the destructive possibilities of nature. We should be in a better position to predict these disasters. The people in Pakistan should have been able to avoid some of the destruction. We should have been able to predict the tsunami. We should have had better dams and better planning for Katrina. That is one aspect of our relationship with God, that he has put us on this earth and given us a special responsibility that other creatures don't have. It is our religious duty to understand the way God works in the universe and the ways we can interact with the universe using the powers he has given us.

Imam Zaid Shakir/Looking Beyond This Life

The questioning of God that took place after the tsunami was perfectly reasonable—from the point of view of anyone who makes the mistake of focusing on this life instead of the next life. Imam Zaid Shakir drove home this point repeatedly when we spoke. During the first few minutes of our talk, he put it this way:

> When you get trapped into a this-world centric paradigm, it becomes difficult to deal with God's involvement in a disaster. Then, it's God who oppressed those people, caused them to suffer. When you deal with a paradigm that includes this world *and* the next world, then any suffering in this world is just a means to complete freedom, liberation and bliss in the next world. Suffering has to be tied to rewards in the next life for it to make any sort of sense and, to use our worldly terminology, to absolve God of any injustice. It's a whole different calculus that we're dealing with here.

A whole different calculus. A new paradigm. Shakir knows about transformation and what it takes to radically change one's world view. An African American, he grew up a Baptist in public housing projects in several cities. It was after high school that he began a spiritual journey, looking to Christianity, then eastern religions, then communism, for wisdom on how to make sense of inequalities in society. He wound up serving in the Air Force for four years, and during this time found Islam. He became a Muslim in 1977. His Islamic studies would take him to Egypt and, for seven years, to Syria.

Since the civil rights era of the 1960s and the parallel black power movement, Islam has become increasingly attractive to African Americans. Many find a religious model for self-sufficiency, not to mention ties to some of their African ancestors who were Muslims. The Nation of Islam, a black offshoot of mainstream Islam, gets the most media attention because of its separatist positions that are often called racist. But growing numbers of African Americans are finding their way to mainstream Islam, and Shakir has become one of the best-known black Muslims in the United States. After two stints as imam of a mosque in New Haven, Connecticut, he moved to Hayward, California, in 2003 to become scholar-in-residence at the Zaytuna Institute, an Islamic school. He lectures around the country and writes essays on how Muslims should view the major issues of the day, including natural disasters.

In an essay about the tsunami, he wrote that only God could have made it happen (drawing the same immediate conclusion as Lutzer, the evangelical pastor). And yet, Shakir wrote, even Muslims were questioning why God did it, why the innocent suffered, why so many of the victims were Muslims. The Quran promised a world of trial and tribulation, good and evil. The prophet Mohammed even warned that earthquakes and other natural disasters would be among the tests to come. "These narrations call our attention to the fact that the believer's brief stint in this world is a preparation for eternal life," Shakir wrote. "Our understanding of suffering, justice, the trials of this world, and many other issues integral to any meaningful assessment of the human condition, are incomplete and inevitably misleading when they are divorced from consideration of the next, eternal life."

When I talked to Shakir, he had just returned home from a speaking engagement at the famous Phillips Academy in Andover, Massachusetts. In the post-9/11 world, everyone wants to know what Muslims think and believe. So Shakir is in steady demand, even at an elite prep school known for the affluence and influence of its students and alumni. Shakir doesn't water down his message. He speaks directly about the daily demands made by Islamic practice and about the vast divide that sometimes exists between the Muslim point of view and the quasi-secular, materialist lifestyles of many

Americans. He told me that he isn't surprised that many Americans of different faiths react to natural disasters by questioning either God or the victims.

Those who question God, he repeated, are fixated on their stature and accomplishments in this world and can't imagine anything worse than losing them because of a random, meaningless calamity. "A lot of people question God's justice, why there is suffering in the world, because they don't look at the big picture," he told me. "Their thought processes, their analysis, is limited to this world, what is immediately perceivable through the senses. The extent to which we consider the hereafter, or fail to do that, or lack the ability to do that, is a barometer of our spiritual station."

Others, in order to defend God, blame groups of sinful people for drawing God's wrath. God can certainly punish humankind, Shakir said. But those who try to identify evildoers are stepping way beyond their bounds by trying to understand God's will. "In these days and times, it can be directed at any of us," Shakir said.

> It is real. God does punish sinners. But God also has mercy on righteous people. And he ultimately is the judge of those whom we might deem to be sinners. There might be good deeds in a person's life that we don't know about that make them candidates for God's mercy. I prefer to emphasize his mercy.

No one escapes suffering, Shakir told me. It's not as if the victims of the tsunami or the Pakistani quake lost out on their chance for pure happiness in this world. This life is destined to be imperfect for all. Everyone experiences pain—physically, emotionally, and spiritually. It's all part of our preparation for the next life. This life, as Shakir put it, is trouble:

> I don't think anyone comes into this world and doesn't struggle. Someone might be blessed with every creature comfort, with loads of money and a huge bank account, but can struggle with depression. Even though physically they might not have suffered, they've suffered psychologically. That's the nature of the world. This world is trials, tribulations and struggle. So don't get too comfortable here because this is only a preparatory stage for something that is much greater. These disasters are periodic reminders. Loud ones. Saying that, while we're here, we are not relieved of the responsibility to comfort the afflicted.

People want to find meaning when a major disaster strikes, Shakir told me. But such meaning can be found each day, when individuals suffer quietly, overcome challenges of all sorts, and maintain their faith. The lessons just keep coming at us, as they always have and always will. Even the impression many have that natural disasters are erupting more often than in the past is untrue, Shakir said. We are more aware of them only because of the dominance of the media in our lives. People who are trying to understand God's role or message in the tsunami are asking the same questions that people asked when news of a disaster did not go beyond a few villages. "If the tsunami happened a few hundred years ago, we might not have learned about it in our lifetimes," he said, making an insightful point that I don't recall being offered by anyone else.

> It would have occurred and would have been equally devastating, but we would have known nothing. Globalized communication gives us the impression these things are happening with greater frequency or greater intensity. But the reality is that they've always been here and will always be here. We just have to prepare ourselves spiritually to deal with them.

How should a Muslim react to news of a major catastrophe in another part of the world? The answer, Shakir told me, is by chanting *Inna lillahi wa inna ilayhi rajioon.* It means "We belong to God and unto him we shall return."

DR. IBRAHIM B. SYED/GOD'S SECOND LAW OF THERMODYNAMICS

After talking for a while with Ibrahim B. Syed, I couldn't help asking if he had any hobbies. I was pretty sure I knew the answer. "I do not spend my time smoking, drinking coffee, playing tennis, moonlighting or playing hanky panky," he said, amused. "I am a very busy man, day or night. But if there is a will, there is a way."

Syed is a clinical professor of medicine at the University of Louisville School of Medicine, where he specializes in medical physics and nuclear cardiology. The purpose of medical physics (it might be obvious to some) is to apply physics to medicine, largely through the use of radiation. So Syed is a man of science. He is also the president of the Islamic Research Foundation International, which he cofounded in 1988 to "revive" the intellectual advancement of Islam. He has written hundreds of articles about the Islamic approach to questions of science, including genetics, human cloning, obesity, fasting, breast-feeding, quantum physics, string theory, the second law of thermodynamics, and yes, hurricanes and tsunamis. So Syed is a man of science—and faith. He gets little rest, preferring to do what he can to revive Islam as a religious culture of science and educational advancement, values that he believes once drove Islam but have been lost to ignorance and superstition.

He also wants to do all that one man can to slow the effects of entropy.

Entropy? Syed has a fully formed vision of the connection between physics and faith, between the laws of the universe and Islam. He believes that both the beginning of the universe—the "Big Bang"—and the end of it all are described in the Quran and that science is therefore in perfect harmony with Islam. And he sees natural disasters as part of the universal journey that was previewed by the prophet Mohammed. Once an earthquake is set in motion according to God's design, as it is explained in the Quran, God will not step in to interfere with himself. In other words, we may not fully grasp God's intentions, but the laws of science—the laws of God—give us a pretty good outline of God's plans for this world. Syed put it this way:

> God has set the laws, and once he sets them, he does not violate them. There is gravity. If you fall from a mountain, you will be killed. That law cannot be violated for the sake of a prophet or anyone. People talk about miracles and all such things. But there is explanation for everything. There are things that we did not understand in the past that we now know. It is important for people of religion to know that everything can be explained, even if we don't know right now. If something supernatural happens, a miracle, we may understand it in the future.

In his article about the second law of thermodynamics, Syed explains that the law deals with the natural dispersion of energy through all processes in the physical world. Energy inevitably winds down as it is dispersed as heat, a process known as *entropy*. Science holds that the universe is gradually running down like a cosmic battery as energy is slowly lost. Syed agrees with another man of science, George Coyne, the Jesuit astronomer, that entropy may lead to the end of the universe as we know it. Syed holds that entropy is the enemy of life and is hastened by inattention, laziness, and greed. So Islam fights against entropy—the loss of energy—by building discipline and peace of mind, qualities needed to stay active and productive. "Without these one cannot achieve success in life and will easily succumb to the temptation of life or entropy," he wrote.

Natural disasters, then, are symptoms of entropy, of heat bursting from the earth's core or from the atmosphere. It's part of God's system. The Quran describes the day of judgment as "When earth is rocked in her last convulsion; when earth shakes off her burden." Perhaps God set the system up, Syed told me, so that if humankind tampers with the laws of nature, it will set off more disasters as a lethal alarm system.

> Natural disasters are God's creation, but human beings may contribute to those tragedies. Look at nuclear weapons, global warming, things created by man. We take uranium and concentrate it to make nuclear weapons. We use too much gasoline and create pollution, dangerous for our health. You destroy nature recklessly, then you have to pay. Nothing is free. Write it down. This is the universe of Allah. No free rent, anywhere.

Okay, I said to Syed. Let's assume you're right. Natural disasters are part of God's rule book, which he does not rewrite in the middle of the game. Still, what good do they do? Are there moral lessons we should read in hurricanes like some do in tarot cards, or must we be content to understand the science involved? Right off, he belittled the popular easy answer: that God is punishing particular groups of sinners. "If you don't know the depth of physics and many things, it is a good answer," he said.

> It is best to tell a layman that is punishment from God, because he may not be able to understand my explanation. The prophet was teaching the people in Arabia, who were illiterate, so he gave simple examples. But, no, there is no punishment for people who worship more than one god. Allah continues to grow the corn, the rice, the wheat, for them.

Instead, Syed offered three general lessons to be taken from natural disasters. The first was that God gives many, many warnings to humankind before taking any punitive action and that disasters may serve as periodic warnings—not to mention reminders of the day of judgment. Second, God tests everyone. Syed told me about Imam Abu Hanifa, who founded one of the main schools of Islamic jurisprudence. He became famous for uttering *Alhamdulillah*—Praise Be to God—in all circumstances, good or bad. "The Muslim must always say *Alhamdulillah*," Syed said. "Praise Be to God. *Alhamdulillah*. Praise Be to God. In every condition, we say *Alhamdulillah*. The prophet said that we must give thanks for every breath we take."

The final message of a great disaster, Syed told me, is that each of us must do what we can to help our fellow human beings and to address the social and moral failings of our societies. Failing to confront evil can cancel out much of the good that an individual does.

> One can be a Muslim, go to the mosque, pray, fast, give charity. That's fine. He is fulfilling all the five pillars of Islam. But he can be failing in his actions to correct society. It is the responsibility of every religion— whether you are Christian, Jew, Muslim, whatever—to correct the evil. Otherwise, the evil spreads fast. When an earthquake comes and many good people die, one must wonder what they can do to improve the world around them.

It's no surprise that Syed calls Satan the personification of not only evil but entropy.

Imam Yahya Hendi/God Is No Puppeteer

To be a person of faith, to be a Muslim, does not require reading God's mind. This point is blatantly obvious to Yahya Hendi, who sometimes sounded exasperated when we spoke. The problem is that so many people are obsessed with finding specific signs of God's presence in their lives—and trying to determine whether God is happy or not—that they unwittingly become God's palm readers. They have some mighty long lines to trace and interpret, if indeed they can find them.

Hendi, the first Muslim chaplain at Georgetown University and an acquaintance of many of Washington's most powerful figures, is a very modern man of faith. When we spoke, he was constantly trying to separate God's broad, central teachings from the unreasonable leaps of faith that many people are eager to take on all sorts of subjects. A fine example, he said, is the belief that God is directing each earthquake or tornado as a puppet master sitting above the clouds:

> Let's call these things by their name: natural disasters. There is science in this world, and science explains these phenomena. Whether it's the movement of winds or something that happens within the center of the earth that makes an earthquake happen, science explains it. Does God have anything to do with it? Of course. But in what way? God is the creator of this nature. His rules govern it. Does the Quran speak about destruction coming upon a town for its sins? Yes. But not by God coming down to earth and saying "Listen guys, I hate your guts now. I'm going to destroy you." Absolutely not.

God tells us what we need to know, Hendi told me. That's why he has given the human race his Scriptures and sent prophets to spread the word. The Quran includes norms—rules—that govern creation and that explain the way people should act. The whole set-up is quite plain. When people fail to meet God's standards, there are consequences. "When the norms are well-practiced, things should go the right way and we should be in harmony with nature," Hendi said. "When those norms are not well-practiced, bad things happen. It's very much like traveling on the highway. The norms in America say you drive on the right side, and if you try to do it on the left side, you wind up in trouble." He said that global warming and other examples of environmental malfeasance may be throwing the world out of balance—and violating God's norms in the process. Other widespread violations, such as the oppression of one people by another or any systemic disregard for the poor and sick, can also throw our world out of kilter in ways we don't understand.

Hendi referred to chapter 30 of the Quran, which talks of the fall of nations and cultures that were once mighty but lost sight of God's expectations and their own cosmic smallness. The Quran says to "Roam the earth and see what was the end of those who flourished before you." Islam's holy book also says, and later repeats, that "God did not wrong them but they wronged themselves." The bottom line, Hendi told me, is that we should not blame God without first considering what people have done with God's world. "If we obey his commands, things will go right," he said. "And if we don't, things will go bad. Is it because God comes down and destroys us? Absolutely not. If we go against the rules that he has *inserted* into creation, things will go badly."

Hendi believes that God's norms are part of natural law. When we violate those norms, the laws of nature react. But he sees this link in very broad strokes and doesn't think that we can decipher the movement of tectonic plates to find clues of God's mind-set. Hendi told me that it is his opinion—and this surprised me—that the stories in Scripture, including the Quran, that describe God's particular punishments are probably metaphors, not recitings of actual events:

> You go to the Old Testament and you have the story of the exodus, a very revealing story about God punishing the Egyptians. It is a very clear story. God hardened the heart of Pharaoh. God destroyed the cities. God destroyed the Egyptians. What can you say? The message is obvious. The story of Noah, as well. They are in the Quran. But I think we should understand those narratives as having metaphorical meaning, not literal. Historically speaking, 2,000 or 3,000 years ago, people could not explain the scientific facts. People could not make sense of science. People did not know why an earthquake happens or why, within a few minutes, you have dark clouds come in and a flood kills many people. Their minds could not come up with more than that there must be a higher power who is angry with someone who did a sin. But I think we live in 2006 here, when we have the scientific means to tell us exactly the way things happen and why they happen the way they do. For it to make sense in religious language, we still come up with analogies.

I told Hendi, somewhat apprehensively, that I did not know of many Muslims who read the stories of the Quran metaphorically. He said that it was not an unusual position among scholars, although others may be more circumspect before sharing it. "We have our right-wing, fundamentalist Christians in the Muslim community, you know," he said with a laugh. God's judgment, as described in the Quran, will be delivered at the end of time, not on a day-to-day basis like changes in the stock market. "For me, Mohammed was previewing for us what will happen at the end of time," he said.

I'm sure that Hendi has been described often as a "moderate Muslim." If you ask me, commentators now use the term to label any Muslim who is not a fundamentalist. I think that *moderate* has to be carved up into at least several, more nuanced descriptions. I'm not sure what they should be, but I would call Hendi a modern, Western Muslim (which I realize is too long and uncatchy a tag). He said the opening prayer in Congress on November 19, 2001, when he must have felt tremendous pressure to say exactly the right thing. His Web site shows him with President Bush and President Clinton, as well as with Archbishop Theodore McCarrick, the retired Archbishop of Washington. Hendi puts a lot of time into interfaith work, often visiting synagogues, churches, and mosques with priests, ministers, and rabbis. He is the Muslim chaplain at Georgetown, a Catholic university. And he is working toward his doctorate not in Islamic studies but in comparative religion.

The ultimate message of the tsunami, which washed away Muslim village after Muslim village, and other such catastrophes can only be *humility,* Hendi told me. It is the message for people of all faiths. "This universe is not about us," he said. "We are not the center. The center is God. We have to be humble. What matters is that we do justice, stand up for goodness and respect God's creation—particularly the harmony that God inserted into his creation. For us, death is very close."

In other words, if we heed God's rules, everything will work out. Earthquakes may still erupt, but we won't blame each other, we'll take care of the victims, we'll repair and care for God's green earth the best we know how and we'll keep in mind the limits of this world. "At the end of the day, what matters is the life to come," Hendi said. "The pain in this life can be sad. But God will pay us much more in eternity than we have lost in this world."

IMAM FEISAL ABDUL RAUF/GOD IS EVERYWHERE, BUT HARD TO FIND

The most prominent Muslim leader in America couldn't help but laugh as I explained the goals of this book and what I was hoping to learn from him. Granted, he was tired from having just returned from Malaysia, where he was starting a chapter of the Cordoba Initiative, his pet project to change the world. But Feisal Abdul Rauf knows something about aiming at elusive targets, and the idea of trying to explain natural disasters tickled him. "Even insurance policies refer to Acts of God," he said. "Already the concept has been introduced into our understanding."

I said earlier that each of the Muslim scholars profiled in this chapter have become spokesmen for their faith since 2001. Rauf has become an international statesman, a theological diplomat, a best-selling author, and as likely an architect as we have for better future relations between America and the Muslim world. He didn't envision this for himself when he came to New York in 1965 at 17 after living for an extended period in Malaysia with his Egyptian parents (his father was a religious scholar who ran Islamic centers). After teaching in public high schools and working in real estate, he was asked to lead a Sufi mosque in New York, Sufism being a mystical and often apolitical branch of Islam. His mosque, Masjid al-Farah, was 12 blocks north of the World Trade Center. In 1997, a prescient vision inspired him to start the American Society for Muslim Advancement to build bridges between Islam and American culture.

Then came September 11 and the new world. Rauf is articulate, cultured, funny, and astute about both Islam and how the West sees Islam. Within weeks, he was all over television, a "moderate Muslim" who could explain what was happening. He also started the Cordoba Initiative, an interfaith group that wants to heal the breach between Islam and the West. So when we spoke, he had just returned from a mission to expand the initiative to Malaysia as a framework for international growth.

Rauf was well acquainted with the public discourse about natural disasters. Rather than dillydallying by, say, talking about the moral responsibility to raise money, he went straight to the heart of the matter: the role that God plays in our world. When people wonder about God's presence in a tornado or an earthquake, they are raising much larger questions of how God touches our limited consciousness at all. In what sense is he part of our world? Rauf dove in:

> I believe that God is conscious and aware of everything that happens. I think there are levels at which the divine presence operates, both at a macroscopic level and a microscopic level, and that there are moments when one is very much aware of a divine intervention in one's personal life. One feels a deliberate intervention to prevent a particular thing from happening. That sense is there. God being at the boundary at both the macroscopic and the microscopic is, in fact, very much part of the Islamic world view, as I see it. The very name of God encompasses the outer and the inner, the one who predates time and post-dates time, who overlaps the boundary between space and time, both in the largest distances of interstellar space and the microscopics of subatomic spaces.

So, if God is conscious of our world in ways we can and cannot understand and permeates every subatomic particle of our lives, does it simply follow that an earthquake *is* God or that God and a hurricane are one? Can a natural disaster or any apparent accident that turns one person's life upside down happen without God's will or desire or involvement? Here, things become far more unclear, Rauf told me. If Islam, like other theistic faiths, holds that God is all-present, there is still no way to identify or measure this divine presence. And then there is the most difficult question of whether humankind's actions can blot out parts of God's design, a dilemma that Rauf defined better than anyone else I interviewed. "If nothing happens without the creator's knowledge, there are many nuances," he said.

> God created the laws of physics, of gravity, of chemistry. What we call the laws of nature are, in fact, divine laws, not separate from divine laws. The question now becomes how we, human beings, manipulate these laws for certain things. To what extent does our intervention have an impact on what happens?

In other words, God set up the rules for the physical world, but corporations, developers, and politicians—given free will and desiring profits—do not have to play by those rules. Humankind can go around them at times. Or bend them slightly. Then it becomes even harder to discern God's role in a physical event. On the day we spoke, Rauf and I had each read an article in the *New York Times* about something known as "methane burps." "The idea is that if global warming is taking place, certain methane gases can suddenly burp through (the Arctic tundra) and create catastrophic end-of-the-world scenarios, real apocalyptic visions," Rauf said. "Again, the notion is that if we intervene in the ecological balances in certain ways, we can make things happen. Is it an *Act of God* or the vector sum of the laws of nature with our own interventions?"

Then Rauf boiled it down to the simplest human terms, showing me how adapt he had become in communicating difficult theological points to a vast audience. Suppose, he said, that he dropped a hammer on his foot. Ouch! There's momentary pain. Maybe a red mark or a bruise. Can God be held responsible? "Certainly the laws of gravity are placed there by God, but did God will that hammer to fall on my foot?" he asked. "Or was it the sum total of the laws of nature, in this case of gravity, *plus* my own action? That is the question that faces us as humanity."

I asked Rauf about the possibility of divine punishment. In particular, I wanted to understand the significance of passages in the Quran—like in the Bible—where God warns people about their immoral behavior and punishes them when they do not heed him. I asked about the cultural influence of the story of Noah (*Nuh*).

> The great flood? Oh yes, there is a historical tendency in the Quran, where God warns people not to reject him, lest they be stricken with divine punishment. That is definitely part of the narratives in our Scriptures. God sends a prophet or a messenger to warn the people, and when they reject the divine message, they are visited with some nature of calamity as punishment for their intransigence. I could see people making the jump. But I would be leery of that. I try to discourage that because calamities happen all the time. How do you know?

If you live on the San Andreas fault, is it God's will that the tectonic plates are sliding past each other? Yes, indeed, but if you choose to reside there, and an earthquake is going to happen one of these days, well, it doesn't mean that God is angry with you. While there are narratives in the Quran like that, there are also statements of the prophet that say whoever dies in an earthquake, from drowning, a woman in childbirth, are considered to have died the death of a martyr and will be rewarded with paradise. So it's not that straightforward that anybody who dies in a calamity is a recipient of God's wrath.

Rauf continued telling me about the Quran, citing passages that talk about the end of time, "when the oceans shall surge, when the mountains shall move like clouds." He said that it is inevitable that people will see contemporary events as the possible fulfillment of such prophecies. But, again, he himself was not willing to make such a leap. The end of time will come when the end of time comes. In the meantime, the clear message of a history-changing tsunami is a reminder of our mortality. "The lesson is that the creator is almighty and we are nothing compared to infinity," Rauf said.

We should care for each other and care for the planet, utilize our smarts and our resources to take care of the planet so it takes care of us. We should be reminded of our primal relationship to the creator and of the two basic commandments of the Abrahamic religions: to love God with all of your heart, mind, soul and strength; and to love your fellow human beings.

THOUGHTS

This life is a life of tests, suffering, and disappointment. The next life is *real* life, when we are reunited with God and worthy of bliss. Evangelical Christians believe this. So do Muslims. They disagree, of course, on how to get to heaven or paradise. But when it comes to how they view this broken old world, they have much in common. Muslims see this world as a brief and erratic trial before God's eternal verdict.

Mainstream Islam has only one recognized understanding of the Quran, that it is God's revealed word, passed through the angel Gabriel to the prophet Mohammed. Muslims revere the Quran as more than a sacred text but as God's very words. And the Quran puts tremendous emphasis, in passage after passage, on paradise. We live in this world as preparation for the next. That's it. So it makes sense that Muslims cannot look at the tsunami or any instance of human suffering without considering the larger context. They can't look at anything in this life without considering the next.

Shakir told me that one's "spiritual station" is linked to the degree that you keep in mind the next life. To focus on the tsunami as some sort of injustice is to lose sight of what really matters. Syeed said that all disasters are reminders of how brief, uncertain, and finally meaningless this life really is. Even Hendi, who takes a very modern view of things, ended our talk by saying that what really matters is the life to come.

This focus on the next life doesn't tell us very much about what God was doing when a massive earthquake left millions homeless in Pakistan. It doesn't tell us much about God's role in this life. But it did not take me long to understand that Muslims do not feel the need. The Quran says what it says, and Islam is about complete submission to God's will. Syed, the professor of medicine, sees God's will in the laws of science. Entropy is God's great challenge, a long-term test. He sees it as the Muslim's duty to take up the challenge by countering entropy, the threat of natural disasters, and all forms of injustice. Rauf, too, told me that God is in the laws of nature and that we are likely getting in the way of God's will by tampering with nature.

Whatever mistakes we make, though, the victims are taken care of. This was the main message of Islam that stayed with me. Muslims believe that the victims of the tsunami—or any car accident—are rewarded in paradise for their suffering here. The greater the suffering, the more sins that are forgiven. So people should grieve mostly for those of us who are left, especially those who worry too much about this life.

9 THE HINDU PERSPECTIVE

Moving from the Abrahamic religions—Judaism, Christianity, and Islam—to the main religions of the East—Hinduism and Buddhism—requires a radical change in mind-set. The eastern understanding of humankind's place in the universe could not be more different. Hindus and Buddhists do not see themselves as being the focus of God's love and attention. Rather, they see themselves as minuscule beings in a transitory, hopelessly complex universe. The tsunami and other agents of suffering are not surprises. Suffering is seen, in fact, as a certainty, although it is not directed at anyone. The path away from suffering and toward something like salvation comes through meditation, yoga, and hard-earned self-awareness. Hindus believe that God is not a separate or an exterior force but is present in all things. Certain aspects of God's presence may take the form of lesser deities, but many Hindus consider themselves monotheistic because the local gods are only reflections of the universal God. Since Hindus don't see God as a personal God, they have difficulty even considering God's role or intentions or actions. Our fates, instead, are believed to be determined by karma, a universal system of cause and effect. Karma determines how much joy and sorrow one will experience in future lives, thanks to reincarnation. The only way to break free from the cycle of birth and death is through detachment, which is attainable after years of meditation, yoga, and study. Suffering, from natural or moral evils, is believed to be part of the cycle of life and death and rebirth.

PROFESSOR ARVIND SHARMA/AVOIDING THEODICY THROUGH KARMA

In the days leading up to our conversation, Arvind Sharma told me, he couldn't help thinking about a famous debate that took place in 1934.

It was between Mahatma Gandhi, the legendary promoter of Indian independence and nonviolent protest, and Rabindranath Tagore, an iconic writer and intellectual in India, if largely unknown elsewhere. On January 15 of that year, a terrible earthquake struck Bihar, India, killing thousands. Gandhi felt that the quake was some sort of divine retribution for India's tolerance of the barbaric oppression of low-caste people, the *untouchables*. "To me, the earthquake was no caprice of God nor a result of a meeting of mere blind forces," Gandhi said. But Tagore countered that "physical catastrophes have their inevitable and exclusive origin in certain combinations of physical facts." He said that "elements of unreason," like Gandhi's argument, would actually hurt the cause of freedom.

Sharma, one of the world's leading Hindu scholars, told me that the conflict between Gandhi and Tagore continues to illustrate two main schools of thought within Hinduism about not only natural disasters but how to explain much of what happens in the world. "Right there, you get the basic division on whether you are going to offer a religious and moral explanation or are you going to offer a scientific and natural explanation," Sharma said.

> Of course, both have their limitations. Science can always tell us how, but has a hard time telling us why. On the other hand, if we start attributing moral causes to all kinds of random physical events, then that reasoning becomes chaotic and superstitious. There are dangers on both sides.

Most Hindus, he said, would probably side with Gandhi and assign some degree of moral blame for catastrophes such as the tsunami. But then things get even more complicated. Because *karma* comes into play.

In the weeks after the tsunami, and then again after Hurricane Katrina, many media "round ups" of religious reactions took the same approach to the religions of the East. They conveniently lumped together Hinduism and Buddhism, reporting that both faiths pretty much attribute all suffering to their belief in karma: payback for misdeeds in prior lives. Two or three paragraphs. A couple of lines on television. And that took care of the eastern religions.

I would grow to understand during the course of working on this book that there are vast differences between Hinduism and Buddhism (more on Buddhism later), that Hinduism is an incredibly complex system of widely varying philosophical and theological beliefs, and that the principle of karma itself is subject to countless interpretations. In the broadest terms, karma is a principle that governs energy and motion, in the form of our actions and thoughts. It is understood as a universal, unavoidable system—like the law of gravity—that oversees cause and effect, action and reaction. Keeping in mind that Hinduism holds that souls are reincarnated in successive lives, the principle of karma insists that one's actions in past lives will affect their lives today and that one's actions today will touch their future lives. But—and here is where it becomes complicated to the uninitiated—it is all but impossible to unravel the connections between causes and effects. There are just too many factors at play. "Whereas in the western traditions, God is the main judge of what is good and bad—that's why we call disasters *Acts of God*—in the Hindu tradition, although God exists, the role of moral judgment is enshrined in the doctrine of karma," Sharma told me. "God is there, but he is like a judge's supervisor. You really have to undergo—enjoy or suffer—the consequences of your own karma, depending on the situation. The explanation very often turns out to be karmic."

So what karmic conclusions can we draw about the tsunami—its location, its timing, and most importantly, its victims? Sharma explained that there are many types of karma and that each could play a role in a given disaster. In the simplest terms, there is individual karma, collective karma, and a combination of the two. Individual karma gets the most attention because of its implications for salvation. "Salvation is achieved by an individual, like you or me, so the dimension of karma most discussed is individual," Sharma said. There is much disagreement within Hinduism about the existence of collective karma, karma that affects a group of people at once. "Some scholars miss this point, but it is there in the Hindu texts," he said.

Sharma concluded that the karma at work in a natural disaster is probably a blend, individual karma "in a collective context." Then he gave me a rather painful example:

> If 100 people come together and kill 1,000, in a sense it is individual karma because you are involved, but it also has a collective nexus because you are working with others. In such a situation, it would make sense if those 100 people who perpetrated the initial act were subjected to a common tragedy. I'm just giving you one strand of karmic reasoning. But there are many interpretations within the tradition.

I said it was a painful example. Cold and calculating. And the victims are past murderers who arguably deserve their fates. Of course, in real life, people don't know what they did, good or bad, in past lives, so they may appear perfectly innocent when struck down by cancer or a car or a tornado. "It can be very puzzling," Sharma said, reacting to my queasiness. "You can say it was some evil karma in my past life, but not know what it was. You see, the duration of past lives in Hinduism is indeterminate. We've been around for a very long time, in the cycle."

Sharma has studied not only the dimensions of karma but the study of karma itself. He's written and edited more than fifty books, including *Classical Hindu Thought: An Introduction* and *The Study of Hinduism.* But he's a scholar of other faiths, so he understands how hard it can be for Westerners raised in the Judeo-Christian mind-set to grasp the concept of karma. He is the Birks Professor of Comparative Religion at McGill University in Montreal, having held posts at other prestigious universities around the world, including Harvard. One of his specialties is the role of women in world religions.

When I spoke with Sharma, he was deep into preparing for an international conference on the role of religion in the post-9/11 world. As president of the conference, which would feature luminaries such as Deepak Chopra, Huston Smith, and Karen Armstrong, he wanted to examine the fact that after 9/11, "the word religion was launched on a semantic trajectory, which would make it a byword for evil, aggression and terror."

As a scholar of many faiths, Sharma is well acquainted with questions of theodicy, of why God allows the innocent to suffer. He said that karma allows people to sidestep the question, at least in part, by giving people the power to affect their future lives through their actions today:

> In Hinduism, theodicy to a certain extent is softened by the doctrine of karma. A crisis can be traced back to your own actions. A colleague of mine, Elaine Pagels (a renowned scholar of early Christianity), made an interesting remark when she heard me explain the doctrine of karma. She said she would rather feel guilty than helpless. At least, in some opaque way, you brought it on yourself. Otherwise, you are living in a world of random evil and you have no control. Anything can happen to you at any time. Both positions are mainstream in Hinduism, that God acts directly—the more western position—and that karma is in control.

Even if the principle of karma holds that the victims in a natural disaster must have had bad karma, there is no way to know how the bad karma was collected. So blaming the victim is out of the question, even though it is a common conclusion by those who do not understand the role of karma, Sharma told me. "You wonder what must have been the karma, what brought this about," he said. "In any case, we can't know. What we do know is how to respond, that the victims must be immediately helped. And remember, by blaming the victim, one is accumulating bad karma. Really bad karma."

In the end, anyone who seeks a fulfilling answer to the problems of suffering is bound to be disappointed, Sharma told me. Then he hesitatingly told me about a metaphysical point of view shared by many Hindus that does address suffering, and natural disasters, in a very different way. I'll let him explain it:

> According to some schools of Hindu thought, this world is really a world of make-believe. Like a dream or a magician's trick. It is an appearance, not ultimately reality. Now, if you stand in front of a mirror, your face is a reality and your reflection in the mirror is only appearance. If you have a concave mirror or a convex mirror, then your face will appear distorted. So long as it is only appearance, appearance is under no obligation to be consistent or logical. Reality has an obligation to cohere. But not appearance. So from this very fine metaphysical point of view, you may consider that catastrophes remain inexplicable because, if you could explain it all, it wouldn't be appearance. Reality has to add up. Appearance does not. If the world has the nature of an appearance, it does not have to add up.

SWAMI TYAGANANDA/SEARCHING FOR THE INNER SELF

Having lived as a Hindu monk in India, Swami Tyagananda was in for some surprises when he came to the United States in 1998. He was raised to believe that there is truth in all religions and was stunned to learn that many Americans—many Christians—were insulted by this position. "For me, there can be many ways to learn the truth," he said. "But I met people who were appalled at the idea that all religions are valid. For me, it was quite an education." He had come to Boston to lead the regional Vedanta Society, a branch of the Ramakrishna Order of Hinduism, based in India. He would soon begin a Hindu program at Harvard, with weekly meetings of prayer, meditation, and study of Hindu texts.

Tyagananda spends a lot of time explaining Hinduism and himself, starting with his name. Swami is a title for Hindu monks that means "master" (of oneself). And Tyagananda essentially means "the joy of detachment." They are two Hindu ideals: self-mastery and letting go of the nonessentials in life.

He also has to explain Hindu conceptions of God, which are so different from the Judeo-Christian sense of God. When something bad happens to Americans, they want to understand God's intentions. When a natural disaster kills innocent people, they ask "Where was God?" Tyagananda has been asked these questions many times and has become quite good, to my ears, of explaining how difficult it is for him to even address the question:

> The problem is with the word God. The word God has a specific theological meaning in the Judeo-Christian tradition. When we use the word, it comes with all that baggage. When we say "Where is God?" I would say from a Hindu perspective that God is all that exists, God is everywhere. God is there in the

hurricane and God is there in the people who are affected by the hurricane and God is there in the people who are helping the hurricane rescue effort. It's almost like the sunlight. When the sun rises, the sunlight shines on everything, good or bad. We don't hold the sun responsible for good things that happen in sunlight and bad things that happen in sunlight. God is like that. Things happen everywhere, but don't blame God for it.

Later in our talk, Tyagananda told me that the Hindu conception of God is so vast—all-consuming, really—and so varied that it is difficult to even explain what it means to pray to God. "Hindus pray to God and seek God's help and guidance," he said.

> They are answered and do get help. The question that is asked—"From where does that help come?"—can be answered in many ways. When people say that God is there and God helps them, there is no reason to dispute that, but it may not be the answer for everybody.

He also brought up Sharma's philosophical point about the Hindu belief that this world is only *appearance* (to my fascination and frustration, I have to admit). Hindu tradition says that everything we experience in this world is temporary. Nothing is lasting. And if it vanishes, it's not there. So it's only an appearance, the swami told me. "If there is anything real behind this whole universe, that real being is God," he said. "If there is anything real in me as an individual, that is my true nature, the real self. Then Hinduism makes this assertion: that the real in me and the real behind this whole universe are not two different things. God is never the other."

So God is never the other, is not separate from us, but is somehow infused in this world through whatever *reality* we can glimpse. This omnipresent God is known as Brahman, although Hinduism also recognizes many lesser deities that are seen as aspects of Brahman. There seems to be little sense in questioning Brahman—absolute infinite existence—when a volcano erupts and villagers scatter. God is always there but doesn't dictate what happens in our lives. Karma does that, the swami told me, in ways we can hardly understand. Karma determines how much happiness and sorrow each person will experience but does not dictate the form it will take. The physical world operates accordingly. But karma gives us an opportunity that the God of monotheism may not—to focus on ourselves instead of wasting energy looking for something to blame:

> If an individual experiences pain or sorrow, the question is "Who do I blame it on?" Or we can say that people and things may have been instruments to bring me this pain, *but I would not have gotten it if I had not deserved it in some way.*

The advantage of thinking this way is that if I am somehow responsible for what is happening to me, I can also undo it. But if somebody else is responsible, then I am not empowered. I become a plaything in the hands of external forces and I have no control over my own life. Karma puts our life back in our control.

Future lives, that is. Karma gives people the chance to improve their lot in future lives. The challenge for this life is to accept that and to greet suffering in productive ways, not through self-pity, excessive mourning, or anger at those deemed responsible. "We have free will," Tyagananda said. "If something terrible happens to me, I can be overwhelmed by it and become depressed. Or I can look at it positively, learn from it and grow and mature. I make that choice. Karma doesn't make that choice." Hindus, through meditation and yoga, seek to break free from worldly attachments and to gain knowledge of their inner selves. They see this process as the key to transforming themselves and the world. Tyagananda told me that Hindus, ideally, should see no point in asking "Why me?" in times of suffering because they understand that suffering is inevitable. Everyone will become ill, grow old, and die. The pain associated with mind and body is impossible to escape:

It is possible for me as an individual to rise above my limitations of body and mind, and touch a deeper core of my being. That deeper core is free from all these existential sorrows. If I touch the core of my being—call it spirit or soul or whatever you want—then I begin to experience existential joy. The Hindus believe that the spirit within is blissful in its very nature. If I can touch that, I am in direct touch with the blessed self, the source of all bliss. We all have the capacity to do that. That's what gives hope. That's why I try to remind people when they get depressed, when they see or experience tragedy, that everyone has the capacity to transcend their limitations. Hinduism doesn't have a special class of beings like angels. Everyone has the capacity to be an angel.

The day before I spoke with the swami, he had walked 20 miles in Boston as part of a fund-raiser to fight hunger. He was joking about his soreness ("The body wonders what happened."), while grateful to have taken part. But he also told me that he cautions students about the limits of "activism," of trying to improve the conditions of day-to-day life. You must seek to help those in need, but suffering can never be completely relieved. The world remains impermanent, in transition, a chain of successive lives, except to those who find their inner selves. "All efforts to change the outside world have necessarily got to be limited," the swami told me.

Reformers have come in every generation, in every century, and they have done great things, no doubt. But how much of what they did has had a lasting value?

Even those whom we see as prophets or saviors or incarnations, they come and are able to bring about a much greater force or power into the world than smaller reformers, but even for them, the whole nature of existence is such that, within time, everything gets diluted.

Feel sad for the victims of catastrophe, Tyagananda said, but know that they will be reborn in future lives. What's important from the Hindu perspective is to find inner peace and eventually leave the cycle of death and rebirth. "The Hindu goal of life is not spoken in terms of salvation, but freedom or *Moksha*," he said. "We can go endlessly in this round of birth and death. But those who say 'No more, I want to be free from all this,' can get out of the circle. They can do it. Then there is no rebirth. We become one with eternity, one with life itself."

PANDITA INDRANI RAMPERSAD/FREE THINKING ABOUT GOD AND KARMA

Only a few hours before I spoke with Indrani Rampersad, we both learned of a terrible earthquake in Indonesia. It was May 26, 2006. More than 5,000 people had died in the heavily populated central Java region, and it was reported that hospitals were unable to care for thousands of seriously wounded people. So I dove right in. I asked Rampersad, a Hindu priest, what she was feeling. What was her immediate reaction? What would she say in a Hindu temple days later? "It is terribly sad," she answered. "Loss of life is always sad. But this had nothing to do with blaming God, if that's what you want to know. It is a result of geography. It is about the earth, the world, the environment, the geography of Indonesia. Many simple religious answers are escapist, I think."

I would quickly learn that Rampersad has more than a touch of rebel in her. In 1993, she had been ordained the first officially recognized female Hindu priest—a pandita—in her home country of Trinidad, despite opposition from some high-ranking male figures. She had studied Hindu philosophy in India and worked as a journalist in Trinidad, comparing the quest for truth in journalism and Hinduism. When I spoke with her, she was living in Queens, New York, and working as a full-time high school teacher, teaching English and journalism, while serving as an adjunct professor at the City University of New York. She was still doing reporting when she had the time and giving sermons on weekends at Hindu temples around the New York City region.

When we spoke, she repeatedly described herself as a freethinker who tries to jar people from accepting orthodox beliefs without exploration. She joked about how male clergy take their influence for granted and abuse their authority and how maybe the world would be better off, or at least more peaceful, without religion. She ridiculed the prepackaged explanations for natural disasters that people from many faiths serve up with absolute certainty, as if they understand God at all:

> Many of us are not prone to asking sensible questions, even within our own faith. We are afraid. We hide behind faith and God when we should be asking questions. The whole thing with religion is that when you go way, way back, we didn't understand the world, so we looked up to God in heaven. There was somebody up there doing everything. But in Hindu belief, it's not like that. We see the world as cyclical, with beginnings and endings that you can't avoid. It's an intimate faith, a relationship with God's energy. We say that one quarter of God's energy is creation. And three quarters is transcendent. It is not manifested. This world is only one quarter of it. People don't deal with the science of natural disasters, in many cases, because our priests themselves do not encourage free thinking. Lots of religions have to be freed. I don't want to cast blame, but I want to say "What are you hiding behind? You want to lock people into little rooms and not give them the freedom to think." How's that?

Rampersad believes in a world where God set up the playing field and the rules but then lets the games be played. God's presence is all but incomprehensible. People have responsibility for their own actions and must accept that what they do affects their neighbors and the world around them. Natural disasters happen because of physics and, in some cases, poor behavior by the world's inhabitants. It's a world, ultimately, that is in constant flux. Everyone is going to die and be reborn, so death shouldn't be feared. She believes that even the idea that this world is imperfect, a notion that spreads after a natural disaster, is deeply presumptuous because no one knows what a perfect world would look like. Rampersad is a hard-core realist with a sense of humor, a priest of practicality as well as Hinduism.

She told me that some streams of Hinduism believe in miracles but that her sect—the reformist, anti-caste system Arya Samaj—does not. Like Rabbi Kushner and the Reverend Campolo, she believes that God does not intervene in our daily lives. "We believe that when the world was created, the principles of science were put in place. Day and night. Motion. We believe that even God does not intervene to change what God has set up as the principles of this universe. God is not a shopkeeper." A few weeks before we spoke, there were news reports that the earth's north magnetic pole was drifting away from North America and toward Siberia. I don't recall any talk about whether God was causing the shift, which could result in Alaska losing its famous northern lights. "God didn't do that," she told me. "It is the principle of motion put in place. Things are going on. The earth is cooling. Processes are ongoing. Things will happen if you live in certain places. You can't blame God."

Rampersad was in New York City on September 11, 2001, and was as stunned as anyone by the attack on the World Trade Center. But she found herself put off by people saying that God had saved those who got out. "How can someone say 'Thank God I was not there. God loves me.' Does God not love the people who died?" she said. "That kind of prayer is very selfish."

Even on the question of karma, it was tough to pin Rampersad down. Certainly, she recognizes that the principle of karma is at work in our lives. But she believes that it is impossible to separate and identify all the karmic streams that come together in one soul's current life. There is short-term karma and long-term karma. There is karma that affects one person, for sure. But there is also karma that touches that person's environment and everyone in it. There are likely regional and national karmic forces that wash over vast groups of people. There is global karma that affects every person in the world. In Hindu tradition, Rampersad told me, no one is empowered to identify or chart the kaleidoscope of karmas that may carry a soul through this life. "I believe that God has given us a vague blueprint, but no details," she said. "I don't like the fatalistic view of karma, that you get what you deserve. God has given us willpower to affect the world, so we should focus on our own actions."

Rampersad told me—and this was a point that she stressed over and over—that it is a terrible mistake to try to understand karma so that individuals can try to change their karma and improve their fortunes. "Hindu belief is that it is your duty to work for good, not for the fruits of the action," she said, noting that this teaching comes from the Bhagavad Gita, one of the fundamental texts of Hinduism, ca. 400 BC, which deals with selflessness, duty, devotion, meditation, and other subjects.

> In the Gita, they tell you, just do your duty to the best of your ability. Don't focus on the fruits of the action. That is for God. It is not a human give-and-take situation. You cannot blame the people in Indonesia. You cannot blame 9/11 victims. Don't worry about their karma.

As a general rule, Rampersad told me, Hindus don't react to misfortune like many in the West. Hinduism's fundamental emphasis on the transitory nature of life, on the role of karma, and on reincarnation produces a cultural mind-set that accepts, more or less, the unpredictability of life and the inevitability of death. Hindus who lived in close proximity to the tsunami, even those who lost loved ones, certainly felt grief and went through the normal course of human emotions. But they probably spent a lot less time asking "Why?" than others, Rampersad said. Hindus know that the real question is *When?* and not *Why?*

"The Hindu thing is we are not afraid of death," she said. "We face death. Many cultures can't face death. They are afraid of it. We deal with it and we know we are going to go one day. In America, it's a big thing. You can't even deal with aging. Forget about death. In Hindu tradition, you age gracefully." She laughed. "Of course, that is changing too. It's okay to use a little dye now."

Professor Vasudha Narayanan/Destruction Is Part of the Cycle

I belong to the Religion Newswriters Association, a national group of journalists who write about religion (we use the awkward term *newswriters* to distinguish us from writers with a sectarian point of view). The group holds an impressive conference each fall, featuring religious leaders who take advantage of the chance to address many top journalists in one big room. In September 2005, the same year that the conference featured Rick Warren, the superstar evangelical pastor and best-selling author, I listened to a panel discussion on Hinduism. I believe it was called "Beyond Castes and Cows." The tag was pretty telling, as most Americans—and most American religion writers—probably know little about Hinduism outside of the most generic stereotypes. One of the panelists was Vasudha Narayanan, a professor of religion at the University of Florida. I was struck by how grateful she was to have the chance to speak and how important it was to her to help people understand Hinduism, at least in a basic way. I remember her saying that Hinduism had already touched Americans who were studying yoga, meditation, and Eastern philosophy and that Hinduism's profile would only grow in the United States.

When I contacted Narayanan to talk about natural disasters—and karma, suffering, and the meaning of life—she was grateful that I was including Hinduism in my book. She implied that not to do so would be a serious mistake (I was convinced of this long before I called), but she is never surprised when Hinduism is overlooked. Narayanan is a past president of the American Academy of Religion, a prestigious group of theologians, historians, and other scholars who study religion, so she knows what place Hinduism holds in the American mind. She founded the Center for the Study of Hindu Traditions at the University of Florida, showing how committed she is to increasing public understanding of the Hindu world.

"One of the first reactions we have to a natural disaster is absolute helpless-ness and humility," she told me. "That coincides with the awe of seeing other people extend their hands and help. It all seems to go together. There are multiple responses, sometimes held by the same people at the same time. It's all very contextual and very poignant."

What a classically Hindu way of approaching the subject: speaking of multiple responses and the importance of context. Narayanan told me about an article in *Newsweek* magazine after the tsunami that sought to briefly explain how each major religious group affected would cope with the disaster. The article said that Hindus along the coast of South India tend to worship local deities who are believed to have the power to create and destroy. It said that the locals would take part in rituals to calm the anger of the ambivalent gods, including the ocean god itself. Narayanan told me that this article caused much consternation among Hindus in both India and the United States, largely because it presented the most low-grade or superficial version of Hinduism as mainstream, even among the poor and uneducated. This is not the case, she said. "When the fishermen went back to fish, when they resumed normal activities, the families who had lost many people started off with what's called a propitiating ritual to the ocean," she said. "But it was not to calm down an angry god, as the magazine said. It was about restoring harmony, thinking of peace." She said that even peas-ant Hindus in India have been raised to understand the religion's teachings about flux and constant change in the world. They may carry out traditional rituals or use traditional expressions about the power of the gods, but they share an inherent cultural grasp of Hinduism's focus on impermanence and rebirth. "Yes, these people do believe in gods, but they do not necessarily attribute all evil deeds to the gods—even if they take part in a healing ritual," she said.

Like the other Hindu scholars I spoke with, Narayanan said that Hindus have a hard time talking about God's role in our daily lives:

Is God involved? Yes and no. In India, we think of the supreme being in a number of ways, both as the supreme power of the universe, who is beyond human words, ineffable, and simultaneously, as local deities. But I think the people who suffered from the tsunami think of it as something that happened in the most natural way. Natural disasters have happened over and over again, all over the world. No one is singled out in any way. Even people in local villages, I think, will see it not necessarily as chastisement, but simply as an act, something that happens. It is an act of nature. Yes, nature is divine, and the supreme being does pervade nature. But it is not seen as an act which *seeks* to cause suffering.

Still, I wanted to know about Shiva's role in all of this. Shiva is the third deity in what is often called the "trinity" of great Hindu gods: Brahma (not the same as Brahman) is the creator, Vishnu is the preserver, and Shiva is the destroyer. These three gods are considered the most important manifestations of Brahman, the universal God or divine force that permeates everything in existence. It seemed like common sense to me that if Shiva is known as the destroyer, he would be involved in the bringing of suffering. But Narayanan explained that Shiva's role can only be understood in the context of the central Hindu belief that everything is in constant flux, moving from creation to destruction, creation to destruction. "Shiva is portrayed as actually destroying, but functionally the concept misleads," she told me.

> In Hinduism, each deity, Brahma, Vishnu and Siva, is seen as creating, preserving and destroying. Each is identified with part of the process, but the whole process is part of the cycle of creation and destruction. Destruction is seen as an act of *grace* because it leads back to creation.

In Hinduism, Narayanan told me, creation and destruction are understood as equally natural, equally inevitable. "The universe lasts for millions and millions of years, so the tsunami is seen as a little blip," she said. "It creates untold suffering—we're not being insensitive by dismissing the suffering— but *as* an act of destruction, it *is* an act of nature. Why does a tiger eat its prey? We all suffer the consequences of nature."

Narayanan dismissed a simple reading of karma's role in human suffering. The principle of karma is a broad philosophical approach to life, she told me. It cannot be understood in such a way as to draw conclusions about people from what happens to them. Because Hindus believe that karma is at work, though, there is a level of acceptance that runs through the religion. Instead of thrashing about to understand God, Hindus understand that life flows according to a structure (even if we can't see it or identify its parameters). "Hindus look at evil, natural or otherwise, with a kind of acceptance," Narayanan told me. "It's not fatalism, but acceptance. Karma functions as a framework through which we perceive things, not as a scapegoat. Since everyone has some bad karma, those of us who are suffering are getting rid of our bad karma faster. It's taken for granted."

There is so much emphasis on bad karma in times of suffering, like after a natural disaster, Narayanan told me, that it's easy to forget that all karma is bad (yes, even good karma). The object of life is not to avoid bad karma so that you won't get washed away by a tsunami or get diagnosed with cancer. The goal is to release yourself from all karma and to work toward *Moksha*, liberation from the cycle of birth and death. Hindus refer to good karma as "golden handcuffs," Narayanan said, because good karma may set one up for temporary happiness but will keep one from developing the detachment from worldly emotions that can lead to Moksha. She explained it this way:

> Hindu tradition says to do whatever good you can, but to not seek to enjoy the fruits of that labor. Do good for its own merit. You study hard as a student, not because an A will get you a better job and a Mercedes, but for wisdom. You do volunteer work not to be the person of the week, but because of the rightness. In that sense, if you do it, the karma will just fall off you, off your soul, like water off a lotus petal or leaf. The lotus flower is frequently depicted in Hindu and Buddhist art. The lotus petals are like Teflon. The mud slides right off it. It doesn't stick to it. Although human beings are born in slush, experiencing terrible suffering, the karma should slide off us. We know it, but it is very hard to do.

DR. FRANK MORALES/FINDING A PHILOSOPHY THAT FITS

As someone who has been on an unusual lifelong quest for truth and understanding, Frank Morales understands well the existential questions that people feel they *must* ask when faced with suffering and evil. Morales began asking such questions when he was hardly a teenager, more out of curiosity than anything. His parents were nominal Catholics but weren't raising him in the faith. And he happened to be very interested in the meaning of life. He read the Bible, Confucius, Eastern philosophy, and finally the Bhagavad Gita, the main Scripture of Hinduism. He began doing yoga and meditating. At 14, he traveled alone from his home in Brooklyn, New York, up to Queens to visit a Hindu temple, coincidentally the first in the United States. He was home. "There are universal questions that, regardless of one's culture and era in history, always arise in people's minds," he told me. "Science can explain how something happened, but not why. Hinduism made sense to me."

Morales is now one of the top Hindu scholars in the United States and one of the few who are not of Indian descent. He is academically minded, insisting that Hindus seek the highest levels of scholarship. He has lectured at dozens of American universities and understands how difficult it can be for Westerners to grasp the Hindu concept of God, an important starting point if one is to understand how Hindus see the tsunami and other forms of suffering. He describes Hinduism as being *panantheistic,* a rarely used word that means that God is all existence. Not just that God created all existence or that God oversees all existence, but that God is one with everything. "In Hinduism, God is both present in the world, since he is the source of all things, including the laws of nature, but at the same time, he also transcends the laws of nature," he explained. "This is something that makes Hinduism different from the

Western religions, from the Abrahamic religions. This may be a little difficult to understand, but God is seen as being present even in the tsunami, in that the laws of nature would not exist without God." I couldn't help thinking that many, if not most, Christians, Muslims, and Jews have a similar implicit understanding of God's multidimensional presence in the universe, even if they use very different scriptural language that makes God seem more knowable.

Morales told me that it would be unnatural for Hindus to try to blame God, or the lesser deities that reflect aspects of God, for events in this world that are limited to a particular time and space. To do so would be to radically change God's nature. Since everything, good and bad, is saturated with God's presence, to try to pin certain, minute events on God would mean not just scaling back God's presence but completely changing what Hindus believe God to be. "More than anything, in all of Hinduism, God is seen as the sustainer of all reality," he said.

> God sustains all the laws of the universe. God sustains life. God sustains all things with his presence. As a result, his presence is even seen in the laws of nature, which sometimes can be bad, in the tsunami, but also can be extremely good—like the food we eat, like the beauty of nature. The laws are operating independently.

Morales stayed on this path, focusing on the divinely inspired majesty of the physical world, of which natural disasters are but one small part:

> Think of disasters as the mirror image of the positive laws of nature, like gravity. We don't blame God for the earth rotating around the sun on a perfect track. If we were a bit off that track, the earth would be burned to a crisp or freeze. We never complain about the good laws of nature. That's the nature of nature. Hindus don't look at nature through rose-colored glasses. You can go on a hike and see the most breathtaking, beautiful scenery and see mountain ranges that are so powerful that you can feel God's presence. At the same time, you can see a mountain lion kill some rabbit. There is good and bad in nature. We can't just praise the good and complain about the bad. If we were to speak to a geologist, they can explain why the planet earth has to have earthquakes if it's going to function properly. Same with volcanoes, tornadoes, all these things. Hindus try to take a realistic view of suffering, and at the same time, a very metaphysical view.

God is above all temporal suffering, Morales said. Suffering is caused by human misdeeds, nature, or both. God is infused in people and nature but is not driving the small events that take place every moment. "If anything,

God is seen as, potentially, that which can end suffering," he told me. "And that's a lot more complicated."

Morales juggles a packed schedule of lecturing, writing, and consulting to companies on South Asian affairs. He believes that Hinduism could find a vast audience in the United States if the Hindu community was better prepared to explain itself. To that end, he helped establish the American Hindu Association in Madison, Wisconsin, where he lives. He runs a Web site, www.dharmacentral.com, that offers his writings on many subjects. And he even started in 2004 the Dharma News Network, an online database of international news from a Hindu perspective. Morales is generally frustrated with how poorly Hinduism is portrayed in the American media, even writing to ABC News to protest a report on the tsunami that dispensed with Hinduism and Buddhism by briefly mentioning karma.

The popular understanding of karma, not surprisingly, leaves Morales cold. He told me that many Westerners who know little about karma, and even some Hindus, boil karma down to a formula for payback. I thought of the bad guy in the old westerns finally losing a draw and taking a slug because of karma. "It's not simply retribution," Morales said. "In the West, people will stub their toe and say 'Oh, it's my karma, from when I hurt someone,' and that's as deep as their understanding will go." He emphasized what other Hindu scholars told me—that karma, far from being a recipe for fatalism, is a pathway to radical freedom. "With every activity we do, with everything that we think, everything that we act upon, every word we say, with every ethical choice, we are *creating* our future," he said, straining to make the point. "We are creating, on a day-to-day basis, our future consciousness, our attitude towards life. We are creating who we are." People often think of karma affecting what happens to us physically—do we move toward or away from shelter before an earthquake strikes?—but karma is also shaping each person's consciousness. "We are determining how we will be born in future lifetimes, to wealthy parents or parents in poverty, for instance," he said. "But that's not all. Why is it that some people seem to be born very bad? Why is it that some people seem to be born very good? They seem to be incorruptible. More than anywhere else, that is where karma is operative."

The important thing, Morales told me, is that Hindus focus on the future and not the past. The goal is to act ethically and faithfully, thereby shaping positive karma or even moving toward liberation from the cycle of birth and death. There is no point to worrying about how past actions have affected one's karma today. "For Hindus, knowing about their past lives is nothing of importance," Morales said. "This is more of a New Age thing. Americans love to look for their past lives."

He repeated that Hindus should not do good deeds in order to stockpile good karma, although some certainly do. Of course, people of all faiths sometimes have mixed motives for doing good works. They may start with pure, selfless reasons for doing acts of charity but find that they like the attention that it brings and figure that it can't hurt when it's time for their day of judgment. But wanting to bankroll good deeds or good karma should not motivate a truly religious person, Morales said:

> What motivates them is wanting to please God. In Hinduism, we have the concept of *Bhati,* of devotion. All good activity should be done as an act of devotion, without any attachment whatsoever, not even the attachment of good karma. In Hinduism, when someone is truly a servant of God, their attitude is "God, I want to serve you out of devotion and I don't care if I have to go to hell and serve you there, if that's your will." Absolute non-attachment to rewards and punishment.

When you come down to it, Morales said, people of all faiths, and none, bear the brunt of tremendous suffering. People of all nationalities, all ethnicities. "That tsunami was very democratic," he said. "It killed Christians, Muslims, Hindus, Buddhists. Locals and tourists. It didn't care what your religion was. If you were in the way, you were finished."

Morales became quite philosophical. I could almost imagine him as a boy, browsing through the faiths for something that would fit. He told me that karma explains, as well as any idea he has come across, why there is so much sorrow in the world—and so much joy. He said that humankind has come up with no better explanation, as far as he can see. The cycles of birth and death, happiness and sorrow, just go on and on:

> The truth of the matter is there has to be some explanation. While karma might seem like a cold, calculated, very rigid, logical sort of explanation, there does have to be *some* explanation. From a philosophical perspective, the questions have to be asked. Why are children born without arms or born blind? Why is it that good people will suffer? Why does a Hitler arise? Why does Indonesia have to face another earthquake? There has to be some sort of theological explanation. For Hindus, as well as Buddhists, the concept is karma.

THOUGHTS

The truth is, after months of talking to Jews, Christians, and Muslims, moving on to Hinduism and Buddhism was more difficult than I expected. The toughest part, I think, was letting go of the Western idea of God as a personal God. The Jews have a covenant with God, a relationship. Christians believe that God sacrificed his own son—for us. Muslims believe that the Quran is God's very word, a gift to humankind. Each group's narrative was written or provided directly by God. So God's accessibility is something of a given when considering the general question of suffering and the specific question of natural disasters that slay the innocent.

Not so with Hindus. The Hindu conception of God, like everything else in Hinduism, is extremely complex and multifaceted. An outsider to the faith has to let go of everything you thought about God. For the Hindu, the universal God is so vast and so immersed in every crevice of the universe (and beyond) that God is impossible to get a handle on. You can't try to isolate God as a separate entity that acts in our lives, for good or bad. The laws of nature, for instance, represent one sliver of God's countless forms, so trying to weigh God's involvement in a single act of nature is a pointless exercise.

At the same time, Hindus accept that there are many lesser gods who reflect aspects of the universal God and may act in our lives. But it would probably be hard to find two Hindus who have the same view of which gods are acting in which ways. There are countless interpretations of *everything* in Hinduism, making the journalist's search for widely accepted explanations even more harried than usual.

Once I started to grasp the Hindu conception of God, my job became to understand the way Hindus see the world. If I could get a feel for their world view, I could find my way to their understanding of nature and suffering. The key was understanding karma in more than a superficial way. God may be unknowable, but karma is not. It plays itself out in our lives, year by year and minute by minute, and gives us the opportunity to change our (future) lives for the better. The fundamental idea that we have the power to shape karma and change the world was deeply important to the Hindu scholars I spoke with. I found the notion that we should forget the past and focus on changing the future to have a certain attractiveness. But I've wrestled with the implication that we cannot know how our present karma was determined. We cannot know what we did in past lives to determine our current fate. We must just go with the flow. Honestly, I wonder if such broad acceptance, such stoicism, is best suited to cultures where personal freedoms are not emphasized and where suffering is commonplace. Most Americans, I think, would be uncomfortable giving up their personal God for a system that says that our fortunes in this life have already been determined.

I was impressed with Morales' refreshingly honest appraisal of karma: Something must determine our fate and karma is the best explanation that he's heard. Karma does jive well with the Hindu understanding of our lives and the world—that everything is in flux, that we are trapped in a cycle of creation and destruction, that suffering is inevitable, and that liberation is only possible by removing oneself from the endless whirlwind of multiple lives. As Tyagananda told me, the only escape is inward, through yoga and meditation.

The tsunami, then, fits quite well into the Hindu world view. It is seen as part of the cycle of creation and destruction. Karma was at work in countless ways. Suffering was unavoidable, perhaps serving as a reminder that acceptance is the best way to deal with the pain inflicted on us in this life. As Rampersad said, Hindus should be better prepared to face death.

Finally, it is hard to shake off the Hindu idea that this very world may be an illusion, an appearance, separate from the reality of God. It is a disconcerting notion on many levels but would explain a lot. As Sharma told me, an illusion does not have to make sense. The horrifying reality of the tsunami might be less horrifying if—somehow, some way—it wasn't real.

10 THE BUDDHIST PERSPECTIVE

There are many traditions of Buddhism, but they share a central, 2,500-year-old teaching of the Buddha: that the world is in constant flux and that suffering is unavoidable unless one seeks true liberation. Only meditation, compassion, and the overall transformation of one's attitude about life can move an individual—and the world—toward detachment and enlightenment. The goal of extreme self-awareness and wisdom is difficult to reach, requiring many years of study and meditation. In the meantime, it is given that bad karma will mold the unpredictable physical world to have its way with us. Nature operates independently, apart from any divine powers, and its destructiveness is not intentional. There is no point in dwelling on suffering. Rather, it is up to each individual and each community to practice the Buddha's teachings, known as the dharma, and to move toward detachment. One must strive to be above it all.

LAMA SURYA DAS/GAINING CONTROL OF OUR LIVES

Public opinion polls always show that the United States is a very religious nation. More than 90 percent of Americans say they believe in God. Large majorities believe in an afterlife. Houses of worship of all kinds dot the landscape, from start-ups in storefronts to arena-size megachurches, and attendance is reported to be quite high among most groups. But Lama Surya Das thinks that Americans, by and large, are less prepared to deal with tragedy than people in many other parts of the world. It's not just that they are more used to having the luxuries of daily life—housing, quality medical care, good schools, law and order in most communities. It's that religious practice in the

United States tends to be kind of thin. Many people who consider themselves religious, Surya Das believes, attend a house of worship for an hour or two each week and separate their religious observance from the rest of their week of family life, work, and entertainment. Surya Das is no outsider. He grew up in Valley Stream, Long Island, where he celebrated his bar mitzvah at 13. Only after he protested the Vietnam War and went to Woodstock did he begin his path toward becoming one of the best-known American Buddhist lamas.

"The religious impulse is there," he told me.

> The light is shining, the love is there. Sunday school and the good book. All the messages, to love thy neighbor, the Sermon on the Mount. But my question is always: Are we really practicing or are we just joining? Believing in health doesn't make you healthy. Being a member of a health club won't make you healthy. It's all about depth and continuation.

Surya Das believes that anyone who practices their religion with depth will be prepared when tragedy strikes. Prayer and meditation, when combined with a commitment to a code of ethics, will give one a rich, organic sense of his surroundings and a new appreciation for the cycles of life that touch us all. With this self-knowledge comes inner strength. But to move in this direction requires a rigorous and focused lifestyle, that is, the antithesis of a routine of shopping, watching TV, and keeping up with the Joneses. As a teacher of meditation and yoga, he emphasizes *practice*. Meditate every day. Do yoga several times a week. Pray every day. He believes that people must practice what he calls transformative spirituality, as opposed to simply joining a congregation, if they want to be able to contend with all that life brings them:

> Sometimes you have to accept that there are simple messages that people need to hear: that your loved one is in the afterlife or, when people lose a child, that God has taken that child back to his bosom. Maybe that's the best thing a parent can hear. I've never lost a child. Maybe any soothing message is good. But transformative spirituality requires a commitment, day to day, hour to hour, moment to moment. We have such a materialistic country, and the religion is very on the surface. As a Buddhist lama, as someone dedicated to helping others, I feel like prayer and reflection are lacking in response to the problems we have in the world today. There are too many other things going on: blame, short-term solutions, cliche Band-Aid answers, us and them. We can learn from the sufferings and difficulties and crises of life. We can make it into a higher education—that everyone dies, that loss is part of life, that change is part of life. We need to understand the universal principles, not just philosophically, but by noticing what goes on around us everyday. We can't

think that we can gain control of the universe. Control-freakism doesn't work very well, even though it is a very popular religion.

People should not be blindsided by most tragedies, Surya Das told me, because they happen over and over. Right before our eyes. Buddhists should have been less taken back by the tsunami. Americans see that tragedies and problems have causes but prefer to react than to change their behavior. "We have all this pollution, and chemicals and additives in the cafeteria food, and suddenly all the kids have ADD," he said. "What a surprise. We see the effects of TV, but suddenly all the kids have short-attention spans, and we feed it with Ritalin like it's a disease." He told me that if people slowed down their lives and reflected more on their real needs, they would be able to do without lots of things that are no good for them. The whole time, I was thinking something like "Easy for him to say." As a working parent of two boys, I knew there was something to what he was saying. It's just that life today is fast-paced and sometimes overwhelming. We take advantage of modern conveniences—preservatives in food, kids' shows on DVD—because we feel like we have to. But Surya Das was talking from the perspective of someone who's been studying Zen and yoga for three decades. "We can be more prepared, less blind-sided and surprised as things happen," he said. "More masters than victims of our fate. Not just control-freaks, but masters. We can be autonomous rather than totally helpless before conditions and events."

At several points, Surya Das told me about the power of prayer. He talked about being prayerful and reflective. One thing I wanted to understand was this: If Buddhists do not necessarily believe in God—they can, but it's outside the practice of the faith—who are they praying to? "Buddhists pray just like anyone else, but not necessarily to God," he answered.

> But Buddhists pray. Buddhists pray to Buddha. Buddhists pray to a higher power that we don't call God. Buddhists pray for peace, for healing, for the departed, for souls to go to a better life, a better way. Buddhists pray for the grieving and the grief-stricken and those left behind.

Surya Das—who was born Jeffrey Miller—teaches and leads meditation workshops around the world, sometimes for weeks at a time. He has organized three conferences in India where Buddhist teachers from the West have gotten to study with the Dalai Lama. He has written several popular books for a general audience, with titles like *Letting Go of the Person You Used to Be: Lessons on Change, Loss, and Spiritual Transformation*. I could tell when we were speaking that he wants to reach as many people as possible, even in small ways. He talks often about spirituality in general, instead of promoting

Buddhism, because he believes that people can gain much just from bits of Buddhist practice. "We're in the West," he said. "We get five priests and ministers, two rabbis, talking about something. Maybe a Muslim. And that's it."

When it comes to karma, most people in the West don't get it, he told me. Americans are conditioned to look for someone to blame, so they understand karma to be a deliverer of cosmic justice. But that's not it. Surya Das told me that karma is simply a system of causation—and if one knows nothing more about it, that's fine. Causation. Everything has a cause. All actions are interconnected. If people behave unselfishly, they improve their own karma, their neighbors' karma, their community's karma, and all karma. But there is no way to know how various streams of karma merge to produce an earthquake or a glass of spilled milk. Surya Das put it this way:

> Buddha said it would take an omniscient one to know why any one thing happens. An example was the color of a peacock's tail. We can't know why each color is there. That's an old-world image. What he means is that behind any one thing, there are myriads of causes and conditions, main causes and minor causes. Why did my next-door neighbor's mother get breast cancer on Long Island when I was growing up, while my mother didn't get it? There's individual karma. Who knows what her diet or stress level or genes were. Who knows? But a lot of women on Long Island got breast cancer, so there's group karma. There's gender karma. There's environmental karma, like why certain things happen in certain places and not others. There's collective karma, like species karma. The dinosaurs came and went. It wasn't because one dinosaur stole some meat from another dinosaur. We all die, so it's part of a bigger karma. It's not about blaming the victim. Karma is a very interesting brush. It's broad, but also very meticulous.

Then Surya Das said something that really surprised me and made me think for days afterward. He said that religious beliefs and impulses are not all that different in the East and West, even if Buddhists and Hindus use vastly different language to codify and express their faiths than do Christians, Jews, and Muslims. "We understand causation as meaning that nothing happens by accident," he told me. "Most Western religions think the same thing, but that God is behind it. What does the good book say: *We reap what we've sown.* That's a form of causation. That's karma. It's a broad understanding of causation, but Western thinking is not all that different."

Clearly, many Jews, Christians, and Muslims would disagree, arguing that a mere system of cause-and-effect is not religion if there is no creator and no Scripture to reveal the creator's intentions. But I think that Surya Das had a point in that most people of faith have faith in the idea that nothing happens by accident. There is a plan—even if everyone disagrees on whether there is a planner and who that planner may be. It comes down to this: *What goes around, comes around.*

Finally, Surya Das pointed out that many people of different faiths have the same inherent belief in an afterlife. This is not the end. "As a Buddhist, I don't believe death is the end," he said.

> We believe in rebirth, blah, blah, blah. Other people believe in heaven. Hell we won't mention. But people believe in *continuation.* Even the idea that how you live your life is important. Some people die and leave a lot behind that carries on in their children and grandchildren and everybody they came in contact with. The idea of continuation seems to be there.

Bhante Uparatana Maha Thera/The Tsunami Was No Surprise

The tsunami was a local tragedy for the many Sri Lankans and others from Southeast Asia who worship at the International Buddhist Center in Silver Spring, Maryland. Although they were living and working in one of America's most vibrant communities, the greater Washington, D.C., region, their hearts and minds were back in their native villages and towns, many of which were hit hard by the tsunami. Some learned that their relatives and friends had died. Not long after the tsunami, the center held a candlelight vigil at which mourners sought to offer *merits* for the tsunami's victims—positive thoughts and prayers to affect their karma in future lives. The center's Web site said of those who attended: "May you all attain *Nibbana.*" (That is, a state of non-attachment, free from lust, hatred and ignorance.)

I spoke with Bhante Uparatana Maha Thera, the founder, head monk, and spiritual director of the International Buddhist Center, on May 27, 2006, only a few hours after Indonesia was hit by a major earthquake. He asked me how many people had died. I told him that the early estimate was 3,000 (the death toll would top 5,000). "Oh my goodness," he said softly. Then he was silent for some time. Finally, he said:

> I feel sympathy, basically. According to my Buddhist discipline and my learning and my understanding, I feel not only for the victims, but for the world. People have too many bad qualities. It affects everything, even the sun and moon (meaning the universal environment). That's my feeling. This kind of thing happens because of, well, our nasty behavior.

I was a little perplexed. Bhante Uparatana was reared in Sri Lanka, and his English wasn't the best. But what was he saying? Who was he blaming? It took me the course of our conversation to get his basic gist: that all people except those who have reached *Nirvana*—freedom from the cycle of birth and death—are flawed and contribute bad karma to the universe, producing natural disasters and other negative consequences. And some people are worse than others, cranking out bad karma. He cited national leaders—politicians—several times. "It's not only the victims; it is the responsibility of the whole universe, the rulers," he told me. "As a result of all this bad karma, it happened at that moment, a certain date and time, that place. But it happened to them, the victims. Those people, they didn't know about it. When bad karma happens, you can't hide anywhere."

Bhante Uparatana has served as the Buddhist chaplain at the American University since 1989. He teaches meditation there. He faces a lot of questions from students when terrible things happen, about the effects of karma and the lines that connect past actions and current actions. They are the kinds of questions, I suppose, that I asked him. Bhante Uparatana tells his students what he told me, that there is no way to know about an individual's karma and the role that it played in a collective tragedy. "We can't really know," he said. "We Buddhists believe in previous lives. We believe that whether we do good or bad, and our intentions, can come back to you later or be wiped out in this life or later on. When people's behavior is good, tragedy may not come to you. But we cannot know."

Bhante Uparatana stressed, to a degree that surprised me, that we may be able to ward off bad karma by living an ethical, reflective life today. Nothing is certain when it comes to karma. A meditative and pure lifestyle can still be knocked asunder by bad karma—in the form of a natural disaster, for instance. But we can start affecting our short-term karma—say, 5 minutes from now—by living well at this moment. "Rather than having material attachment to the world, you must do charity, do wholesome things, do good things," he said.

> Christians have to share the Christian faith properly. Muslim people have to properly conduct their faith. Hindu people, Buddhist people, rather than cheating in their faith, must do the same, you know? When people have good discipline, good practice, loving kindness, equanimity, sympathetic joy, generosity, good behavior, if they have it, evil things keep away.

All faiths provide this path, he seemed to be saying, but many people cut corners and try to cheat karma. They seek to ensure that they can live long, prosperous, and pain-free lives, shunning the realities of this world. Then—Bam!—reality strikes. And they are ill-suited to deal with it. We cannot change the impermanence of our lives, he explained:

According to Buddhist teaching, all conditional things are impermanent. When we know the teachings, we don't worry about it. Things happen because they happen. We have to live the best way because at any moment death can come to us. We have to prepare for it. We need wholesome karma. We need to do wholesome deeds, with loving kindness, with sympathetic joy, with community, generosity. We have to share with our neighbors and our religious communities because we are subject to die at any moment. We must keep this in our mind, our entire life. If you know it, you can survive. Emotionally, if you expect bad things, you're not surprised that it happens. The Buddhists talk about the negative side, suffering and pain. This is the pain, the reality. It may seem pessimistic to talk about, but this is what's happening. In New York (on 9/11), we didn't see the bodies that much. But the tsunami, we saw the bodies. It is a lesson to us. Feel that it can happen to us, not only Indonesia. I feel it can happen to me or my community. People don't pay attention about it until it happens to them. Then it's too late.

The sad reality, Bhante Uparatana told me, is that too few people learn from what's happening around them. They distract themselves from reality. Look at New Orleans, he said. The nation was furious and disillusioned for several weeks, demanding action and answers. But then it passed, like a season of concern. "It was a lesson, impermanence happening to us," he said. "People try to explain it away, cover it up."

Bhante Uparatana's message, what he left with me, is that the whole world is a steady, low-grade tsunami or hurricane—unpredictable, always dangerous, and prone to flare-ups. We need to be disciplined, to stay calm, quiet, and still, to keep our bearings. It is the only way to see and hear the waves of chaos and disruption that circle our supposedly ordered lives like vultures that must eat eventually. In the big picture, we are no different than leaves on a tree. So we must be selfless and detached, not giving in to the temptation to believe that human beings are the center of the universe.

"The world is full of bad things," he said.

Bad things happened a long time ago. We had the wars. Many were killed. It comes back. But now, we are rich and medicine is saving our lives and gaining long lifetimes. But we can't expect it. These kinds of natural disasters could be balancing the population, keeping balance in the universe. That is my feeling.

So when a natural disaster strikes, what should a Buddhist do? Meditate on the future instead of dwelling on the past. "We do good karma, whole activities, and transfer it to the victims," he said. "We transfer it to them where they exist until their rebirth. The tragedy happened to them, but we don't want it to continue into their next birth."

KUSALA BHIKSHU (THICH TAM-THIEN)/LAUGHING AT THE PAIN

I had a good feeling about Kusala Bhikshu (Thich Tam-Thien). And not just because of his name. Kusala means "skillful." Bhikshu is a word for monk in his particular Zen tradition, which is from Vietnam. And Thich Tam-Thien, the name given to him when he received full ordination as a Bhikshu in 1996, means "heavenly heart mind."

He was raised as a Lutheran and later became an agnostic before finding his way to the International Buddhist Meditation Center in a Korean section of Los Angeles in 1980. He never left. He now leads meditation and discussion groups there; talks about Buddhism in local high schools, colleges, and churches; and is a member of the official Buddhist-Roman Catholic dialogue in Los Angeles. He's a chaplain at UCLA and does a tremendous amount of community work, including as a ride-along police chaplain. Kusala also rides a motorcycle and plays blues harmonica. And in November 2005, he supplemented his user-friendly Web site—www.urbandharma.com—with his first Buddhist podcast, available on iTunes.

So he sounded like a pretty outgoing monk, hip even, when I decided to contact him. He exceeded my expectations when I asked him his reaction to news of a terrible natural disaster. "My reaction is not one of surprise," he said. "It's just confirmation of the first noble truth: that life is ultimately unsatisfactory. Everything that's born will exist for a while and then it comes to an end. So I'm surprised when the world *is* doing fine. I haven't been surprised lately, have I?" He laughed heartily, as he did often during our talk. The bleaker the picture, the more he laughed (or at least that was my impression). He seemed to know what I was thinking and went right at it:

> People oftentimes look at Buddhism as being pessimistic. But to me, it's realis-
> tic. It is a way of approaching your everyday life in a down to earth, practical
> manner. If you think the world is just a big bowl of cherries, without the pits,
> you're going to be disappointed. That's for sure.

A big bowl of cherries—with big, annoying pits. Kusala's idea of life. That's how he talked throughout our interview. Direct and passionate. He told me that the obvious lesson of a sudden and devastating natural disaster is that people are deluded if they think they can ensure their happiness. "We can create the perfect house, the perfect family, and in a moment, it's all gone," he told me, as matter-of-factly as if he were talking about a tough opponent in an upcoming football game.

There is no security in this world of ours, in this world of *samsara,* the place where birth and death occur. So Buddhists would say the only true refuge is the dharma, the teachings of the Buddha. We see how cruel the world can be. And yet, the world has no intention. It's not punishing anybody. It's simply in process.

In process. Nobody's in charge or calling the shots, other than the uncaring, dispassionate system of karma. We talked about an essay that Kusala wrote after the tsunami, in which he outlined the five *niyamas,* "the five reasons why stuff happens," as he put it. He described the five universal reasons as, more or less, physics, biology, karma (or ethics), spirituality/transcendence, and psychology. These five interconnected niyamas determine the cosmic order, but do so independently, with no divine creator pulling the strings. "Because we're living in a monotheistic culture, our mind wants to find one thing to give us peace," he said. "For Buddhists, it's never one thing." Then Kusala told me about the first niyama, which is the rule of physical matter, the laws of physics:

> There is no one or no thing behind them. They are simply a process. Because they are a process and there is no one behind them, there is no intent. A lot of people, when they have this idea of monotheism, seek out the creator's intent. As a Buddhist, I can't do that. The universe, as far as we're concerned, has no intention. Which makes us pretty insignificant, which isn't always bad. I asked a Catholic friend of mine, does God have an intention? Can you have God without an intention? He said no. From a Buddhist perspective, I think our burden is much lighter. Something I found interesting as I reflected on this is that Buddhism doesn't have justice. Because justice requires a divine lawgiver, and Buddhism is non-theistic. Not atheistic, but non-theistic. Instead, we have karma, cause and consequence.

So life is a series of imminent sorrows set in motion by neutral forces that are neither looking out for human beings nor taking aim at us. But we have a say in our fate thanks to, of course, karma. It's embarrassing to admit this, but the whole time I was reading up on Hinduism and Buddhism and speaking with scholars of Eastern religion, in the back of my mind I was thinking about a TV sitcom called *My Name Is Earl.* The show debuted on NBC in 2006, centering around a good-natured if dim-witted character (that's Earl) who decides that he has bad karma and sets out to improve his life by righting his past wrongs. Earl often refers to karma, and sometimes talks to it, so it's almost as if karma is part of the cast. I often wondered what Buddhists think of the show, but I would never have dreamed of bringing it up—until Kusala did. "It's humorous and insightful," he said. "When karma makes it into mainstream comedy, Buddhism is becoming part of the culture."

He thought that *Earl* was a truly important development because if people understand karma, they can do something about their lives. "We can do something about the consequences of the future by our religious practice," he said. "We can do something about the consequences of our lives right now. It requires personal responsibility. A lot of people don't want to accept that." A Buddhist, he told me, can affect her future by living an ethical life and cutting down on bad karma. And she can improve her state of mind and move toward harmony and detachment through meditation.

Kusala told me that he talks about these concepts in a general way when speaking at schools. He's not seeking to convert people to Buddhism but to make them think about basic things: the impermanence of our lives, the inevitability of suffering, and the benefits of ethical behavior and meditation. He said—laughing—that no one has come up to him to say that he inspired them to become a Buddhist. Kusala was so inspired by reading Huston Smith's *The Religions of Man*. "I was at a gathering and he was the keynote speaker, and I went up to him and said 'You're the reason I'm a Buddhist.' He looked at me with these wonderful eyes and just smiled."

Kusala did recall, though, a seventh-grader in a history class in Glendale, California, who really got what he was trying to say. "Her name was Esmeralda," he told me. "She said 'Rev. Kusala, I now understand the difference between pain and suffering. Suffering happens when you don't want to have the pain.' At her young age, how did she know? Suffering stops when we come to a profound place of acceptance with the way things are." He said that many religions focus on suffering but that only Buddha did anything about it, teaching the way to Nirvana. I couldn't help objecting, pointing out that Christians would likely say that Jesus did something about suffering as well. Didn't he suffer on the cross for humankind? "Well, you get salvation after you're dead," Kusala said. "Until then, you suffer. The Buddha said you don't have to suffer. You can find release right now in Nirvana."

DR. ALAN WALLACE/THE PURSUIT OF A MEANINGFUL LIFE

Many of the people I interviewed for this book would, at some point, veer away from the theological challenge posed by natural evil and start talking about the somewhat easier challenge put forth by human evil. I say somewhat easier because man-made crimes can be pinned on people with moral and ethical deficiencies. Bad people. We may ask why God allows evil rulers to run roughshod over the innocent. It's hard not to. But it's a very different question than asking whether God is responsible for a destructive earthquake that even totalitarian governments can't make happen. So, in most cases, I would try to steer my interviewees away from the Holocaust, as mind-boggling as it remains, and back to the tsunami.

Alan Wallace, however, connected the two worlds of evil—natural and human—with a link I had no reason to break. A scholar of Tibetan Buddhism who has been teaching Buddhist theory and meditation since 1976, Wallace talked to me in great detail about the roots of suffering as diagnosed by the Buddha. These three roots—anger, greed, and delusion—are said to be the main engines that drive human misery. Anger encompasses malice, hatred, cruelty, the desire for vengeance. Greed leads to addiction, excessive desire, selfishness. And delusion covers the always dangerous belief that an individual, a group of people, or a nation doesn't have to play by the same rules as others but is *entitled* to more.

As Wallace explained it to me, these sources of misery make everything sick. They shape many forms of karma. Not only do angry, greedy, and delusional people hurt their neighbors and the environment, but they spew forth so much pain that countless evils may snap back at them, today and in future lives. One way that a build up of bad human karma may manifest itself is through a natural calamity. "We ask why we have to suffer so much. Nature dishes up so much—aging, sickness, natural calamities. That is enough to deal with it," he said.

> On top of that, we humans compound an immense amount of suffering, as if we were impoverished of suffering. We don't have enough, so let's make up more, so we have a bounty of suffering and misery. That bounty, that excess of suffering, nature is not responsible for. But we are.

And what about when nature is responsible, I asked him. Can we learn anything by trying to pull out the strings of human misbehavior that fed into a big ball of bad karma? No, he said. The only way to deal with natural disasters is to move forward—to take care of the injured, rebuild infrastructures, and do what we can to prepare for the next big hit. Doing these things will produce positive karma. Gazing at one's bellybutton while pondering the past will do nothing. "There is a range of human suffering," Wallace told me.

> Earthquakes happen. And tidal waves. There are many forms of illness for which human beings are not responsible. What can we do? We say it's a natural event and respond the best that we can, with care and medicine, while taking whatever actions we can to prevent these things from happening in the future—better levees, better vaccinations, greater distribution of goods during a famine.

I've interviewed who knows how many people over the last 20 years, including many big-name intellectuals. But only a few have left me in the dust, hoping I could keep up with them. Wallace gave me an hour-long lecture (I hardly got a word in) that was so organized and fluid that he seemed to be reading from a lectern. But he was speaking extemporaneously, moving from broad subjects like karma and the sources of happiness to logical subsections, which sometimes moved laterally into other categories before smoothly returning to their spot. It was all very linear, very rich, and almost hypnotizing.

A native of Pasadena, California, Wallace cut short his Western education in 1971 to study Buddhism and Tibetan language in India. He later translated Tibetan texts and taught throughout the United States and Europe. For the last two decades, he has focused on the connection between Buddhism and brain science, a subject that is garnering much attention these days. When we spoke, Wallace was the president of the Santa Barbara Institute for Consciousness Studies, which he founded.

Wallace told me that karma, like physics, is all about causation. But we can't see the patterns of cause-and-effect like we sometimes can in the purely physical world. In order to begin to understand karma, he said, one has to get a sense of the vast range of connections between actions and effects. A husband says something unkind to his wife and she becomes unhappy. That's short-term karma. How parents raise their children produces longer-term karma. "Our past motivations, habits, conduct, are defining to a large extent the quality of our lives now. That is karma," Wallace said. "In terms of the trajectory of an individual's life, through our thoughts, behaviors, attitudes, impact on other people, we are *recreating* ourselves each day of our lives."

When it comes to our relationship with the world, small and seemingly innocent actions can produce, over time, a tremendous sweep of bad karma. As an example, he cited the use of pesticides:

> We find some good bug spray, some nifty thing we can spray on weeds so we can say "I don't need to get down there and pull that weed. I can shoot it dead with a chemical." Your neighbors see that it works and start using it. Except maybe the chemical slips into the ground water. Maybe it's poisoning the soil. You're 60 years old and never feel the repercussions. But as that ground water accumulates, your grandchildren are being born with problems. You may find that cancer is becoming more prevalent, people's immune systems are shot. You may find it in your crops, in your food. But this may not show up for two or three generations. There are long-term effects that ripple out into the environment and slowly but surely ripple back—and may hit you 5 or 10 or 150 or 200 years later. That's karma. Our actions go into this network of causal interrelationships. If those actions were detrimental to us and others, damaging

to other species and our own, those actions—using a bug spray—were unethi-cal. Wrong behavior manifests itself later. Actions that are conducive to our own and others' flourishing are virtuous, ethical. This way of looking at ethics, at karma, gives us a sense of moral responsibility.

Wallace focused on what the individual can do, minute by minute and through the course of his or her life. Ethical and reflective behavior can instantly improve one's life and begin to produce good karma that will touch the lives of loved ones, neighbors, and the world. The right outlook and behavior will not only send out positive waves but prepare one as best as possible for the sorrows and miseries that still await each of us.

To begin to put oneself in this position, Wallace told me, you must first focus on the meaning of happiness. The key is understanding that hedonic pleasure, the everyday goal for many of us, is different from *eudaimonic* pleas-ure, or what Wallace describes as genuine well-being. Hedonic pleasure comes from contact with outside stimuli—not only base things like food, sex and wealth, but music, literature, intellectual pursuits, and even daily contact with loved ones. "There is the joy of seeing my grandson grow up, happy and healthy; it's virtuous and good," Wallace said. "There is certainly nothing immoral about this, or base or crude, and yet, it is driven by stimuli." Eudai-monic pleasure, though, is a different plane and doesn't come easy. It has been the goal of contemplative and spiritual traditions since the ancient Greeks. It is a state of mind that comes from difficult, ongoing meditation and contemplation and actually removes one from the effects of outside stimuli. As Wallace put it:

> It is a quality of well-being that's not stimulus driven. It persists in the absence of pleasurable stimuli and persists in the presence of adverse stimuli, like the loss of a loved one, ill health, the loss of financial acquisitions, loss of money and goods, loss of reputation and status, and so forth. Also the adversities of warfare. The question that has been raised for centuries in these great spiritual traditions and the deepest philosophical traditions is how may we flourish not only in the good times, but in the absence of pleasurable stimuli and even in the presence of adverse circumstances. This is eudaimonia, genuine happiness.

For the Buddhist, the pursuit of eudaimonia is how best to deal with suffer-ing, such as a natural disaster, and is the natural route to produce positive karma that will limit suffering. The pursuit is, at once, how to react and—to use a popular term in modern culture—how to be proactive.

The pursuit of such genuine happiness is one of Wallace's three keys to a meaningful life. The second is the pursuit of understanding—of oneself, other people, and the world. The third key is the pursuit of virtue—compassion, generosity, patience, and tolerance. Wallace told me that these three pursuits have been broken apart in the modern world. "Virtue is for religious people, understanding is for science and happiness is for everybody," he said. "But that is a fragmented life. The reunification of these pursuits—as they were unified before the rise of modern science, before the Enlightenment, before the secularization of the world—can produce a meaningful life."

And living a meaningful life, Wallace told me, is the best way to ward off pain and prepare for suffering. It is a Buddhist alternative to praying to God and asking questions of God in the wake of unexplainable pain.

Wallace is doing his part to bring together the components of a meaningful life by studying the effects of Buddhist philosophy and meditation on brain science. He has a deep appreciation for science (and a background in physics). But he told me that what drove him from Western civilization as a young man was the separation of ethics and meaning from science. He is still deeply frustrated by modern science's fixation on the physical world. Wallace believes that science could have a role to play in exploring religious beliefs about consciousness—even the widely held belief that our consciousness continues after death:

> Modern science is so utterly fixated on the objective and the physical, it has never gotten down to any deep exploration of the nature and dimensions of consciousness. There are many things that are not physical—love, numbers, mathematical equations, laws of nature, justice, time, so many things crucial to our existence. To declare that only physical phenomena are real strikes me as a case of severe myopia. This whole issue of the continuity of consciousness is a very legitimate area for scientific inquiry, but will require that we develop rigorous scientific methodologies for exploring subjective phenomena. It could happen. For those who do affirm a continuity of consciousness and the possibility of re-embodiment in future lifetimes, here is the really, really long-term playing out of our behavior.

ROBERT A. F. THURMAN/STOP WHINING AND FOCUS

Of all the interviews I did for this book, the fastest by far was with Robert Thurman. It took all of 14 minutes, 12 seconds. The funny thing is, I asked a lot of questions and we covered a lot of ground. He simply spoke incredibly fast. I could see right away why Thurman has become the most prominent Buddhist in America. He didn't need to warm up, get his thoughts together. He knew what point he wanted to make and he made it. As it says on his Web site, "Robert A.F. Thurman lives to make the teachings of the Buddha interesting and meaningful to people from all over the world." He has accomplished a great deal, on both the scholarly and the popular levels, because he has the focus that influential people often do. Even as we spoke, he was thinking ahead, telling me that he needed to expand on his book *Infinite Life* by writing another book dealing with biological theory.

Thurman was polite and gracious, qualities that a journalist learns to appreciate in famous people who deal with the media often and have a lot of demands on their time. But he had a clear distaste for how Buddhism is often portrayed in the United States, even by those who call themselves Buddhists. "All Buddhist theories about the relative universe are only relative theories," he told me at a rapid pace.

> Even the biological theory of karma is not promoted by Buddhism—by knowing Buddhists; that is, philosophically *educated* Buddhists—as an absolute dogma. All scientific theories are hypotheses that account for the evidence at the moment, but can be falsified by some other data. No theory of Buddhism that purports to describe the events of the relative universe claims to be absolute in nature.

When the Western media need to go to a Buddhist scholar on the issue of the day, Thurman is usually the first choice. He is, after all, a close friend of the Dalai Lama and was the first American ordained as a Tibetan Buddhist monk (although he gave it up after several years for academia). In the celebrity-obsessed United States, he is also well known as a friend of Richard Gere and as the father of Uma Thurman. So he was a go-to guy in the days after the tsunami and willingly wrote and spoke about the meaning of karma. When we talked, he briskly summarized his personal reaction to a natural disaster this way:

> My reaction is concern for the people who died, but not in the sense "Oh dear, they're dead." There is that, but it *happened.* So then I'm thinking "Where are they going?" I have a view of the continuity of life, which is a traditional Buddhist view, which over many years I have come slowly to adopt. You don't have to do that when you become a Buddhist. But when the Buddhist world view grows on you over many years, it comes to seem like common sense. You wonder what happens to the people as they go into a post-body state, an afterlife state. I have great concern of that sort, while I feel for the bereaved and those left behind.

Thurman described karma as Buddhism's theory of evolution. One action leads to another, producing an evolution of events. Like others I spoke to, he insisted that the theory of karma is empowering, giving people even in dire straits a chance at a new beginning, starting right away or perhaps in the next life. "You don't sit and whine, 'God did it.' 'Mother Earth did it.' 'Why me?' 'It's so unfair' and blah, blah, blah," he told me. "Because people are dying all the time and disasters happen all the time. You say 'I am going to use this disaster to make myself immune to doing anything negative.' You can consciously take control of your own evolution, and make even death and rebirth a positive process."

Thurman did use some rather harsh examples of how karma may work. For example: "When people lose their life in an untimely manner, it may relate to their own taking of life in previous lives in an untimely manner." Yikes. Must we conclude that someone who is victimized in this life committed murder in a previous life? And that all 320,000 people who died in the tsunami did something equally terrible in previous lives? Thurman said that, yes, the possibility is there, staring us in the face. But it does not matter. It is not important, he told me. The goal is to focus on one's present behavior and how it may affect future karma, and not to waste energy wondering about what happened in past lives. Why? He gave this very logical and very cold explanation:

> If someone comes and kills me or tries to kill me, I can't remember ever having done anything to them, or to anyone else even, in previous lives. But if I say, logically speaking, using the theory that seems to account for things, that I must have done something bad or negative to this person or to someone close to them at some previous time, I become aware that I put out into the universe a negative thing which is coming back at me. What this does for me is A) it says I'm glad I'm getting it over with by now having suffered this, and B) I don't want to do like that again to anybody, because I want to break the vicious cycle. The knowledge gives the impetus to change.

While I was listening to him, and later when I was typing my notes, I kept thinking that most people—most people I know—can't remove emotion from the equation. Anger. Fear. A feeling of injustice. Why should I suffer for an action I can't remember? What was missing from Thurman's explanation, probably because it was so obvious to him, is that the Buddhist must develop, through meditation and discipline, a very detached way of seeing the world. How else can one make sense of, even be thankful for, being mugged?

Even if we accept that our suffering is cosmic payback, there is no place in Buddhism for blaming others, Thurman told me. "If you say about a victim, 'Oh great, he got what he deserved,' you are in a way taking their life, mentally, and continuing the cycle," he said. There is also no place for self-pity.

In fact, the Buddhist who is suffering should point the finger at himself. "Blame yourself," he said.

> Say "That's my karma." Take responsibility. By being aware of my own complicity in any action that seems to be coming from outside, randomly, by becoming aware of my own involvement and responsibility for it, I can turn the suffering, the disadvantage for me personally, into a source of energy to make it better. You follow?

I asked Thurman about the role of collective karma. Might everyone at one place and time be touched by the same stream of karma? It would be easier to understand, in a way. But he dismissed the idea, using as an example the Chinese persecution of Tibet, something that is very close to his heart. "The Tibetans were invaded by the Chinese and 1 million were killed in the communist class struggle, turning society inside out," he said.

> People may say that it is the Tibetans' collective karma. It doesn't really make sense because the people who were Tibetan and lost their lives in the Chinese invasion and occupation of Tibet were not necessarily Tibetans in the previous centuries when the Tibetans attacked China and killed a lot of Chinese people.

He concluded his argument by saying this: "It really is the sum of the individual evolutionary paths of the different people." So even the Tibetan people who died—and those who cannot practice their faith at home today because of persecution—must have done something awful in their prior lives.

But if we must be so detached and logical that we can accept whatever happens to us, even welcoming suffering as a necessary result of past behavior, can we raise our voices at sources of evil? Is there a reason to protest injustice? I tried to put this question to Thurman. The Dalai Lama campaigns for Tibetan independence. Shouldn't he be thankful, I asked, that his people are being oppressed because their suffering is the next link in the karmic chain? Should the survivors of the tsunami be unemotional about the fact that there was no warning system in the Indian Ocean that could have saved thousands of lives? Thurman understood my question and seemed to appreciate my willingness to trudge ahead. He answered me by using a recent example of political failings that inspired many voices to rise up in protest:

> If some morons refuse to recognize global warming and refuse to cut down carbon dioxide emissions and refuse to do anything about the levees and refuse to do anything about the wetlands, and your house gets destroyed in New Orleans, you can very much be critical of them and try to vote them out or express your criticism. You can and you should. However, when you do that

as a creative contribution to prevent this kind of disaster from happening to you or anyone else in the future, it is different than cosmically blaming the other party, shaking your fist and going all berserk about it. You can have righteous fury against external circumstances that you analyzed as being causal. But there's a different edge to it when you have taken primary responsibility yourself. Cosmically.

There you have an explanation for being politically involved and spiritually detached, simultaneously, from a man whom *Time* magazine chose as one of the twenty-five most influential Americans. I wasn't sure that I could fully grasp, or accept, this idea. And yet, I found myself thinking that the people of Indonesia could do worse than following Thurman's two-sided theory. Rail at the powers that be for failing you and your loved ones. But try to shield yourself from the tempting but debilitating effects of anger, self-pity, and hopelessness by accepting what is and moving on.

THOUGHTS

Any religion that promises a loving God will have at least some difficulty explaining why innocent people suffer (even if they do put forth an explanation, i.e., original sin, preparation for the next life, etc.). Hinduism has an easier time, since its adherents believe that the world is in constant flux and that God is not necessarily looking out for us. Buddhism has an easier time still. In fact, the Buddhist view of the world is predicated on inevitable pain and suffering of all kinds. The Buddha's teachings are *designed* to help us face the onslaught that this life brings. Survival is the whole point. As Kusala told me, Buddhism is not pessimistic, but realistic.

This realism would seem to mesh well with the questions we faced after the tsunami or any calamity. Buddhists are free to believe in God or a godlike divinity, but Buddhism does not call for a god. It deals with what is. And life is hard. Good people do suffer. Horrible events take place out of the blue, changing thousands of lives in an instant. We can't run from this life. But we can detach ourselves from the daily rush of fleeting emotions and sensations—not only grief and sorrow, but materialism, temporary pleasures, concerns about status, and the denial of death. Surya Das said that Americans, by and large, are not willing to face these realities. He's probably right, although the growing popularity of Buddhism in America would appear to show that at least some Americans are intrigued by a promise of salvation that does not come from God.

It remains to be seen whether *My Name Is Earl* will increase the Western curiosity about karma—and even inspire the kind of reflection and ethical behavior that might produce good karma (wouldn't it be the American way to grow through television?). But karma remains an awfully cold system for determining our lot in life—and lives. When Thurman told me that a victim of a violent crime must accept that he did something equally awful in a prior life, I winced. Who wants to give up a loving, personal God for such a calculating system of retribution? The problem is that karma does explain an otherwise unexplainable act of violence, even if you can't accept the answer. A religion centered on a loving God has a much harder time.

Both Bhante Uparatana and Wallace emphasized the big picture that every action we take is connected to something greater. This is a terribly appealing idea, no matter what one's faith. Each said that one can start to improve their short-term karma right now, immediately, through ethical behavior and compassion. I think that most people of faith feel that they are connected to something larger, even if they can't explain what or how. So the notion that we can *recreate* ourselves daily, as Wallace said, and touch in small ways our acquaintances, loved ones, and communities is somehow empowering and consoling. Buddhism says that there is something we can do—that anyone can do—to face tragedy and to prepare for the next hit. It doesn't promise the absolute salvation and fresh start that monotheism does. It seeks, instead, to help us face what lies before us and what will come next.

11 THE NONBELIEVER'S PERSPECTIVE

For the atheist, the agnostic, the secular humanist, and other skeptics, the question of why natural disasters occur is almost too easy. It's science, pure and simple. Physics. No one is pulling the strings. The answer, then, is to learn more about these disasters so that we can predict them or minimize their consequences. Religious explanations tell us nothing, even if we want to believe that they are true. (Note: I profile only three people in this chapter because they cover the skeptical bases quite well.)

DAVID SILVERMAN/WHY PRAY TO THIS GOD?

Not long after the tsunami, David Silverman took part in a "debate" with evangelist matriarch-in-waiting Anne Graham Lotz, the best-selling fundamentalist author Tim LaHaye, and Shmuley Boteach, an outgoing Orthodox rabbi with a growing interreligious audience. It was three against one, but I have no doubt that Silverman loved the odds. The way he sees it, his three opponents were twisting in the wind, trying to explain their God's mysterious behavior. All he had to do was poke holes in their flimsy cover-ups for God's violent actions or their plain inability to answer questions about the God to whom they have dedicated their lives.

For Silverman, the national spokesman for American Atheists, the playing field was stacked in his favor. He absolutely relishes the chance to take on religionists, as he calls them, when they're forced to defend a God whose supposed actions can't be defended. "Anne Graham said not to think about it too much, and just to pray, pray, pray," Silverman told me. "In other words, turn off your brain. Tim LaHaye was talking incessantly about this being a sign of the end times. This is something Christians have been saying about every natural disaster for the past 2,000 years." He had a bit more respect for Boteach but not because Silverman is a (nonbelieving) Jew. "The Old Testament God is not necessarily a nice God," Silverman said.

> Think about Noah's flood, think about Job, think about the tree of the knowledge of good and evil. Shmuley came out and said that this is something God did and we just have to accept it. That stands logically—as long as you give God the ability to be mean and malevolent, which Judaism allows. But then you get to the point of why are we praying to this guy?

If there is such a thing as a mainstream atheist group in God-fearing America (and you can make a good case that there isn't), it would have to be American Atheists. The group has been defending the civil rights of atheists since 1963 and lobbying, not surprisingly, for the complete and total separation of church and state. American Atheists was founded by Madalyn Murray O'Hair and her family after they successfully challenged prayer in the public schools in a case that went to the U.S. Supreme Court. O'Hair, her son, and her granddaughter disappeared in 1995 and it was later learned that her son had stolen money from the group. This news was well received by many O'Hair haters—and there are many—but American Atheists has forged ahead. Silverman was leading the group's New Jersey chapter when he was tapped several years ago to serve as national spokesman, thanks to his irrepressible defense of atheism and his love of talking.

Silverman *loves* talking about natural disasters. He believes that they form an airtight case against the common notion of an all-powerful, all-loving, all-present God. "If you combine benevolence with omnipotence and all-powerfulness, you can't have natural disasters," he said with something close to glee.

> Either God sent the tsunami, which means he is not a nice guy, or he didn't know it was going to be there, so he's not omnipotent, or he couldn't stop it, which means he isn't all-powerful. You can't get all three. If you think about it, natural disasters disprove most religion, especially Christianity.

For Silverman, the predictable question of whether there is a God is old hat. Boilerplate stuff. He prefers to go at religionists from another angle: Even if there is a supreme being, why would you pray to a God who causes or allows so much suffering?

The biggest challenge they have is proving not just that he exists, but that God is worthwhile. That he is worth praying to. If you have a God who sends in tsunamis, why in the world are you going to pray to him? They'll say "Oh, this is a warning from God, this is a statement from God." As far as an atheist is concerned, God could make a much more articulate statement. According to the Old Testament, God can speak—and speak clearly.

Silverman says he became an atheist at 6 years of age. His first independent thought, he told me, came while sitting in the backseat of his mother's car. "I realized that God is fiction," he said. "I kept asking questions and getting non-responses." Today, his blog—the nogodblog on the American Atheists Web site—gets about 15,000 hits a day. It's not a bad number in a country where atheists are one of the few groups who are publically ridiculed. But Silverman realizes that the community of organized skeptics—atheists, agnostics, secular humanists, etc.—has virtually no voice when compared to organized religion. "We are dwarfed by the amount of time and money that religion gets," he said. "What a shame."

Silverman is a careful observer of what is said and written after a natural disaster. It's all a big circus, and he's sitting with his cotton candy, watching the theological jugglers and tightrope walkers. He is most bothered by the efforts of religious leaders to use a calamity to build support for their beliefs or to attack others. "They all said, coincidentally of course, 'This all completely agrees with my religious belief and is actually a warning against behaving any way but my way,'" he told me. "It's funny that there weren't any Christians out there who concluded that this was a warning not to pray to Jesus." Since religious leaders can't really admit that certain tragedies contradict their most basic teachings about God, they almost have no choice but to concoct a formula for explaining suffering as part of their belief system. "This is repugnant to me," Silverman said. He used that word—*repugnant*—repeatedly during our talk:

When someone says "Look, a disaster struck an area that's a Muslim area or a Buddhist area, so that's a statement against Muslims or Buddhists because God wants you to be Christian," that is so repugnant to me. It is repulsive. It is repugnant when religious leaders come out and point the finger at gay people, at atheists and say "Oh, this is a warning against being like that. Instead, you should be like me. And by the way, you should give us more money." It's bad enough that people say it. But they actually have *followers,* people who say "Yeah, my God is in control and he sent that tsunami to commit first-degree murder of thousands of people." The same people who say it's a sign from God say in the next breath that God can't really reveal himself because it eliminates free will. That's a bogus argument. It's either a sign or not a sign. If it's a sign, it's a lousy sign.

Silverman's wish is this: Instead of giving money to religion and praying to God, people would put their time and money toward preventing future calamities and dealing with them when they occur. This means developing better technologies and improved means of communication. It's all we can do. But the problem is, Silverman told me, that people are not satisfied with what they can do in *this* life. They want endless life. They don't want to die. "When you accept the fact that the laws of physics and mathematics govern the universe, that there's no guiding force, when you go to the atheism place, you lose a meaning of life separate from your own personal meaning," he said. "And you lose your immortality. That's a big thing to lose. Every religion that's ever been invented by man has had some degree of immortality—because people have an innate fear of death."

Silverman told me—and this point made me sit up straight—that he thinks most people are atheists. They innately understand that life doesn't make sense and that no one is in charge. But they pretend to be believers so they don't have to face the truth. "They don't want to deal with it, so they pretend that they believe in the invisible, magic man in the sky," Silverman said, clearly satisfied with this most provocative position. "That's why when you challenge them on it, they get so defensive, angry or withdrawn. Prayer is a form of self-hypnosis so that people can convince themselves they're not going to die. A natural disaster is a shot of reality. People doubt mythology when they're confronted with reality."

DR. MASSIMO PIGLIUCCI/EVIDENCE FIRST, THEN HE'LL TALK

When I spoke with Massimo Pigliucci, he was days away from hosting an international conference of evolutionary biologists at the State University of New York at Stony Brook, where he runs a lab that studies the evolutionary genetics of plants. More than 1,500 scientists from around the world—hardcore evolutionists—were on their way to Long Island, and more than a few of them were likely to lament the growing call for the teaching of "intelligent design" in public classrooms. Pigliucci ridicules the idea that intelligent design has anything to do with science. It's a common theme on his Web site about positive skepticism, one of several Web sites he maintains (others cover science, philosophy, and a blog about whatever strikes him). "I tend to take on way too many things," he said with an Italian accent that goes well with his name, but not with his highly un-Catholic lack of belief. "I'm agnostic—or a moderate atheist," he told me.

Pigliucci's Web site promoting skepticism, www.rationallyspeaking.org, says it is dedicated to the idea "that reasonable belief in something has to be proportional to the evidence favoring such belief." Sounds like a good motto for scientific inquiry. Whether it works for the religious quest depends on what one means by evidence. Pigliucci sounds like a good-natured soul, a scientist who likes to laugh and act a bit silly, but he can't find it within him to take most religious belief as more than a goof:

> The whole thing seems to me a left over from an earlier age, when human beings really had so little understanding of the cosmos and of nature that we automatically projected some kind of will onto natural phenomena. This is one of the origins of religion. Religion is of course very complex. It has many different connotations and many different forces bring it into being, but certainly one of those, if you look at early religion, was the need for an explanation. When you have no idea how something could happen, lightning for example, the ancient Greeks thought that lightning was Zeus getting upset because he couldn't get his way with a human female he was interested in at the moment. These were not exactly explanations, but stories. They really had no idea how to account for these very strong phenomena. But after science told us what lightning is and how it comes about, it really seems naive to attribute any purpose or any direction to natural processes.

As someone who demands hard evidence before reaching even tentative conclusions, like a gumshoe detective with a doctorate, Pigliucci was not inclined to see a natural disaster as anything more than a disaster that's natural. He got right to the point before I could even bring it up. "When I see a natural disaster, I see it as one of the prices to pay for living in a universe that is regulated by physical laws that were not designed with human beings in mind," he told me. "They are essentially neutral. I don't see either evil or good when I see a natural disaster. A man-made disaster is a different matter. But that's not what we're talking about."

Pigliucci grew up in Italy, where he took 5 years of religion in high school, taught by priests, and remembers doing quite well. But he was far more influenced by his science classes and by the three years of philosophy that Italian students were required to take. I asked if it was hard to call himself an agnostic in Italy, where Roman Catholicism is woven into the culture, the bread and wine. Yes and no, he said:

> Italian society, European society in general, is much more secular than American society. The United States is the only western country where religion is so prominent in public life. It is a very interesting situation, which goes back to

the country being established largely by religious minorities who were fleeing Europe.

Pigliucci tried to be kind when talking about religion. He probably thought he was doing so when he told me that he was impressed with recent research that showed that the religious impulse may be a result of biology. Hard wiring. I told him that people of faith would scoff at the idea that their prayers and devotions are set up like their sex drives. He agreed. But he couldn't come up with another reason that people would see God in an earthquake. The explanations and deflections that religious people offer after natural disasters—the contents of this book—struck him as utterly ridiculous. "These so-called explanations don't actually explain anything," he told me.

> They are just stories put together after the fact. It would be nice if whatever supernatural entity is in charge of these things would warn us ahead of time, like "Look guys, if you don't change this particular behavior, I'm going to send a tsunami on you." That I would pay attention, too.

Of course, Pigliucci zeroed in on the many inconsistencies, contradictions, and outright mysteries regarding natural disasters that puzzle even people of deep faith. He took aim like at a row of plastic ducks at a carnival:

> If, in fact, these are supernatural retributions for bad behavior, clearly God is not very particular about who he picks. We all heard that Katrina in New Orleans was to punish the gay community there. But what about the people who are not gay and perished or whose houses were destroyed? Is God really that careless? If I wanted to see any real intention, any real design, behind those things, I would be much more impressed by selective targeting, which you would think a supernatural being would be able to do. We cannot aim our bombs at particular minorities—at least not yet—but certainly God could do better than a cluster-bomb kind of retribution. And of course there are plenty of instances in which perfectly good people who believe in God, who are not homosexual or guilty of the alleged sin of the day, get struck down by one of these things. We get reports of churches hit by hurricanes, tornados. How do you explain this? Logically, you can't. Finally, why would God need a natural process to do whatever he wants to do? Why not just kill people overnight in their sleep? A natural disaster is a wasteful and highly imprecise method for achieving that purpose. No?

Like other nonreligionists, Pigliucci is amused by most religious perspectives on natural events. But he's angered by the attempts by religious leaders to portray disasters as divine warnings against a particular group. "The problem is the next step, when they use these catastrophes to attack or belittle this or that minority, this or that lifestyle," he told me. "As if the catastrophe itself were not enough of a problem. Not only have the people in New Orleans lost their houses, but they have to hear nutcases going around saying it was their fault."

Pigliucci saved one of his favorite arguments for the end of our talk. It is intellectually lazy for a religious person, he told me, to see God's influence when things go well but to say nothing when things go badly. He used the example of when someone who survives a fatal airline, train, or boating accident or a car wreck praises God for his or her survival. "What this person implies, perhaps without realizing it, is that everybody who died in that accident somehow was not in the grace of God," he said, incredulous. "That's pretty self-centered, I would think. Talk about having an ego."

To Pigliucci's way of thinking, trying to find meaning in a natural disaster is what philosophers call a *category mistake.* He told me that it's like trying to figure out the color of triangles. "It may be the kind of question a New Age guru would ask, but in fact it's nonsense," he said. "Color is not one of the attributes of triangles. You're misunderstanding what a triangle is."

DR. PAUL KURTZ/THE DEFECT IN THEOLOGY

He is widely known as "the pope of unbelievers." It's a title that many might want to save for the Antichrist or at least a lesser devil. But Paul Kurtz has earned it. He has spent the last half-century making the case against God—and against all beliefs that cannot stand up to factual evidence, the scientific method, and critical analysis. He is believed to have coined the term "secular humanism," a philosophy that centers around the human capacity to improve society, without divine help. It is a philosophy, of course, that is considered a threat by many people of faith, who see its influence pervading the culture like an amoral mist.

Kurtz, who turned 80 in 2005, had not slowed down when I spoke to him in mid-2006. He had quickly responded to my inquiry about an interview and sounded eager to talk about natural disasters. Indeed, he spoke with the passion of the faithful, even if his faith has no room for an unknowable divinity. "I am a non-believer; I don't believe in God," he told me proudly. "I find no evidence for him—or her." Before I could complete my first question, Kurtz went straight to the famous dilemma framed by the first scholar profiled in this book:

> It's the classical problem of evil, when bad things happen to good people. I don't think the religious believer has responded to it. All their arguments are rationalizations. If God is good and just, how do you explain a just and beneficent God

allowing 200,000 people to be washed away in the tsunami, including innocent children and babies, and surely virtuous people as well as good people? The case of the tsunami is even more difficult than why God allowed the Holocaust to occur. Either case raises questions about God. That's why I'm a skeptic of the God concept. It is a defect in the whole theology. A tsunami is a natural event. Tectonic plates shifted. An earthquake occurred. The universe doesn't have purpose. Nature doesn't have purpose. It just is. If people or animals are killed in the process, it's because nature is indifferent. It's indifferent to what happens to humans.

It says a lot about the importance of religion in America that Kurtz is a hero in the small community of committed nonbelievers but is largely unknown in the wider culture. He has founded or played a leading role in most of the groups that make up the nonbelieving community. He is the chairman of the Council for Secular Humanism and the Committee for the Scientific Investigation of Claims of the Paranormal, two capitals of nonbelief. He is founder and chairman of Prometheus Books, which has published more than 1,500 titles on critical thinking and other subjects. He is the longtime editor-in-chief of *Free Inquiry* magazine (the June/July 2006 issue included numerous tributes to Kurtz, "humanism's philosopher," for his 80th birthday). Kurtz is also professor emeritus of philosophy at the State University of New York at Buffalo. In the interest of full disclosure, I should say that I took a class with him during the early 1980s. It was a low-level philosophy course that was called "Knowledge and Reality"—or something like that. Looking back, I think I was far too young and far too focused on chicken wings and beer to follow a word Kurtz was saying. I recall sitting toward the back of a small auditorium and watching a professor who was quite intense about something.

For Kurtz, the only way that believers can even talk about natural disasters is to avert their eyes from their central challenge: If God is all-powerful, he either made the tsunami happen or let it happen. If believers do not acknowledge this truth or have no way to explain, they are done. There is nothing else to say. "If God created the earth, he could have prevented the tsunami, held it fast so it didn't happen," Kurtz told me. "There are chance events in the universe: the collision of galaxies, the violence of an earthquake, a terrible storm. They have bad fall-outs. It has nothing to do with God. That's how nature operates. The skeptic has no problem."

Kurtz understands the lure of religion. It gives comfort and solace to people who cannot otherwise face the inexplicable. He said that he has little problem with nature's cruelty because in addition to being an atheist and a secular humanist he is also a *stoic*. "I say, well, we have to resign ourselves to the fact that these things sometimes happen," he said. "We must do all we can to avoid them in the future, if we can." So he looks to science. Kurtz, like many non-believers, believes that humankind should seek to advance scientific knowledge as greatly and as rapidly as possible in order to prevent and deal with the onslaught of natural challenges. "The whole human effort, since we left our primitive caves, has been to develop science and reason," he told me.

> I can remember when people died from pneumonia, 60 years ago, before we developed antibiotics. People died from spinal meningitis. So you find the causes and develop technologies and therapies that will void them. I take my comfort from reason and understanding, and from the human courage to deal with these things.

Of course, science says nothing about our souls or what happens after death. For Kurtz, there is nothing to say. "We can pray for someone to save us," he said. "I don't think anyone is on the other side listening."

Kurtz comes from a line of freethinkers. He considers himself blessed not to have any religious baggage. When he surveys the growing intensity of religious faith, both in the United States and around the world, he is distressed and bewildered. "For 40 percent of Americans to believe in the rapture, the notion that Christians will be plucked out of their shoes and everyone else will be left to die, is stupefying," he told me. "But I think it's our fault. We have not submitted these beliefs to criticism. I think the public needs to be exposed to the critical examinations of these beliefs."

In early 2006, his magazine, *Free Inquiry,* published several of the controversial cartoons of Islam's prophet Mohammed that had inspired violent protests around the world when they were published the year before in a Danish newspaper. At least one major bookstore chain would not stock the issue of Kurtz's magazine, out of fear for the "safety and security" of its customers. "People said it was terrible because it would offend the Muslims," Kurtz said.

> They should be offended. One cartoon had to do with suicide bombing, a Muslim standing on a cloud and saying "We've run out of virgins." I mean, suicide bombing is the best illustration of a religious belief which has no foundation in fact and is very destructive and *ought* to be publically criticized. The public needs to hear a critical examination of these wild claims.

That is what Kurtz has always wanted, a public examination of claims that he considers to be unverifiable. Of course, most religious people already know that their beliefs are unverifiable and choose to hold them anyway. People of faith who try to make sense of a natural disaster, like many people quoted in this book, are often left silent. But they continue to pray and to keep the faith. Just as Kurtz will keep his.

THOUGHTS

For the nonbeliever, a natural disaster is *proof.* Case closed.

Silverman was just about gleeful to talk about natural disasters. Not only does a sudden catastrophe that kills thousands contradict the idea of an all-loving, all-powerful God, but it supports his favorite claim: that any god who is overseeing the universe could not be worthy of our praise. Such a god must make a disaster happen or let it happen or—at best—can't stop it from happening. So any god running the show can't possibly be the God that so many worship. Kurtz made many of the same points: that if God is all-powerful, God must create our suffering; and that if God is all-loving, the innocent should not suffer.

Of course, these are the central questions of theodicy, which people of faith have been wrestling with since the beginning (and which are the focus of this book). The difference is that people who believe must reach into their scriptures and traditions to try to come up with explanations. Nonbelievers don't face such a challenge. They insist, quite simply, that there is no divine answer.

From a strictly logical point of view, it's hard to argue with the nonbeliever. Pigliucci wants proof of God's existence, and there is no proof that will satisfy the scientific method. So he dismisses religion as an outdated form of myth, replaced in the modern world by science. A natural disaster happens because the laws of physics demand it.

Still, the religious impulse is undeterred. The tsunami happened. The world watched in horror. Hurricanes followed. And earthquakes. People are killed and maimed in accidents every day. Others are diagnosed with incurable illness. Innocent people suffer, while less innocent people appear to prosper. But people still believe.

The nonbeliever may feel content and self-satisfied, convinced that he's won the argument over God's existence and that the tsunami is all the proof you could ever want. Most of the world, however, has not been swayed.

FINAL THOUGHTS

S o what's the answer? Where was God in the tsunami?

It depends on who you ask. That's no cop-out. As a journalist, I'm not about to pick the best answer. But I will sort through the many explanations I heard—most of which evolved from sincere meditations on the questions at hand—to try to make some sense of it all.

Going in, I suppose that I knew that the major religious traditions would offer very different explanations for God's role in the tsunami and, more generally, in our world. As my journey evolved, I was repeatedly struck by how the various traditions *understand* the question in radically different ways. The key thing to realize is that they have utterly disparate notions of who God is and how God (or, in some cases, karma) interacts with humankind and with the physical world. A given scholar's religious training and sensibility inevitably gives shape to his or her approach to dealing with the sudden and horrific deaths of 230,000 people.

Consider the lens through which each tradition sees the world—and the threat of that world swallowing up its human inhabitants. Evangelical Christians focus on original sin and the fallen nature of the world. Muslims try to keep their eyes on the next life. Hindus understand God as being so vast that the very idea of God manipulating our daily lives sounds absurd. Hindus and Buddhists believe that people determine karma, which controls the ebb and flow of nature. Mainline Protestants see God's face in the victims of disaster and their rescuers. Jews have a range of notions about God's presence—and what it means to argue with God. Roman Catholics leave room for mystery as they hold to their faith. African American Christians are too focused on human evil to even worry about it.

Some groups, by their very nature, are more confident in their explanations than others. Muslims and evangelical Christians, for instance, are alike in that each tradition clings to an unshakable understanding of God's place in the world. They may not have the details on why a particular calamity took place, but followers of each tradition are inclined to insist that God has a reason. Zaid Shakir and Erwin Lutzer, who have little in common on most matters of faith, are each very comfortable stating that God made the tsunami happen. To deny it, they say, would be to deny God's complete power. African American Christians share a similar certainty about God's presence, even if they are far more eager to await the promise of salvation than to justify whatever blows they have been dealt.

Then you have mainline Protestants, Jews, and to a lesser degree, Roman Catholics, groups that know what they believe about God and the world but are less insistent on making sense of it all. They generally don't make the case that having faith requires having all the answers. They see the challenges posed by the tsunami, understand the contradictions between their image of God and the terrible facts on the ground, and are willing to say that there are some things we just can't know. These traditions offer so many views on the fundamental questions about God's presence that it is very difficult to generalize about their explanations for suffering.

Then you have Harold Kushner, Tony Campolo, and even Anthony B. Pinn, three men who I suspect share the innermost thoughts of many Americans who are silenced by tragedy. Kushner and Campolo both hold that God cannot be all-powerful because there is just too much suffering in the world. Kushner believes that God cannot stop the suffering, Campolo that God has chosen to reduce his power. Pinn, overwhelmed by the suffering endured by African Americans, has not devised a formula to explain God's coexistence with tragedy. Instead, he has turned away from God, preferring to focus on human responsibility than to even consider the possibility that God is not all-loving. I can't help believing that many people privately wonder how an all-loving, all-powerful, all-present God can watch over so much senseless pain. If I'm right, many people face questions of theodicy late in the night—even if they've never heard the term.

Even though religious traditions think of God in such different ways, there are certain bedrock beliefs about suffering and the nature of our world that kept coming up as I worked on this book. The more scholars I talked to and the more research I did, the more I began to see blurry but unmistakable commonalities between and among the faiths. Someone would be explaining a particular point to me from their tradition and I would start to hear echoes of a similar point from another tradition. I began to draw lines connecting the faiths, lines that I now think may provide the truest lessons about the dark realities of this life that religion has to offer.

Here are the five lessons I could see:

The first is probably the most obvious. It is the responsibility of human-kind—of individuals and of communities—to do everything possible to protect the vulnerable and to come to the aid of the victims of disaster. Each tradition holds that to do so is an ethical and moral imperative. Not to do so means that humankind is failing itself and whatever divine force that you believe in. The reality, of course, is that we are failing, perhaps miserably, on this count. There was no warning system in the Indian Ocean. The levees of New Orleans were doomed to fail. Relief organizations had trouble raising money to care for the throngs of homeless after the Pakistan earthquake. And somehow, after each major natural disaster, the challenge of international cooperation raises its ugly head. Even in times of gravest need, government leaders—sometimes spurred on by religious figures—feel the need to rule on who can help and who cannot. The victims be darned.

The second point on which serious scholars from across religious lines seem to agree is that it is impossible to know whether God (or karma) directs a natural disaster to strike at a given population or target. This is an important point because after each major disaster, the media report that Jerry Falwell or Pat Robertson or local clerics at the site of the tragedy are insisting that God was *aiming* for a particular group of sinful people. This notion captures the public's attention and angers many people of faith. But it's been my experience that few serious scholars actually believe this. This isn't to say that many religious people don't believe that God will lash out at the sinful. The idea that God will punish the wicked is part of many traditions. But the scholars I spoke to generally held that we cannot read God's mind. We may believe that we understand God's broad plan for us. A given religious group may even be certain of it. An evangelical Christian or a Muslim or someone else may believe that God had to be behind the tsunami because God is behind everything. A Buddhist or a Hindu may believe that karma is responsible for an earthquake. But we can't read God's mind or determine whose karma is responsible. It is up to each individual to determine what message a disaster holds, if any.

The third point that crossed religious boundaries had to do with the nature of this world. It's a mess. The world is unpredictable and dangerous at best, hopelessly broken and riddled with sin at worst. Add in the fact that our lives are temporary—death is unavoidable and can come at any time—and you have good reason to focus on what is really important. And yet, too many are distracted by materialism, stature, and the false hope that day-to-day happiness can be secured. As a result, people are far less prepared to deal with sudden tragedy than they might be. Each religious tradition, in addition to offering a path to salvation or transcendence, also offers opportunities in this life for silent prayer, communal prayer, meditation, contemplation, yoga, deep study, and other pursuits that can lead people toward higher wisdom and a more grounded happiness. But people must choose to take such a path. Otherwise, it will take a sudden tragedy like the tsunami to make people consider how fleeting our time in this world really is.

The fourth point did not come across in as many conversations but came up enough to have a great impact on my thinking. The more you understand about science—about the vastness of the universe and the intricateness and complexity of the forces at play—the less likely it seems that natural disasters are directed at people. The scholars I spoke with who are scientists or have backgrounds in science seemed to have a much broader and deeper understanding of what the tsunami represents in the universal scheme. It was a history-changing tragedy for humanity, for sure, but only a blip or quiver in the context of billions of years of bangs and crashes across the universe. Even if humankind was made in God's image, we appear to be less central to the universal plot than many people imagine.

The last point is at once obvious and easy to overlook. It is simply this: true understanding of humankind's place in the world will come only after death, if at all. Unless God is revealed in the form of a messiah, a messiah's return, or some form of modern-day miracle, science is not likely to be able to certify or measure God's presence in this world. The great questions of theodicy—raised so poignantly by the tsunami—will go unanswered until one reaches the afterlife or the next life or the continuation of consciousness or some kind of oneness with the universe. If you're a nonbeliever, of course, you can only outrun nature for so long. In the meantime, it will be up to preachers, clergy, theologians, and everyday people of faith to try to apply what we believe to what we cannot know. There will always be another tragedy, caused by humankind or an *Act of God,* to raise ancient questions about God's presence and God's desires with new urgency and desperation.

Days before I completed this book, in July 2006, another tsunami hit a 110-mile stretch of Java island in Indonesia. At least 650 people were killed.

NOTES

INTRODUCTION

1. Reuters, "To God, an Age-Old Question," *Telegraph,* Calcutta, India, December 31, 2004, http://www.telegraphindia.com/1041231/asp/foreign/story_4195540.asp.

2. Bill Broadway, "Divining a Reason for Devastation," *Washington Post,* January 8, 2005, B9.

3. Reuters, "To God, an Age-Old Question."

4. Rowan Williams, "Of Course this Makes Us Doubt God's Existence," *(London) Telegraph,* January 2, 2005, op-ed.

5. Albert Mohler Jr., "First-Person: God and the Tsunami," Baptist Press, January 4, 2005, http://www.bpnews.net/bpnews.asp?ID=19827.

6. Agence France-Presse, "God Signed Name in Tsunami, Claim Clerics," *Sydney Morning Herald,* January 10, 2005, http://www.smh.com.au/news/Asia-Tsunami/God-signed-name-in-tsunami-claims-clerics/2005/01/10/1105206024347.html.

7. Associated Press, "Obeying Lore Saved Island from Tsunami," *(White Plains, NY) Journal News,* March 1, 2005, 8A.

8. John Garvey, "Is God Responsible? The Tsunami and Other Evils," *Commonweal,* January 28, 2005, 10.

9. Leon Wieseltier, "The Wake," *New Republic,* January 17, 2005, http://www.tnr.com/doc.mhtml?i=20050117&s=diarist011705.

10. David Bentley Hart, *The Doors of the Sea* (Grand Rapids, MI: William B. Eerdmans Publishing Company, 2005), 101.

11. Associated Press, "Franklin Graham Sees 'Revival' for New Orleans," *(Greensboro, NC) News-Record,* October 4, 2005, http://www.news-record.com/apps/pbcs.dll/article?AID=/20051004/NEWSREC0101/51004004.

12. CNN.com, "Late Edition (trans.)," October 9, 2005, http://transcripts.cnn.com/TRANSCRIPTS/0510/09/le.01.html.

13. Larry Cohler-Esses, "Nature's Wrath, Or God's," *Jewish Week,* September 16, 2005, 1.

14. Edward Rothstein, "Seeking Justice, of Gods or the Politicians," *New York Times,* September 8, 2005, E4.

15. C.S. Lewis, *A Grief Observed* (New York: HarperCollins, 1961), 27.

16. Union for Reform Judaism, "Against Indifference: A Conversation with Elie Wiesel," *Reform Judaism,* Winter 2005, http://reformjudaismmag.org/Articles/index.cfm?id=1074.

17. PBS.org, "Faith and Doubt at Ground Zero," *Frontline,* Winter 2002, http://www.pbs.org/wgbh/pages/frontline/shows/faith/interviews/griesedieck.html.

CHAPTER 1: THE DAY AFTER CHRISTMAS 2004

1. Associated Press, "Pope Prays that Peace Efforts Will Prevail," *(White Plains, NY) Journal News,* December 26, 2004, 15A.

2. Associated Press, "Anger Piles Up Along with Baggage," *(White Plains, NY) Journal News,* December 26, 2004, 8A.

3. Roger Bilham, "A Flying Start, Then Slow Slip," *Science* 308 (May 20, 2005): 1127.

4. Ibid., 1126.

5. Center for Oral History, "Tsunamis Remembered," University of Hawaii at Manoa, http://www.oralhistory.hawaii.edu/pages/historical/tsunami.html.

6. Institute of Computational Mathematics and Mathematical Geophysics, Novosibirsk, Russia, http://tsun.sscc.ru/tsulab/tgi_5.htm.

7. PBS, "The Wave that Shook the World (doc.)," *Nova,* aired March 29, 2005, http://www.pbs.org/wgbh/nova/tsunami/.

8. Ibid.

9. Kaz de Jong, "Addressing Psychosocial Needs in the Aftermath of the Tsunami," *PLoS Medicine,* June 2005, http://medicine.plosjournals.org/perlserv?request=get-document&doi=10.1371/journal.pmed.0020179.

10. J.P. Narayan, "Effects of Medu and Coastal Topography on the Damage Pattern," *Science of Tsunami Hazards* 23, no. 2 (2005): 9.

11. Bilham, "Flying Start, Slow Slip."

12. Tim Stephens, "Massive Tsunami Sweeps Atlantic Coast in Asteroid Impact Scenario for March 16, 2880," *UC Santa Cruz Currents Online,* June 2, 2003, http://currents.ucsc.edu/02-03/06-02/tsunami.html.

13. *(London) Times,* "Could an Even Bigger Disaster Strike in Our Lifetime?" January 2, 2005, http://www.timesonline.co.uk/article/0,,18690-1422952,00.html.

14. Kevin Krajick, "Future Shocks," *Smithsonian,* March 2005, 40.

15. George Pararas-Carayannis, email to the author, July 12, 2005.

CHAPTER 2: THE FLOODS OF THE PAST

1. Jan Brett, *On Noah's Ark* (New York: G.P. Putnam's Sons, 2003).

2. Andrew Elborn and Ivan Gantschev, *Noah and the Ark and the Animals* (Natick, MA: Picture Book Studio USA, 1984).

3. *Tanakh: The Holy Scriptures* (Philadelphia, PA: Jewish Publication Society, 1984), 11.

4. Richard Elliott Friedman, *Commentary on the Torah* (New York: Harper-Collins, 2003), 37–38.

5. N.J. Dawood (trans.), *The Koran* (Baltimore, MD: Penguin Books, 1956), 21.

6. Karen Armstrong, *In the Beginning* (New York: Alfred A. Knopf, 1996), 40.

7. Dawood (trans.), *The Koran,* 22.

8. Muhammad Shaykh Sarwar, *The Complete Idiot's Guide to the Koran* (New York: Alpha, 2003), 56.

9. Armstrong, *In the Beginning,* 46.

10. Ibid.

11. Norman Cohn, *Noah's Flood: The Genesis Story in Western Thought* (New Haven, CT: Yale University Press, 1996), 32.

12. Augustine, *The City of God* (New York: The Modern Library, 1950), 516–17.

13. Stephanie Dalley (trans.), *Myths from Mesopotamia* (New York: Oxford University Press, 1989), 30.

14. Ibid., 112.

15. Ibid., xviii.

16. David Leeming and Margaret Leeming, *A Dictionary of Creation Myths* (New York: Oxford University Press, 1994), 95.

17. F.H. Woods, "The Deluge," in *Encyclopedia of Religion and Ethics,* Vol. 4 (New York: Charles Scribner's Sons, 1968), 554.

18. Robert Wexler, "Ancient Near Eastern Mythology," in *Etz Hayim: Torah and Commentary* (The Rabbinical Assembly, New York: Jewish Publication Society, 2001), 1346.

19. Chas L. Souvay, "Noah's Ark," in *The Catholic Encyclopedia,* online edition, 1907, http://www.newadvent.org/cathen/01720a.htm.

20. William Ryan and Walter Pitman, *Noah's Flood: The New Scientific Discoveries About the Event that Changed History* (New York: Simon & Schuster, 1998), 251.

21. Jonathan Sarfati, "How Did All the Animals Fit on Noah's Ark?" in Answers in Genesis Web site, March 1997, http://www.answersingenesis.org/creation/v19/i2/animals.asp.

22. Voltaire, "The Lisbon Earthquake," *The Portable Voltaire* (New York: Penguin Books, 1949), 561.

23. Will Durant and Ariel Durant, "The Age of Voltaire," in *The Story of Civilization,* Part IX (New York: Simon & Schuster, 1965), 722.

24. Russell Dynes, "Seismic Waves in Intellectual Current," Disaster Research Center, University of Delaware, http://www.udel.edu/DRC/preliminary/272.pdf, 21.

25. Alfred Noyes, *Voltaire* (New York: Sheed & Ward, 1936), 465–69.

26. Garvey, "Is God Responsible?"

27. *Tanakh: The Holy Scriptures,* 1381.

28. Ibid., 1399.

29. Santa Clara University, "Is God Unjust: The Tsunami and the Book of Job," roundtable transcript, http://www.scu.edu/ethics/publications/submitted/DeCosse/Tsunami.html.

30. Elie Wiesel, *Messenger of God* (New York: Touchstone Press, 1976), 235.

SELECTED BIBLIOGRAPHY

Armstrong, Karen. *Buddha.* New York: Viking Penguin, 2001.

Armstrong, Karen. *A History of God.* New York: Alfred A. Knopf, 1993.

Blech, Benjamin Rabbi. *The Complete Idiot's Guide to Jewish History and Culture.* Indianapolis, IN: Alpha Books, 2004.

Brown, Lawrence. *Bodhi Beautiful: How to Be a Hindu in America.* Mumbai, India: Bharatiya Vidya Bhavan, 1999.

Cohn, Norman. *Noah's Flood: The Genesis Story in Western Thought.* New Haven, CT: Yale University Press, 1996.

Dalley, Stephanie (trans.). *Myths from Mesopotamia.* New York: Oxford University Press, 1989.

Dawood, N. J. (trans.). *The Koran.* Baltimore, MD: Penguin Books Inc., 1956.

God, Why? Teachings from the Tsunami. DVD. Nashville, TN: United Methodist Communications, 2005.

Greenberg, Irving. *For the Sake of Heaven and Earth.* Philadelphia, PA: The Jewish Publication Society, 2004.

Hart, David Bentley. *The Doors of the Sea: Where Was God in the Tsunami?* Grand Rapids, MI: William B. Eerdmans Publishing Co., 2005.

Kushner, Harold S. *When Bad Things Happen to Good People.* New York: Anchor Books, 1981.

Leeming, David, and Margaret Leeming. *A Dictionary of Creation Myths.* New York: Oxford University Press, 1995.

Lewis, C.S. *A Grief Observed.* New York: HarperCollins, 1961.

McCullough, David. *The Johnstown Flood.* New York: Simon & Schuster, 1968.

Neiman, Susan. *Evil in Modern Thought.* Princeton, NJ: Princeton University Press, 2002.

Parrinder, Geoffrey (ed.). *World Religions.* New York: Facts on File, 1971.

Pleins, J. David. *When the Great Abyss Opened.* New York: Oxford University Press, 2003.

Powers, Dennis M. *The Raging Sea.* New York: Kensington Publishing Corp., 2005.

Rauf, Imam Feisal Abdul. *What's Right With Islam.* New York: HarperCollins, 2004.

Samples, Kenneth. *Without a Doubt.* Grand Rapids, MI: Baker Books, 2004.

Steinberg, Ted. *Acts of God.* New York: Oxford University Press, 2000.

Tanakh: The Holy Scriptures. Philadelphia, PA: The Jewish Publication Society, 1985.

Thurman, Robert. *Infinite Life: Awakening to Bliss Within.* New York: Riverhead Books, 2004.

Wiesel, Elie. *Messengers of God.* New York: Touchstone, 1976.

INDEX

ABOUT THE AUTHOR

GARY STERN is a journalist who has covered religion for a decade for the *Journal News* of suburban Westchester, New York. He won the James O. Supple Award from the Religion Newswriters Association as the national religion "writer of the year" in 2001, and in 2005 he won the Templeton Award as National Religion Reporter of the Year. Stern has written about every major religious group in New York and has covered many of the top religious figures of the day. He grew up in Brooklyn and Staten Island and has a master's degree in journalism from the University of Missouri. He lives in White Plains, New York.